Thinking Gender in Transnational Times

Series Editors
Sadie Wearing
Gender Institute
London School of Economics and Political Science
London, UK

Leticia Sabsay
Gender Institute
London School of Economics and Political Science
London, UK

Sumi Madhok
Gender Institute
London School of Economics and Political Science
London, UK

Gender theories have always been important, but no more so than now, when gender is increasingly acknowledged as an essential focus for economics, policy, law and development as well as being central to a range of fields in the humanities and social sciences such as cultural studies, literary criticism, queer studies, ethnic and racial studies, psychoanalytic studies and of course feminist studies. Yet while the growth areas for the field are those that seek to combine interdisciplinary theoretical approaches with transnational arenas of inquiry, or integrate theory and practice, there is currently no book series that foregrounds these exciting set of developments. The series 'Thinking Gender in Transnational Times' aims to redress this balance and to showcase the most innovative new work in this arena. We will be focusing on soliciting manuscripts or edited collections that foreground the following: Interdisciplinary work that pushes at the boundaries of existing knowledge and generates innovative contributions to the field. Transnational perspectives that highlight the relevance of gender theories to the analysis of global flows and practices. Integrative approaches that are attentive to the ways in which gender is linked to other areas of analysis such as 'race', ethnicity, religion, sexuality, violence, or age. The relationship between theory and practice in ways that assume both are important for sustainable transformation. The impact of power relations as felt by individuals and communities, and related concerns, such as those of structure and agency, or ontology and epistemology In particular, we are interested in publishing original work that pushes at the boundaries of existing theories, extends our gendered understanding of global formations, and takes intellectual risks at the level of form or content. We welcome single or multiple-authored work, work from senior and junior scholars, or collections that provide a range of perspectives on a single theme.

More information about this series at
http://www.palgrave.com/gp/series/14404

Nina Sahraoui

Racialised Workers and European Older-Age Care

From Care Labour to Care Ethics

Nina Sahraoui
Robert Schuman Centre for Advanced Studies
European University Institute
Firenze, Italy

Thinking Gender in Transnational Times
ISBN 978-3-030-14396-1   ISBN 978-3-030-14397-8   (eBook)
https://doi.org/10.1007/978-3-030-14397-8

Cover illustration: © MasPix / Alamy Stock Photo

This Palgrave Macmillan imprint is published by the registered company Springer Nature Switzerland AG
The registered company address is: Gewerbestrasse 11, 6330 Cham, Switzerland

To Emilia and Bouchta

Foreword

There is now hardly a major city in any high-income country that doesn't depend on migrant workers from low- and middle-income countries to do its domestic and care work. These workers are mainly, but not entirely, women, and this care labour force also includes first- and subsequent-generation minority ethnic workers. They find themselves caught at the intersection of some of the most significant social, economic, political changes and crises of our time. First is the crisis of care itself. In developed countries this emerges from the combination of the rise of women as wage-earners combined with lower fertility, the increased ageing of society and the effects of social expenditure cuts and austerity. In poorer countries this crisis is no less intense. The growing reliance on a female wage caused by the effects of structural adjustment policies, environmental damage, wars, poverty, unemployment and illness impels adults' migration to seek employment.

By 2016 half of the world's 232 million migrants were women, many of them going into domestic and care work. In doing so, they enter a further crisis—of migration. This is not a crisis of migration per se but of the political responses to it. These have created political discourses in which the economic costs and benefits of migration predominate over rights and citizenship, and have shaped migration policies which are becoming more restrictive not only towards 'unskilled' workers (into which category care workers fall) but also in limiting migrant eligibility to basic welfare provision. It's here that the precariousness of the care work they are drawn into is intensified by the existential precariousness of their lives as migrants and as racialised workers. For, while this is a story of big changes, it's also a story of continuities where the ongoing devaluation of care labour as women's unskilled work combines with a persistent racialised servitude in which minority ethnic women have traditionally been recruited into domestic and care work in homes and residential institutions.

Much of the research into this phenomenon over the past two decades has focused on care and domestic work undertaken in people's own homes. Nina Sahraoui's wonderfully illuminating, analytically profound and sensitive study is based on interviews with migrant and minority ethnic care workers in (mainly) residential homes and institutions for older people in London, Madrid and Paris (conducted by the author in three languages). It provides a hugely significant and original contribution to our understanding of the personal, political and policy dynamics of gendered and racialised care work in postcolonial and neo-liberalised Europe.

The book starts and ends with a quotation from an interview with Fouzia, an Algerian old-age care worker in Paris, who says: 'France is a country with rights. So give me my rights. A little bit of rights, because in a way I'm doing something for France. (...) Who will do it? (...) it's the miserable care assistants. What I do, it's not little, it's really something' (p. 1). The paradoxes in this statement are at the centre of the analysis developed in the book: the way in which care work is devalued and its workers rendered invisible while at the same time being absolutely essential to the well-being of, in this case, frail older people, and a fundamental part of the care infrastructure of these countries. It explores how this devaluation is experienced by those at the sharp end of precarious employment, care privatisation, institutionalised racism and restrictive migration rules. And how, in the face of this, the very acts of caring for older, vulnerable people provide the workers with an expression for their own dignity, affection, generosity and pride.

These contradictions are explored through a synthesis of two conceptual frameworks: the gendered political economy of care and the feminist ethics of care. The first of these enables the author to situate and compare the racialisation, gendering and commodification of care work in each of the three countries within the intersection of their care, migration and employment regimes. The second—care ethics—informs an analysis of the daily practices of care work as well as a critical evaluation of how care work is understood and managed in the care homes in particular and in society in general. In pursuing these two dynamics, each chapter develops new and critical insights.

For example, the author examines the processes of labour market segmentation in the old-age care sector in which workers find different 'routes' into this work. These routes are shaped by the different ways the care and migration regimes operate and intersect in the three countries, and how they are both enabling and constraining. For example, in all countries there are workers who are overqualified for the work they do, a situation which often results from the obstacles (time and cost) related to achieving recognition for care work qualifications achieved in (non-EU) countries of origin. In many cases, employers benefit from qualified workers who are able to take on more complex nursing roles without being paid the rate for such work, while those workers face the difficulty of appreciating being given more fulfilling tasks in the knowledge of the exploitation that this represents. However, this was particularly marked in London, where 80% of workers interviewed were overqualified and this was due to the particularly restrictive point-based system which favours skilled over unskilled and in which care work is designated as unskilled. By contrast, in Spain, it was more likely that migrants were 'channelled' into care work as it gave them an employment foothold (and if they were working in a private home, a place to stay) whilst awaiting legal recognition. In further contrast, the old-age care sector in France invests more in on-the-job training and possibilities for professional training which permitted some of the workers interviewed in Paris, especially the minority ethnic workers, to aspire to their work as a stepping stone into more professional care work. Yet while these differences exist, overall there is a clear disconnect between 'utilitarian' migration rules in which rights are related to the value of labour on the one side and the needs of old-age care sector which is dependent on these workers' labour, on the other. Caught in the middle of this, workers find they are deskilled and often trapped in low-paid work from which there is little escape.

The book offers an excellent illustration of theory refinement grounded in the workers' own experiences. For example, the analysis unfolds the ways in which the workers experience the working conditions in which they find themselves. Sahraoui observes that while old-age care work carries all the objective indicators of precarious employment—temporary, part-time, low waged and lacking collective organisation—it is in the *subjective* experience of that work that precariousness should also be understood. Contemporary employment precariousness is a consequence of the ways care has been commodified. In a situation of reducing public expenditure costs through marketing care provision, care home owners and employers end up transferring the social and economic costs of the insecurities of care as an underfunded or for-profit business on to their workers. However, just as significant is the workers' own subjective existential precarity. In order to analyse the physical and emotional demands of their work, Sahraoui turns to the ethics of care to explain that: 'Precariousness is substantial to life itself, it is thus a condition shared by all, albeit differently. Bodies that are racialised—as are migrant and minority ethnic care workers—are exposed to specific social, economic and political forms of precariousness' (p. 133). She documents the physical toll of work that requires long hours of lifting, turning, carrying (men are often employed to do this). Then there are the needs to be attentive, responsible and responsive (all attributes of the ethics of care) to the frail older people in their care. This is often performed with inadequate or poor quality equipment where managers, for example, cut the costs of meeting incontinence needs. Understanding the complex relational requirements of this work means more than what is conventionally termed 'emotional labour', Sahraoui argues; it involves communication, forms of reciprocity as well as the challenges of residents who can be aggressive or even violent. Yet, being able to meet such relational needs was for the workers a source of pride in their work.

These attributes of the work are set against the lack of collective voice to resist their exploitation and against the conceptions of the professionalisation of care work which was task oriented rather than person oriented. That lack of collective voice is particularly critical in Sahraoui's analysis of the personal, collegial and institutionalised racism that the workers endure. She points out that even where clear anti-discrimination laws exist (in France and the UK), these are insufficient to deal with these forms of everyday racism. In the knowledge that certain overt terms or actions can be constituted as racist, discrimination by colleagues takes more covert forms and is difficult to prove or complain about. In relation to residents' direct racism, this was often not taken seriously; indeed managers saw it as something that workers just have to learn to put up with as part of the job. Sahraoui concludes that a rights framework, while important, is just not enough to deal with the multiple forms of subordination experienced by the workers. Rather, she says, we need to apply the ethics of care that give the workers (both men and women) their pride and dignity to social justice. In other words, a society which values care economically by paying a proper wage, socially by enhancing the value of care and politically by giving a collective voice to those involved in care work as either provider or service user would be one which would begin to remove the invisible injustices with which these workers live and work.

This book offers us an excellent grounded understanding of the diverse effects of the crisis of care and its continued devaluation in postcolonial and neoliberal Europe. The gendered political economy of care now stretches globally and includes the big international business of care provision and agencies working with states to both recruit and send migrant workers. Over the past decade a political space has also opened up where transnational networks of care and domestic work grassroots activists combined forces to push for the International Labour Organization's Convention passed in 2011 on *Decent Work for Domestic Workers*. This sets standards—to be ratified and implemented by its member states— for rights to decent working conditions and collective organisation. It has been a major step forward in enabling local and national mobilisation for decent working conditions. But it is also the case, as this book evidences, that dealing with the crisis of care and its racialised, gendered and geopolitical inequalities, as well as those of age and disability, calls for a longer-term perspective in which care is central to global social justice. In the political discourses of national and global social policy actors, care work is often hidden, subsumed under the duty of paid work for individuals and economic competitiveness for nation states. Ethically, politically and practically, care constitutes the social reproduction activities that sustain society, as much as labour, local, national and migrant, sustains the economy and ecological justice sustains the planet. It is within this framing of justice, sustainability and interdependence that it becomes possible to understand the complexities of the politics of migrant and racialised care work and the struggles around it. This book helps us enormously to think through this transformation.

Emeritus Professor of Social Policy   Fiona Williams
University of Leeds

Acknowledgements

I am infinitely grateful to all the persons who were willing to spend time with me, to tell me about their lives and to share with me some of their hopes as well as worries. If I could not have conducted this research without their trust, these encounters have also transformed me as a person. Just like the blurred boundaries between a labour of care and personal lives that I explore in this book, this research became part of my life in many ways. I am deeply indebted for this unique experience to all those I have met along the way.

This book draws on my PhD thesis conducted at London Metropolitan University, and I want to thank my supervisors Dr Irene Gedalof and Dr Leroi Henry for their valuable guidance and support throughout this research. I had the chance to learn a lot from their respective fields of academic expertise, and I am grateful for the many hours spent together discussing my research. Leroi started supervising my project when I joined the Marie Curie network in 2013, and I am thankful he decided to continue supervising my research even after he joined another university; this continuity meant a lot to me. I am very grateful to Irene for becoming my supervisor in 2014. A couple of months earlier, I had attended a lecture Irene gave and as her talk gave me much food for thought, I asked for a meeting, eager to continue the conversation. I didn't know at that time that a few months later Irene would become my supervisor; I consider myself very lucky to have benefited from many more opportunities to discuss with Irene and to have developed my research with her mentoring. After my Viva, Irene supported the project of this book all the way through, and I am deeply grateful for her decisive accompaniment. I also wish to truly thank Prof. Fiona Williams, external examiner of my thesis, who encouraged me to publish this book and made me the honour of writing the Foreword. I also thank the series' editors for their constructive comments, the reviewer of my manuscript at Palgrave for thoroughly engaging with my research with stimulating feedback and Amelia Derkatsch, Commissioning Editor, for supporting and timely managing the publication project that produced this book.

The financial support of the FP7-PEOPLE-2012-ITN project 'Changing Employment' ('The changing nature of employment in Europe in the context of challenges, threats and opportunities for employees and employers', project no. 31732) made this research possible, and I would like also to acknowledge the crucial contributions all members of this Marie Skłodowska-Curie Action made to my research through the numerous academic events of the network that provided each time an occasion for constructive comments. My deep thanks to the coordinator of the network Prof. Paul Stewart and to other members who provided feedback to my presentations, commented on earlier versions of my chapters and with whom I had the chance to engage in inspiring conversations; though the list would be too long to name everyone, let me thank Prof. Holm-Detlev Köhler, Prof. Julia Kubisa, Prof. Sonia McKay, Prof. Adam Mrozowicki, Dr Cilla Ross and Prof. Violetta Zentai. I was also given incredibly rich feedback by my former fellow doctoral students in 'Team 2' and wish to thank them warmly: Karima Aziz, Ben Egan, Mateusz Karolak and Radek Polkowski. A heartfelt thank you to Dr Olena Fedyuk, who provided precious guidance to individual and collective research activities within Team 2, for sharing with us her enthusiasm for filmmaking and for her valuable insights into migration and care; her work has been truly inspiring.

This book results from fieldworks conducted in three capital cities: Paris, London and Madrid. In each of these cities my research has been enabled by the kind support of researchers, university departments and civil society organisations. In London, my gratitude goes to the trade union organisers who let me accompany them to care homes across the

London region. An immense thank you to the CSU-CRESPPA research centre in Paris for their welcome; I would like to thank Dr Sylvie Contrepois for her support and Prof. Helena Hirata for our conversations and for her precious help in accessing private care homes in the French capital. In Madrid I had the pleasure to be hosted at the Universidad Complutense and thank Prof. Arturo Lahera Sanchez and Prof. Juan Carlos Revilla warmly for their academic hospitality and their support in accessing care providers. I am also infinitely grateful to Dr Paloma Moré, who introduced me to a group of migrant care workers who welcomed my presence in their ranks for a few months and whose friendliness I dearly remember; I enjoyed every moment with them. Along this journey I have met the most amazing women whose strength and creativity provided comfort, inspiration and emotional resources to navigate the thesis adventure.

I dedicate this book to my parents, Emilia and Bouchta. They achieved so much that they opened up for me a whole new world of possibilities.

I thank my life partner, Jordan, for embarking on this adventure with me without a shadow of a doubt.

On a final note, let me stress once again that this book is the outcome of numerous interactions. I am deeply convinced that all forms of knowledge are co-produced in many ways; I thus thank all the persons with whom I talked about migration, care, gender, racism, precarity and so much more, first and foremost the women and men I met during fieldwork, but also colleagues and friends met at conferences across Europe and over coffee breaks in the various institutions that hosted me, and last but not least, friends and family who joined the conversation and shared their thoughts while taking walks or late at night. I am ultimately indebted to all of them.

Note on Previous Publications

Subsections from Chap. 6 build on parts of Chap. 1 in the volume *Gender, Work and Migration: Agency in Gendered Labour Settings* (2018), which I co-edited with Dr Megha Amrith.

An earlier version of a selection of subsections from Chap. 7 is part of a chapter to be published within the edited volume *Politics of Dis-integration* edited by Michael Collyer, Sophie Hinger and Reinhard Schweitzer in Springer Imiscoe Series under a Creative Commons licence (forthcoming). I thank the editors and other contributors to this volume for the inspiring conversations around 'dis-integration'.

Contents

List of Abbreviations

BAME	Black, Asian and Minority Ethnic
CQC	Care Quality Commission
EEA	European Economic Area
ENAR	European Network Against Racism
EU	European Union
HALDE	High Authority for the Fight Against Discrimination and for Equality (*Haute Autorité de lutte contre les discriminations et pour l'égalité*)
HMRC	Her Majesty's Revenue and Customs
IELTS	International English Language Testing System
ILO	International Labour Organization
NHS	National Health Service
NMDS-SC	National Minimum Data Set for Social Care
NMW	National Minimum Wage
NVQ	National Vocational Qualification
OECD	Organisation for Economic Co-operation and Development
SAAD	System of Autonomy and Dependency Care (*Sistema de Autonomía y Atención a la Dependencia*)
SOVA	Safeguarding of Vulnerable Adults
TUC	Trades Union Congress
UK	United Kingdom

List of Tables

1

Introduction: From the Empirical Study of Care Labour to Feminist Care Ethics

France is a country with rights. So give me my rights. A little bit of rights, because in a way I'm doing something for France. (…) Who will do it? It's not François Hollande [former French President elected in 2012] who will do it, it's not his wife, it's the miserable care assistants. What I do, it's not little, it's really something. (Fouzia, 43, Algeria, Paris)

Fouzia had been living in France for 12 years when I met her. She came to France from Algeria and had been working for a couple of years as a care assistant in domiciliary care at the time of the interview. We met in a Parisian hospital: Fouzia did not have much free time for herself, and the only moment she could dedicate to an interview was when the older woman she took care of was being looked after by other healthcare professionals in the hospital. We talked for about two hours in the busy hallway of the hospital where a small cafeteria served visitors, hospital workers and, more rarely, patients. Fouzia seemed to enjoy talking about her job and conveyed overall a sense of satisfaction and pride. She appeared to be highly engaged, with each story she told she reflected on what constitutes good care and shared with me the challenges she was facing to achieve the standards she had set herself. The pride she took in her daily work was, however, disregarded by her friends, family and society at large. Fouzia's trajectory differs in one significant aspect from most of those portrayed in this book. A former ministry employee in Algeria and a former bank employee in France, Fouzia decided to change her profession after the death of her mother in Algeria, guided by her sense of guilt over not having been able to take care of her. Being in this profession out of choice, Fouzia met with incomprehension from her family, friends and sometimes even the relatives of the older persons she took care of. She felt the importance of her work was not recognised, neither by those close to her nor by the state through its policies. Fouzia lamented her low earnings and the absence of supplementary health insurance, which meant that many medical treatments were only partially covered by social security. She deplored the lack of access to further training, which was contrary to the life-long learning opportunities enshrined in French labour law, as well as the absence of paid leave. These are the rights Fouzia referred to in the opening quotation, and their absence constituted for her the symptom of society's disdain for her work. Fouzia ironically spoke of the 'miserable care assistant' to contrast that figure with the actual importance of her work that in spite of being invisible to most people, including her close ones, indisputably mattered: 'it's really something.'

By exposing this paradox with anger, Fouzia's statement encapsulates the research endeavour of this book. While families increasingly need to rely on paid care to provide for the needs of older relatives, the work of sustaining life is devalued, marginalised and widely disregarded. In the context of ageing populations, increasing participation of women in the labour market, frequent geographical mobility within families, growing marketisation of care provision and, most importantly, global inequalities, migration and paid care work tend to be increasingly connected in western European societies. This growing reliance is furthermore inscribed in broader gender inequalities and racialisation processes.

Projections of the old-dependency ratio hint at the size of the challenge that providing older-age care represents for the future of European societies. The old-dependency ratio (i.e. population of 65 years and over to population of 15–64 years) is estimated to increase by 48% in the UK, 50% in France and 125% in Spain by 2050, reaching 45%, 46% and 48%, respectively, according to 2015 Eurostat figures. In the aftermath of the 2008 financial crisis, the number of foreign-born people working in residential care grew by 44.5% between 2008 and 2012 in European countries of the Organisation for Economic Co-operation and Development (OECD 2013). Older-age care represents one of the few sectors experiencing labour shortages; urban centres are especially affected by these shortages and the reliance on migrant and minority ethnic labour is likely to grow. Against this background, working conditions in the sector remain characterised by low pay, long hours, job instability, health implications and lack of career advancement opportunities. The significant role of migrant and minority ethnic workers in the older-age care sector, symptomatic of the multiple inequalities faced by these workers, is related to the workings of various fields of policy, from the restructuring of European welfare states to migration and employment policies (Williams 2011c). Since the care industry is meant to expand, and the role of migrant workers within it is expected to grow, researching migrant and minority ethnic care workers' experiences contributes to deeper understandings of this central challenge for European societies.

1.1   From Feminised and Racialised Domestic and Care Work to Private Residential Care: Ruptures and Continuities

The role of migrant workers in the care industry has been mostly explored in the literature on migrant domestic workers. While residential older-age care remains under-studied in comparison with the domiciliary setting within migration and care studies, theoretical paradigms developed within this literature significantly contributed to this book. Major works in the field include Anderson's *Doing the Dirty Work? The Global Politics of Domestic Labour* (Anderson 2000) and *Servants of Globalization* by Rhacel Parreñas (2001). In the former, Bridget Anderson uncovered the ways in which migrant women performing domestic work find themselves positioned within multiple tensions. The commodification of domestic work and the role of migrant women within these processes reveal how class and 'race' play out within gendered hierarchies. In the latter, Parreñas problematised the global role of migrant domestic workers, notably through the concept of 'international division of reproductive labour' in her study of Filipina domestic workers in Los Angeles and Rome. The literature has been further developed through monographs, like *Black Girls: Migrant Domestic Workers and Colonial Legacies* by Sabrina Marchetti (2014), and case studies, such as those brought together in the collective volumes *Migration and Domestic Work: A European Perspective on a Global Theme*, edited by Helma Lutz (2008) and *When Care Work Goes Global: Locating the Social Relations of Domestic Work*, edited by Mary Romero, Valerie Preston and Wenona Giles (2014). To wit, an important body of literature provides country- and city-specific knowledge about migrant and minority ethnic care workers in the care sector. In the UK, a pioneering report published by COMPAS researchers in 2009 sketched out the contribution of migrant care workers to the care sector (Cangiano et al. 2009). In addition, a series of publications on this theme by Shereen Hussein, Martin Stevens and Jill Manthorpe analysed the relative position of ethnic minority and migrant care workers in the sector (Hussein et al. 2011; Stevens et al. 2012). Sondra Cuban's (2013) volume offered an ethnographic insight into domiciliary and residential care and a detailed analysis of processes of deskilling. Haren Christensen and Ingrid Guldvik (2014), in their comparative study of migrant care workers in Norway and in the UK, focused on care work with disabled persons and shed light in particular on deskilling through migration policies and power relationships in the work setting. Studies on the role of migrant workers within care in France have so far focused on domiciliary care (Lada 2011). Several specific difficulties emerge when studying the role of migrant and minority ethnic workers in the care sector in the French context. The categorisation of 'social care' familiar to the British context, or that of 'cuidados' in Spain, has no direct equivalent in France (Martin 2008). Care is most often apprehended in academic work through the proxy category of 'services à la personne', which encompasses all services performed as paid economic activity in private households. While it mostly concerns care and domestic work, this statistical category also includes activities such as gardening. This makes it difficult to group together all care-related activities and renders the care sector as such statistically invisible (Jany-Catrice 2013). Finally, two major sector-specific publications offer rich context data on the work of migrant care assistants in Spain (IMSERSO 2005) and in the autonomous region of Madrid more specifically (Rodríguez Rodríguez 2012).

This book draws in particular on the theoretical framework of a transnational political economy of care (Williams 2011a, b) that highlights the intersection of various regimes as defined by Fiona Williams: 'a country's *care regime* intersects with its *migration regime* and its *employment regime* which provides the institutional context that shapes the experiences of both migrant women employed in domestic/care work and their employers, as well as the patterns of migrant care work to be found in different countries' (Williams 2014, p. 17, emphasis in original). The edited volume by Bridget Anderson and Isabel Shutes, *Migration and Care Labour Theory, Policy and Politics* (2014), offers for instance ethnographic insights into case studies on care and domestic work, while contributing to the theorisation of the role of migrants in paid care. In addition, the literature on migration and social reproduction is mobilised to conceptualise the political economy implications of my findings. *Gendered Migrations and Global Social Reproduction* by Eleonore Kofman and Parvati Raghuram (2015) offers an overview of the theoretical developments in this field. Such a global perspective is also adopted by the literature on 'global care chains' (Hochschild 2000; Parreñas 2001; Yeates 2009), a major research theme within studies on migrant care and domestic workers.

On the whole, the literatures briefly presented above tend to focus overwhelmingly on migrant care workers and rarely include minority ethnic workers in their analysis, with the exception of several studies conducted in the UK (Cangiano et al. 2009; Stevens et al. 2012). A focus on migrant workers serves the purposes of illuminating the global politics of migrant labour and of shedding light on the relationship between the 'care deficit' in the so-called Global North and the feminisation of labour migration from the so-called Global South. I argue that these analytical lenses, while important, conceal the role of minority ethnic workers in the sector, and thus the post-colonial continuities and the underpinning racialisation processes through which bodies are categorised, not exclusively in articulation with the migration status. Among participants in this research, minority ethnic workers represented a significant share of the workforce in London and in Paris but not in Madrid, reflecting national differences in terms of migration history and policies. With a primary focus on migrant workers, the design of this research nevertheless included minority ethnic workers in order to grasp differentiated patterns of racialisation. The book thus contributes to the existing literature on migrant care labour by illuminating both the commonalities and the divergences that govern racialisation processes and their material implications for migrant and minority ethnic care workers.

Furthermore, the literature on migrant domestic workers and the global politics of domestic work does not place its primary focus on the care industry. While migrant workers in the domestic sector came to epitomise the multiple inequalities faced by migrant women from the 'Global South', less emblematic sites of work remained somehow on the margins of this field of literature. Situated in the 'private' sphere of the home, research into the experiences, trajectories and role of migrant domestic workers often leaves out an analysis in terms of the industrialisation of care and the content of care work in this specific context. This book, owing to a focus on migrant and minority ethnic workers within marketised older-age residential care (and to a smaller extent in domiciliary care), addresses questions that have attracted less attention in academic scholarship. The institutional context of residential care offers valuable insights into the intersection of migration, employment and care policies. This monograph thus provides cross-national understandings of care work within private residential older-age care, while empirical academic research conducted in these settings tends to concern single-country case studies (Rodriquez 2014; Molinier 2013). What is more, a focus on the marketised sector of older-age care uncovers central but under-researched implications of a shifting political economy of care, notably the increasing corporatisation of care in Europe beyond processes of commodification (Farris and Marchetti 2017).

1.2   A Distinct Theoretical Endeavour: Building Bridges Between the Empirical Study of Care and Feminist Moral Philosophy

Beyond these specific gaps that this monograph contributes to address, the theoretical endeavour undertaken is altogether distinct from most previous research on racialised care workers' trajectories and experiences.

Over the course of the empirical research, the more narratives I heard from participants, the more I sensed the need to deepen the initial gendered political economy framework I had started with. This theoretical framing proved to be key in thinking about intersecting policy fields and their interwoven implications in the lived experiences of racialised care workers. Yet, care workers' voices questioned these oppressions in a singular manner, one that the study of the mechanisms that lead to labour market segmentation or the analysis of migration policies that foster arbitrariness at the workplace level did not account for. There was something in their narratives that transcended their position as racialised care workers, that revealed something about the whole of society, but that at the same was expressed from their specific standpoint. I started to familiarise myself with the literature on the ethics of care and its developments within feminist moral philosophy while I was conducting interviews; the longer I was on fieldwork the more it resonated with the voices of research participants. I had initiated this research with feminist methods of enquiry, notably Dorothy Smith's institutional ethnography (see Chap. 2), which already emphasised the specific epistemological standpoint of participants, but feminist moral philosophy illuminated dimensions of the empirical material that would have otherwise been neglected or silenced. It provided me with the tools to hear what research participants formulated in new ways and to distinguish patterns that I did not expect to find. All along, it has been a very grounded experience, with narratives guiding me in this theoretical journey. Even though much food for thought had been provided by the later elaborations around a feminist ethics of care conceptualised by philosophers and political scientists (Tronto 2013; Sevenhuijsen 1998), reading Gilligan's initial contribution, derived from interviews with girls and women in the context of studies in moral development, felt particularly close to heart. Her work enabled my own analysis in its current form in that 'voices' were central to her book and the theoretical reflections were anchored in empirical studies. Further to Gilligan's contribution, moral philosophers and political scientists (Held 2005; Tronto 2013; Slote 2007; Engster 2007; Robinson 2011) have fruitfully engaged with her research from various perspectives, from political theory to international relations to philosophy of ethics (see Chap. 2). It is however striking, how, over three decades after the publication of Gilligan's *In a Different Voice* (1982/2003), the academic fate of 'an ethic of care' has remained disconnected from empirical enquiry in spite of Gilligan's own methodology. Some researchers in social policy have attempted to apply care ethics to their fields (Sevenhuijsen 1998; Hankivsky 2004; Mahon and Robinson 2011), yet their methodologies did not include ethnographies that would have provided a voice to this ethics. One exception to this is the ethnographic study of a care home published in French by Pascale Molinier (2013), who contributed, along with the philosophers Sandra Laugier and Fabienne Brugère, as well as the political scientist Patricia Paperman, to introduce feminist moral philosophy around care ethics in French academic spheres (Molinier et al. 2009; Brugère 2011; Gilligan et al. 2013).

This book thus proposes to combine the gendered political economy of older-age care from the standpoint of racialised care workers with the philosophical lenses of an ethics of care (Gilligan 1982/2003; Tronto 2013) and by doing so to contribute to a nascent field of literature (Mahon and Robinson 2011; Molinier 2013). As mentioned above, this task is carried out from the standpoint of racialised care workers whose position is here considered as constituting a privileged standpoint for the emergence of knowledge, as argued by feminist standpoint theory in reference to the notion of epistemic privilege (Smith 2005). Adopting this standpoint is also informed by the aspiration of a feminist democratic ethic of care (Tronto 2013) to give voice to those actually providing care within society.

1.3   Chapters' Overview

Participants' trajectories are mirrored in the themes that the book progressively explores as their experiences in the older-age care sector unfold, from entering it, to experiencing various dimensions of care work, to moving up or out of the sector and finally to considerations around social reproduction. Alternatively, the book can be read thematically, in terms of the theoretical conversations the chapters develop, bringing empirical perspectives into the theoretical debates within the care ethics literature and relying on the latter to revisit sociological concepts explored in this research.

Chapter 2 recounts the research journey that resulted in this book. I first outline the feminist methodologies that inspired the research design and describe how fieldwork was concretely conducted in London, Paris and Madrid. I then turn to the analytical frames developed by Fiona Williams for a transnational political economy of care and that I here draw upon to analyse the intersections of migration, employment and older-age care regimes. This chapter equally traces the academic genealogy of the care ethics literature relevant to this book in order to clarify how my research is inspired by feminist moral philosophy and what, in turn, it contributes to specific developments of care ethics.

Chapter 3 summarises relevant contextual elements of the gender, migration, care and employment regimes in the three countries and sets the scene for the political economy analysis developed in the following chapters. While presenting similar features of gendered and racialised labour market segmentation, the three cities and their national contexts present nevertheless significant specificities regarding each type of regime. Following Williams' regime characterisation, Chap. 3 provides an overview of the policy contexts of participants' trajectories and experiences, distinguishing cross-nationally some of the main similarities and differences further explored in the rest of the book.

Chapter 4 scrutinises how participants in this research first entered the older-age care sector. I start out by assessing the role of intermediaries across the three cities. The chapter then considers how specific policies impacted differently participants' trajectories into and within older-age care. A typology of these routes into the care sector is presented according to participants' motives for taking up a care job. I examine in this chapter how labour market segmentation occurs empirically against the background of different sets of intersecting regimes. Drawing on participants' trajectories and secondary data, in the final section of the chapter I focus on a cross-national analysis of the discrepancies of utilitarian migration policies that these insights uncover.

Chapters 5 and 6 examine the concept of precarious employment and work within older-age care combining an approach in terms of political economy and care ethics. After inscribing the analysis of precarious employment in the context of neoliberal economies and care marketisation, Chap. 5 examines participants' experiences of precarious employment through job stability, levels of earnings and rights at work. It highlights how processes of employment precarisation transfer socio-economic costs onto workers and demonstrates the limitations of the usual indicators mobilised in the study of economic precarity. The chapter emphasises the crucial relevance of the meanings that participants attach to their situations beyond general indicators for apprehending the lived experience of precariousness.

In Chap. 6, the very content of care work is brought to the fore in order to analyse work precariousness. Building on existing literature on precarious work and drawing on the care ethics literature, the emotional and physical implications of older-age care work are analysed. This chapter interrogates the concept of emotional labour on the basis of participants' everyday experiences as illustrated by their narratives as well as their discourses around the role of emotions. It equally draws on feminist moral philosophy to account for the complexities encountered in participants' narratives around the ambiguous role of emotions in care work. The chapter argues for a renewed understanding of care work inspired by participants' narratives and conceptualised in conversation with specific tenets of the care ethics literature.

Chapter 7 focuses on participants' perceptions and experiences of racism and discrimination at work; it differentiates between the position of migrant and minority ethnic workers and explores the structural conditions that foster such abuse as well as participants' coping strategies. The cross-national comparison reveals how intersecting inequalities are inflected by diverse institutional practices and how these are symptomatic of different forms of institutional racism embedded in three national contexts. The chapter questions the function of anti-discrimination policies in contemporary neoliberal polities considering participants' daily experiences of racism and their perceptions of such legislation as beyond reach. I interrogate how care ethics' relational ontology can serve to productively transform limited understandings of racism.

Chapter 8 investigates participants' professional mobility and aspirations. I first interrogate the articulation between citizenship acquisition and professional prospects on the one hand and between professional training in the care sector and social mobility on the other. This chapter explores whether racialised care workers intend to remain in the care sector and what they aspire to, both within and outside the older-age care sector. It proposes on this basis a typology of participants' professional aspirations that uncovers how they perceive the opportunity structures available to them. The cross-national analysis enables the identification of differentiated outcomes produced by distinct regime and policy intersections.

In Chap. 9 participants' own caring responsibilities are scrutinised. The chapter studies how care activities outside of their employment are distributed and managed in their daily lives. It explores how by being employed to sustain the social reproduction of families—and thus that of societies—in the Global North, racialised care workers find themselves at the crossroads of a double outsourcing. European migration regimes tend to deny workers' own caring responsibilities and needs, creating gendered inequalities that are further exacerbated by the social implications of precarious employment and work. Bridging care ethics literature and the empirical study of care work is crucial, the chapter argues, to combat care's marginalisation and achieve better distribution of care responsibilities in society.

2

Theoretical Framings: Feminist Standpoints, Gendered Political Economy and New Approaches to Care Ethics

This chapter presents the main theoretical endeavour of this book. While I began from the premise of institutional ethnography and its underpinning standpoint theory, the empirical findings of this research led me to reach out for the literature on the ethics of care with the view of engaging to the fullest with the collected data. If the theoretical frame of the political economy of care proved vital to understanding the intersections of various regimes and the structures of relations, experiences and contestations so produced, explaining these experiences and struggles echoed too strongly with the ethics of care for this conversation to be ignored. This chapter thus recounts the theoretical journey of my research, from initial theoretical assumptions to the conversations in which the book intervenes on the basis of my research's findings.

The first section of the chapter presents the methodology adopted in this research, institutional ethnography and the underpinning notion of standpoint theory. It presents how the social location of 'racialised care worker' came to be constructed as an epistemologically privileged standpoint. The section further outlines how the latter translated into concrete methods and how fieldwork unfolded. The second section clarifies the use of the notion of intersecting gender, migration and care regimes

© The Author(s) 2019
N. Sahraoui, *Racialised Workers and European Older-Age Care*, Thinking Gender in Transnational Times, https://doi.org/10.1007/978-3-030-14397-8_2

for the study of a political economy of care, drawing on Fiona Williams' theoretical framings and strands of the intersectionality literature. The third section presents a selective academic historiography of the concept of care ethics, starting with the initial formulations of Carol Gilligan. Acknowledging the significant developments of the academic literature around an ethic of care, and situating this monograph within the relevant research currents, it engages with a broader scope of authors from moral philosophy, political theory and social policy. The chapter argues for the need to link back with empirical research on care work to foster original developments in the care ethics literature. There is still little scholarship in this field that adopts this focus in spite of the empirically grounded initial contribution of Gilligan. The final section presents how this book sets out to conceptualise an ethic of care from an empirical perspective and how this approach, in turn, contributes to the theory of care ethics.

2.1 Feminist Methodological Inspirations and Fieldwork

Institutional Ethnography and Feminist Standpoint Theory

Institutional ethnography, mainly developed by the Canadian sociologist Dorothy E. Smith, has its starting point in the everyday world. Smith argues that this method of inquiry 'works from the actualities of people's everyday lives and experience to discover the social as it extends beyond experience' (Smith 2005, p. 10). This anchorage in everyday lives and practices is central to institutional ethnography as methodology, Smith emphasised in this regard that ideas and concepts are not only out there but are also embodied: 'thoughts, concepts, beliefs, ideology, et cetera, are not allowed to escape into a metaphysical space set up for them in people's heads and outside their doings. They are also people's doings, their activities' (Smith 2005, pp. 209–210). This approach emphasises that sociological enquiry is necessarily situated in space and time so as to relate to people's activities and their materiality. By starting from a particular location, institutional ethnography avoids taking categories of discourse for granted. From a specific standpoint, institutional ethnography seeks to explicate 'social relations generating characteristic bases of experience in an institutional process' (Smith 1987, p. 176). This echoes strongly with feminist standpoint theory, of which Smith's institutional ethnography is one instance (Smith 1997). A key contribution of feminist standpoint theory is that knowledge is situated and consequently chosen social locations offer different potentialities at the time of understanding specific sets of power relations. Analysing power is central to standpoint theories in that they serve 'to observe and explain patterns in the relations between social power and the production of knowledge claims' (Harding 1997, p. 384). Such analysis, by dissecting the mechanisms of oppression, bears the promise of facilitating social change. In Hartsock's words: 'standpoint theories are technical theoretical devices that can allow for the creation of accounts of society that can be used to work for more satisfactory social relations' (1997, p. 370).

Adopting a specific standpoint, here that of the racialised care workers, serves to achieve a deeper understanding of a specific set of power relations and their manifestations. If the research was first guided by participants' perspectives, it aimed at a broader analysis of patterns of inequality by exploring 'with people their experience of what is happening to them and their doings and how those are hooked up with what is beyond their experience' (Smith 2005, p. 41). Combining institutional ethnography with attention to a set of intersecting regimes (as detailed in Chap. 3) allows relating analytically the data collected at the micro-level with a political economy analysis uncovering the workings of specific oppressions, the 'ruling relations' in Smith's terminology. The feminist attention to the everyday world of racialised care workers produces an intersectional account of their experiences and of the structures within which they are inscribed. Precisely, it is from close attention to the daily experiences of care workers, as recounted in their narratives, that the main tenets of an ethics of care emerged 'in practice'. Methodologically, racialised care workers' voices represent here a specific standpoint.

Constructing the Category of 'Racialised Care Worker' as Standpoint

Before the following section exposes the main ideas underpinning care ethics and situates this book within the existing research strands, I here clarify how the feminist premise of this research first led me to engage with this literature. Taking as the starting point of analysis participants' everyday experiences, I sought to bring care workers' voices to the fore. In the process of engaging with their narratives, the 'secondary dialogue' in Smith's words, voices emerged that formulated a specific ethic of care. Building upon insights from my materials, a new direction of interpretation emerged that I did not foresee at the outset of the research. Though embedded in different settings and carrying different meanings (as I will demonstrate), these discursive practices nevertheless resonated with Gilligan's ground-breaking study *In a Different Voice* (1982/2003).

It is no coincidence that feminist standpoint theory and care ethics literatures speak to each other. Although they have each their own genealogy, all of these contributions reflect a broader shift in social sciences. The academic fate of the care ethics paradigm illustrates the deeper questioning of knowledge production from feminist perspectives that standpoint theory attempted to both grasp and accompany by providing necessary theoretical tools. Yet, it seems paradoxical that in spite of the significant developments of both standpoint theories and the conceptualisation of care ethics, few studies have engaged with care ethics from an empirical perspective.

In this monograph I construct the group of racialised care workers, women in their majority, as constitutive of a specific standpoint. This approach shifts the common focus of feminist standpoint theory on women to a feminised profession, that of care workers. Following standpoint theory premises, it is assumed that the social location of care workers, their daily practices and discourses can illuminate specific axes of oppression and inequality within society. Underpinning this construction is the idea that actually 'doing care' daily provides a unique perspective on the place of care in society. Though the workforce in older-age care is feminised as a contemporary matter of fact, identifying elements of an ethic of care in participants' accounts cannot be equated with feminine voices. Constructing the care sector as representing an epistemologically privileged social position, rather than that of women, avoids glossing over the masculine voices among care workers. Beyond the classical critique of gender essentialisation formulated in relation to care ethics (I come back to this debate in the following section, in Chap. 6 and in the general conclusion), positing racialised care workers as a standpoint offers a valuable empirical insight into Tronto's theoretical statement of care as practice, that is, that providing care materially fosters caring dispositions (Tronto 2013). It also transcends the usual association of care ethics with women's voices since many men, in particular migrant men, are employed in the care sector. This should not conceal the gender dynamics that the participation of men in a feminised sector of the labour market triggers (Gallo and Scrinzi 2016), but from the perspective of the debates that care ethicists have engaged in, constructing 'racialised care workers' as a privileged standpoint offers a fruitful displacement. The following section describes the research design elaborated on the above-mentioned grounds and the fieldwork consequently conducted over a period of over a year.

Research Design and Fieldwork Unfolding in Three European Capital Cities

A major choice in terms of research design was the decision to focus on non-EU and minority ethnic workers, leaving aside intra-European migration. This definition of the scope of the research was motivated by three considerations, mainly: (1) that non-EU workers are concerned with specific migration regimes, shaped by European and national policies; (2) that many studies on migrant care workers do not make the distinction between EU and non-EU migrants (Cuban 2013; Christensen and Guldvik 2014) and thus leave out fields of analysis specific to those workers; and finally (3) that in spite of the differences that exist between non-EU and minority ethnic workers, bringing together these two groups is consistent with the study of postcolonial migrations, a historic continuity downplayed by a focus on migrant care workers only. This research design thus served specific purposes, and while EU migrants are not part of this research's cohort, their role in older-age care in these three cities should be acknowledged, for instance, the significant presence of Polish women in the UK or of Romanian women in Spain.

In terms of geographical field sites, the choice of London, Paris and Madrid is related to their shared status as European capital cities and major urban centres. They crystallise many of the tensions present in contemporary European societies, in general, and in particular the 'care deficit' (Fraser 2016). Though these cities are embedded in three significantly different national contexts as to their migration, employment and care regimes (presented in the following chapter), they are at the forefront of care commodification and marketisation due to the economic and socio-demographic characteristics of these territories (Farris and Marchetti 2017).

To strengthen the comparative dimension of the analysis, I also decided to focus predominantly on one work setting: private residential care. Most participants were thus employed by either for-profit or not-for-profit private care homes. A minority of participants working in domiciliary care were included, not to brush over the overlaps encountered empirically as many participants worked both in domiciliary and residential care either simultaneously or at different points in time (often first within domiciliary care and later on in institutional settings). Similarly, the private care industry was growing in both areas. Rigidly separating residential care would thus have resulted in an artificial divide obscuring the actual experiences of migrant and minority ethnic workers who navigate between the spheres of domiciliary and residential care. Overall, the focus of the analysis remains located in the experiences of migrant and minority ethnic workers in the context of residential care; however, when relevant, the findings chapters bring in the differences attached to both work environments.

The time dedicated to fieldwork was divided into three periods of four to six months at each site of fieldwork, first in London, then in Paris and finally in Madrid. In London, in the context of a research placement with a major union in the UK, I accompanied union organisers on their visits to care homes of the London Region and this constituted the first entry point of my fieldwork. Through snowballing I extended the research to workers employed in care homes where unions were not present. I also participated in community events of the Filipino community, notably around the Sunday mass. In Paris, I was granted access to a major private chain of care homes thanks to the contacts provided by an experienced French researcher. This authorisation opened the door to several care homes of that company in Paris and enabled me to meet care workers employed in these care homes. Here again the snowballing method extended the group of participants beyond those employed by the care providers I had contacted. Finally in Madrid, I similarly initiated contacts with care providers on the one hand and researchers on the other. Expert interviews opened up additional possibilities thanks to the contacts these researchers provided to private care facilities and within the vibrant network of migrants' organisations in Madrid. In parallel, I also met participants through the access granted by a large private not-for-profit care provider, which ran many care homes in Madrid.

In the three sites of fieldwork, interviews were conducted at workplaces, in cafés and in participants' homes. Most interviews lasted about one hour, ranging from half an hour to over two hours. With the daily experiences of migrant and minority ethnic care workers at the heart of the research project, semi-structured in-depth interviews appeared to be the most suitable method for data collection. The topic guide covered the following themes: current employment situation; work content; training and career opportunities; managerial relationships; security, stability and protection at work; employment history; migration status and history; bullying and harassment; transport to work; family situation and caring arrangements. At the end of each interview, I also asked participants to fill out a questionnaire in the form of mostly closed-ended questions. The questionnaire gathered information about participants' demographic characteristics (age, gender, nationality) and migration history (migration status, length of residence), as well as information about their employment (job title, employer type, contract, earnings, benefits, job tenure, job stability and union membership). At the end of the fieldwork phase, I had collected 82 interviews with care assistants, 13 with nurses in supervisory roles and care home managers and 18 expert interviews (including industry representatives, trade union officers, researchers, and NGO and migrant association activists) for a total of 113 semi-structured interviews. Importantly, in addition to the interviews, I have spent many informal moments with a reduced number of research participants in each city. I also joined collective activities organised by migrant associations from demonstrations to training sessions to cultural events and informal get-togethers. I conducted interviews in English, French and Spanish. All interviews with care workers were fully transcribed; I coded them in their original languages and translated the chosen quotes into English.

In London, all respondents were employed in private residential care. In Paris and in Madrid, a minority of respondents were employed by private providers of domiciliary care or directly by families (5 and 8, respectively) and the majority was employed in private residential care (25 and 19, respectively). Most respondents were women in all three sites of fieldwork, but the proportions of men and women varied: 19 women and 6 men in London, 26 women and 4 men in Paris and 23 women and 4 men in Madrid. The average age of research participants was the lowest in London, 37, with an age range of 20 to 60. In Paris the average age was slightly higher, 40, and ages ranged from 25 to 59. In Madrid the average was the highest, 42, and ages ranged from 25 to 56. In terms of countries of origin, the methods implemented resulted in a significant diversity of origins thanks to the multiplication of fieldwork entry points (Table 2.1).

Table 2.1 Participating care workers' countries of origin

	London (*n* = 25)	Paris (*n* = 30)	Spain (*n* = 27)
Countries of origin	The Philippines (8)	Cameroon (6)	Ecuador (11)
	Born in the UK (3)	Guadeloupe, FR (5)	Peru (5)
	Somalia (2)	Ivory Coast (4)	Colombia (2)
	Mauritius (2)	Senegal (4)	Morocco (2)
	Bangladesh (2)	Guinea (2)	Cameroon (1)
	India (2)	Born in metropolitan	Nicaragua (1)
	China (1)	France (2)	El Salvador (1)
	Rwanda (1)	Reunion Island (2)	Cabo Verde (1)
	Nigeria (1)	Morocco (1)	Paraguay (1)
	Uganda (1)	Tunisia (1)	Cuba (1)
	Ghana (1)	Algeria (1)	Born in Spain (1)
	Sierra Leona (1)	Myanmar (1)	
		Martinique, FR (1)	

Source: Own data and elaboration

As a woman in my late 20s with a university degree, raised in France to Moroccan and Polish parents, my interactions with research participants were embedded in different power relations resulting from the encounter between my positionality, their own and our perceptions of our respective social locations. In Paris for instance, it seemed that I was in some social situations perceived as 'white' and in others as 'minority ethnic'. My positionality further varied across field sites. On the whole, my position as a foreigner in London and in Madrid contributed, I believe, to creating a more trusting environment. An encounter of different subjectivities, these variations illustrate that knowledge is co-produced through the interview process.

The endeavour to relate everyday experiences to 'ruling relations' requires attention to concrete elements of context and methods designed to analyse the latter: these are presented in the following section. Framing this research within a gendered political economy of older-age care provides a backbone to understand specific structures of relations and the experiences inscribed in these settings.

2.2   Understanding Ruling Relations Through Intersecting Regimes

Theoretical Framing of the Gendered Political Economy of Older-Age Care

This research was guided by a double commitment: attention to the everyday world of migrant and minority ethnic care workers and the intention to provide a political economy analysis of their experiences. For this purpose, I set out to analyse specific 'ruling relations' (Smith 2005) through the theoretical tools of a transnational political economy of care (Williams 2011a, b). This approach relies on the idea of intersecting regimes. Borrowed from Gøsta Esping-Andersen's categorisation of welfare regimes (1990/2013), the term covers 'the organization and the corresponding cultural codes of social policy and social practice in which the relationship between social actors (state, labour market and family) is articulated and negotiated' (Lutz 2008). Included in this definition are 'clusters of policies, practices, legacies, discourses, social relations and forms of contestation' (Williams 2012, p. 371). Importantly, the notion of regime does not imply a top-down analysis but includes grassroots forms of organisation and conjectural mobilisations, be it individual or collective. The migration regime as an analytical tool is for instance concerned both with regulative practices and the attached normative frames as well as with practices fostered by migrants' agency (Rass and Wolff 2018). Table 2.2 presents the indicators attached to each regime as elaborated by Fiona Williams (2012, pp. 371–372). The following chapter sketches out the main characteristics of these regimes for each of the three countries.

In addition to the migration, care and employment regimes, the feminisation of the workforce and its implications requires attentiveness to what Helma Lutz and Ewa Palenga-Möllenbeck name the 'gender regime'. They argue that 'household and care work organization can be seen as the expression of a specifically gendered cultural script in which tasks and responsibilities are coded as either feminine or masculine' (Lutz and Palenga-Möllenbeck 2011, p. 350). Gender regimes are here conceived of as over-arching discursive norms and material practices traversing care, employment and migration regimes. Beyond existing differences, the main tenets of a patriarchal gender regime, relevant to all three countries, are described in the following chapter.

At the heart of a transnational political economy approach lies the idea of intersecting regimes whereby discourse, policies and practices intersect, producing distinct constraints, experiences and contestations. Referring to the literature on intersectionality, I clarify below the use of the notion of intersection and of constructed social categories for the purpose of analysing how multiple patterns of inequality are articulated.

Intersections at Multiple Levels and Strategic Use of Categorisations

The notion of 'intersecting regimes' draws on the literature developed around theories of intersectionality. Within this current, many authors

Table 2.2 Fiona Williams' regime indicators for cross-national comparison

Care regime	Migration regime	Employment regime
(a) The extent of care provision for children under school age, older and disabled people; (b) whether it is provided by the public, voluntary or private sectors and how that mirrors the balance between formal and informal care; (c) the instruments used—For example direct payments, care allowances, cash benefits, tax credits; (d) the gendered and racialised basis of the care workforce, its hierarchies of skill and the relationship of these to workers' remuneration; (e) the histories of care policies and the relational practices of care/domestic work in the home; (f) 'care cultures', that is, dominant national and local cultural discourses on what constitutes appropriate care and who should provide it; (g) Political negotiation and struggle at supranational, national and local policy-making levels.	(a) Immigration policies—Rules permitting country entrance and exit as well as special arrangements such as quotas for care/domestic workers, bilateral arrangements, and rules in relation to skills, gender and family dependents; (b) residency, settlement and naturalisation rules in combination with social, economic, political, legal and civil rights; (c) national norms and practices governing relationships between majority and minority groups and anti-discriminatory laws against discrimination or for multiculturalism; (d) the extent of mobilisation of migrant worker activity through advocacy groups and trade unions as well as international non-governmental organisations; (e) National and transnational histories, for example, colonialism, old trade routes and shared political, economic or religious alliances.	(a) Existing labour market divisions in terms of gender, ethnicity, migration and nationality; (b) the impact of deregulation in shaping precarious employment in the migrant care labour market; (c) how far forms of social protection such as eligibility for unemployment and sickness benefits, pensions, minimum wage and rights attached to care responsibilities are extended to migrant care workers; (d) discourses, policies and cultural practices around work-life balance; (e) the forms of political mobilisation and policy negotiation at national and supranational levels; (f) National histories' dependence on and the treatment of migrant and indentured labour.

Source: Table based on Williams (2012, pp. 371–372)

have stressed the need for methodological clarification, given that the concept has proved to be particularly productive but equally fuzzy (McCall 2005; Choo and Ferree 2010; Walby 2007; Winker and Degele 2011). Intersectionality is born out of the claim that multiple forms of oppression are not additive but mutually constitutive. While this fundamental idea has underpinned some sociological work prior to the emergence of the label 'intersectionality', its conceptualisation and translation into an operational paradigm was put forward most clearly by Black feminists. The term itself has been coined by Kimberlé Crenshaw, who argued that oppression was qualitatively different for women who find themselves in different positions, given that 'race', gender and class intersect (Crenshaw 1989). It is thus the interpenetration of social phenomena that is at the heart of intersectional analysis (Brah and Phoenix 2004) and intersectionality encourages reflection on the use of social categories and its implications (Choo and Ferree 2010).

Failing to question constructed categorisations threatens the analytical enterprise of uncovering the ruling relations; a reflexive approach to social categories is thus key to the study of power. Leslie McCall identifies, within intersectional approaches, the anti-categorical complexity that rejects categories and deconstructs them, the intracategorical complexity that 'focus[es] on particular social groups at neglected points of intersection' (2005, p. 1774), and finally the intercategorical complexity which focuses on relationships of inequality among social groups as already constructed, and makes provisional use of these categories (ibid.). Depending on the level of analysis, a certain use of socially constructed categories is hardly avoidable (McCall 2005). In this book, I make use of several existing social categories such as 'migrant' or 'minority ethnic', while questioning the relevance of these categories in the findings chapters both theoretically (e.g. for a discussion on the concept of 'minority ethnic' and 'racialised' worker, see Chap. 7) and empirically (e.g. for a discussion around meanings attached to migration statuses, see Chap. 8).

Furthermore, while intersectionality is often identified with research on intersecting identities, its contributions go beyond this dimension and are relevant to different levels of analysis. One such approach emphasises processes as focal for analysis: 'The process model of intersectionality places primary attention on context and comparison at the intersections as revealing structural processes organizing power' (Choo and Ferree 2010, p. 11). This resonates with the methodological approach of institutional ethnography that seeks to uncover the 'ruling relations' deriving from everyday experiences, as presented above. In addition, the contextual dimension of such process-centred analysis requires an emphasis on historicity: 'the intersection does not denote specific places occupied by individuals or groups (e.g. working-class black women). It is a process; for example, "class" takes on racialised or gendered inflections for specific people in specific places and times within the arenas of organisation, representation, intersubjectivity and experience' (Anthias 2012, p. 13). Following Floya Anthias, intersectionality is thus here understood as an 'intersectional framing', rather than an 'intersectionality theory', serving the purpose of a 'heuristic device for understanding boundaries and hierarchies of social life' (2012, p. 4). The description of gender, migration, care and employment regimes in the following chapter, constituting the context to a gendered political economy of care, is inscribed within this broader intersectional approach.

In what follows, I summarise some of the main tenets of the care ethics literature and most importantly I present how this book engages with this literature and contributes to the conceptualisation of care ethics.

2.3 Classic and New Approaches to Care Ethics

Gilligan's Initial Formulation of an 'Ethic of Care'

The particular development of feminist moral philosophy relevant to this book is rooted in the paradigm shift initiated by Carol Gilligan in her book *In a Different Voice*. In the field of psychology, Carol Gilligan questioned Lawrence Kohlberg's moral development theory and uncovered the gendered bias of his conceptualisation by shedding light on the unheard voices of women (Gilligan 1982/2003). Gilligan argued that men achieved higher moral development scores due to the gendered scale of assessment that focused on rights and rules while the 'different voice' of women emphasised relationships and responsibilities, a tone illegible to the masculinised theory of moral development prevalent at that time in the discipline of psychology. In her terms: 'though the truth of separation is recognized in most developmental texts, the reality of continuing connection is lost or relegated to the background where the figures of women appear' (ibid., p. 155). Presented with Heinz's dilemma, the two participants of Gilligan's famous case study, Amy and Jack, articulated significantly different answers. Amy formulated a 'narrative of relationships that extends over time' (ibid., p. 28) thinking about the posed dilemma in terms of communication, human connection and relationships, while Jack framed the problem as a conflict between life and property to be mediated by law. Gilligan's study of women's abortion decisions sheds further light on how lived experiences of connection and responsibility shift over time and how care for others and self-care is negotiated, whereby context is everything and no universal principle holds. On this topic, the analysis of a young woman's narrative brings Gilligan to the following conclusion: 'responsibility now includes both self and other, viewed as different but connected rather than as separate and oppressed' (ibid., p. 147). Overall, Gilligan demonstrates how women's moral development, starting from the hypothesis of attachment, negotiates separation arising from the need for personal integrity, while men's moral development comes to question equality and reciprocity by experiencing difference and connection. The subsequent developments of Gilligan's initial formulation of an ethic of care prove the ground-breaking shifts that her arguments triggered. However, fierce critiques have been formulated and continue to be reproduced in scholarly accounts of the paradigm's theoretical lives (Hankivsky 2004; Slote 2007). The major critique concerns the essentialisation of men and women by ascribing feminine and masculine traits and thus fixed gender identities. Most critiques seem however to gloss over the nuances that Gilligan introduced already in the first edition of her study. In the very first pages of the study, she emphasises that if 'association with women is an empirical observation', this interpretation does not 'represent a generalization about either sex' (ibid., p. 2). This nuance is significant: at the time of Gilligan's study men and women tended to articulate different responses to moral dilemmas, which, if one acknowledges the performativity of different socialisations, comes as no surprise. Nothing in Gilligan's study indicates that these discourses might or should be the same over time and generations. Since her research, it is highly probable that men and women's attitudes towards attachment and separation in the USA, where the study was originally conducted, have changed. Rather than essentialising men and women, I argue that Gilligan's study uncovers the psychological implications of gendered models of upbringing and socialisation. Engaging with her findings from a different starting point, that of racialised care workers constructed as a privileged standpoint, neutralises some of the initial critiques and expands on the initial insights.

In the following section, I address some of the debates that have accompanied the development of the care ethics literature and review its contributions to a series of themes relevant to this book.

Beyond Liberal Ethics: Care Ethics Within Feminist Moral Philosophy and Political Theory

The common foundation of political theories and feminist moral philosophy inspired by care ethics crystallises in the critique of the autonomous individual as central to liberal political thought. The relational ontology of an ethic of care achieves alternative understandings of the polity and of society. In *Moral Boundaries*, Joan Tronto considers Gilligan's contribution from the perspective of moral philosophy (Tronto 1993). Her theorisations uncover the political potential of Gilligan's contribution. Starting from the ontological assumption that human beings are not independent but permanently *in relationships*, an 'ethic of care' conceives of all humans as vulnerable and fragile and as both recipients and givers of care (Tronto 2011a). A feminist ethic of care thus argues for 'a recognition of connection and dependence as part of human life and moral subjectivity without, on the other hand, reifying them as "natural", or glorifying them as sources of moral goodness' (Sevenhuijsen 1998, p. 63). In contrast with care ethicists who assume higher morality of care itself (Slote 2007; Engster 2007), I argue with Selma Sevenhuijsen and others (Robinson 2011; Nguyen Minh et al. 2017) that revealing the marginalisation of care in political thought does not equate with assuming higher moral grounds for care. From a feminist perspective, one needs to acknowledge that 'relations of care are not always good or pure' and that consequently 'part of the job of the care ethicist is to consider the conditions under which relations can, and often do, become relations of domination, oppression, injustice, inequality, or paternalism' (Robinson 2011, p. 5). And yet, foregrounding a relational ontology uncovers dimensions of human lives obscured by the liberal assumption of autonomous individuals.

The 'ethic of care', defined on the basis of a relational ontology, thus seems to conflict with an 'ethic of justice' derived from the Kantian philosophical tradition and the Rawlsian model of justice. There is no consensus within the literature on care ethics as to the nature of the relationship between these two ethics. Some argue for an integration of the ethic of care within the liberal framing of rights, so as to temper the shortcomings of an ethic of justice (Okin 1989; Kymlicka 2002; Slote 2007; Engster 2007). Such an understanding, however, fails to address adequately the paradigm shift that a relational ontology operates and only adds a caring touch to a liberal model whose ideal remains individuals' independence and autonomy, understating fundamental differences between the two ethics (Hankivsky 2004). Arguments developed in this book from an empirical perspective demonstrate in this regard the far-reaching implications of the paradigm shift contained within an ethic of care and the missed opportunity that mere assimilation of an ethic of care into an ethic of justice would represent. I illustrate in what follows the differences between the two ethics following chosen tenets of care ethics.

In contrast to the universal principles of a liberal ethic of justice, context, specific relationships and embodied experiences are primary within an ethic of care. An ethic of care is, by definition, situated. Care ethicists concur in emphasising the importance of context within care ethics: the moral agent in the ethics of care stands with both feet in the real world (Sevenhuijsen 1998, p. 59). Applying care ethics to social policy, Olena Hankivsky calls 'contextual sensitivity' an 'attentiveness to the complexity and relational qualities of individual lives' (2004, p. 32). In contrast to a liberal ethic that endorses universal principles, an ethic of care requires the specificity of a given situation to be acknowledged: spatial and time contexts, relationships and materiality.

Another fundamentally different proposition of care ethics when compared to liberal ethics is the idea that individuals are and become through relationships without a 'true self' that could be extracted from social life. Care, in this perspective, constitutes an ability developed in relation to others, to different degrees according to one's given social location. Sevenhuijsen conceptualises this idea with the notion of a 'processual self': 'a self which is continually in the process of being formed; moral identity is continually being developed and revised through this process. The constructing of moral identities is thus, in this sense, inherently a social practice' (1998, p. 56). Caring is thus by no means an essentialised attribute of a specific gender, rather, care is a practice and dispositions are shaped by practices. In her political treatise, Joan Tronto argues: 'attentiveness to needs can and must itself be trained' (2013, p. 49).

Far from conceptualising care as practice, in the neoliberal version of liberal democracies, care is thought of as resulting from individuals' choices. However, neoliberalism's emphasis on individual choices obscures the non-marketised work and relationships that sustain society and its reproduction. The neoliberal society effectively undermines the possibilities for a fairer distribution of care responsibilities, both ideologically and materially, in that it posits individual responsibility as a consequence of individuals' autonomy and independence. This very limited understanding of responsibility reduced to the scale of the individual, as if no collective outcomes were produced by the accumulation of individual choices, fails to acknowledge interdependency and reinforces the illusion of individuals' independence. Hankivsky argues in this regard that an ethic of care entails 'a responsibility to make connections regarding how those around us are affected by our actions. It is about considering how decisions affect *real* people and their lived experiences' (2004, p. 38, emphasis in original).

Finally, coming to the core of the political theory, care ethics is equally productive for thinking about citizenship and democracy. The marginalisation of care in most contemporary scholarship about citizenship is a patent fact (Sevenhuijsen 1998; Tronto 2013). Yet, without an explicit association of care with citizenship, the place of care in liberal societies is deemed to remain marginal. Having engaged with care ethics from the perspective of international relations, Fiona Robinson argues for 'the rec-

ognition of care as the very basis of active citizenship and human security'
(2011, p. 84), a sine qua non condition for changing models of masculin-
ity and femininity more in line with a fairer distribution of care responsibilities and more conducive to sustainable peace. Arguably, the most
comprehensive development of a democratic political thought around
care ethics is proposed in Tronto's *Caring Democracy*. Tronto elaborates
what she calls 'a feminist democratic ethic of care'. Her argument, that
'democratic politics should center upon assigning responsibilities for care'
(Tronto 2013, p. 7), relates the question of the place of care in current
societies to the workings of democracy, sustaining that bringing care into
the centre of society is necessary to satisfy the conditions of a democratic
society. Tronto goes beyond acknowledging an equal contribution of the
language of rights and justice and that of care and responsibilities in the
formation of morality; she draws out the implications of the ontological
shift achieved by an 'ethic of care' to redefine democracy and justice altogether. By stating that leaving care outside the democratic discussion and
assigning caring responsibilities to non-citizens undermines democracy,
she poses the conditions for a renewed conversation around care.

Overall, and strikingly so in spite of Gilligan's empirical endeavour
from which the initial conceptualisation of an ethic of care emerged, few
care ethicists have engaged with empirical studies. In the following
section, I present the theoretical undertaking of this book, at the crossroads of feminist moral philosophy and empirical studies of care work.

Contributing to Care Ethics from Empirical
Perspectives: Building New Research Paths

Apart from studies that have applied this paradigm to social policy
(Sevenhuijsen 1998; Hankivsky 2004; Mahon and Robinson 2011), the
care ethics literature developed entirely in theoretical realms. A notable
exception is Pascale Molinier's book *Le travail du care* (in French) whose
author mobilised the care ethics literature in her ethnographic research
project conducted in a care home for older persons in Paris. Her book
focuses on the voices of care workers, from which an ethic of care
inscribed in their everyday work emerges, but conflicts with institutional

and professional dynamics implemented by management on one level and social care policies on another. Molinier links care workers' discourses with feminist moral philosophy and by doing so she constructs care workers' narratives as epistemologically privileged in that their voices become the beating heart of an ethic of care. Her ethnography constitutes a significant contribution to the conversation between philosophers, psychologists and sociologists around care ethics. This book feeds into this nascent field of literature by continuing the conversation, on the one hand around themes beyond those explored by Molinier, and on the other by situating the analysis within a gendered political economy framework. I argue for renewed contributions to the care ethics literature from the perspectives of those having taken on to provide various forms of care in contemporary societies. I see the two dimensions, carers' own narratives around care and a political economy analysis of the latter, as inseparable to satisfy care ethics' emphasis on context and its conceptualisation of care as practice and responsibility, leading *in fine* to a redefinition of citizenship and democracy altogether. Given the unequal distribution of caring responsibilities within the current political economy of care, the experiences of racialised care workers need to be foregrounded in this enterprise.

First, most obviously, this book links care ethics back to people's doings and practices by engaging with this current of feminist moral philosophy from the viewpoint of racialised care workers' experiences. As stated above, the subsequent developments of the care ethics paradigm have remained theoretical, or if applied, limited to the field of social policy and thus disconnected from daily practices around care with the exception of Molinier's study of a Parisian care home. In this book, Chap. 6 highlights that the care ethic paradigm is to be found in care workers' narratives and argues that their voices need to be brought back into the formulation of the main assumptions of a feminist democratic ethic of care.

Second, this book contributes to the conceptualisation of care as a practice. For the overwhelming majority of participants, including women and men, working in the care sector represented a constrained choice resulting from a lack of opportunities (see Chaps. 4 and 8). Yet, they articulated in their narratives an ethic of care that emerged from their daily activities of caring for older persons. To be sure, my emphasis on these dimensions of their narratives should conceal neither the power relationships that a care interaction might entail, nor the conditions under which care is provided that might be exploitative. Yet, I argue that adopting the specific standpoint of racialised care workers contributes in a unique way to thinking about the relationship between caring dispositions and the daily provision of care. If Tronto insists on the necessity of training one's attentiveness to needs for caring attitudes to arise (2013), little is said about how this is achieved empirically. Analysing care workers' narratives reveals how caring attitudes result indeed from daily practices, that is, changing social locations and fluid gender identities. Care workers' attentiveness to needs is produced by their material practices and, symmetrically, the ignorance of such needs among those groups in society who have extracted themselves from caring responsibilities is equally produced by specific material contexts. Empirical insights into how those in charge of a major share of care provision within society thus not only shed light on the unequal distribution of care responsibilities but also reveal how both caring attitudes and indifference are produced by the material conditions organising care provision.

Third, I revisit specific empirical findings in the light of care ethics. In Chaps. 5 and 6, I bridge the sociological literature on precarious work and life with the care ethics perspective on life precariousness. The notion of the 'precariousness of life' (Perez Orozco 2014) developed in relation to care ethics broadens the scope of analysis of precarious employment and work and illuminates the ways in which paid work in older-age care is specifically precarious. Thus, drawing on the care ethics literature leads to a critique of classical conceptualisations of precarious employment, foregrounding the importance of lived experiences and of the subjective meanings attached to it. In Chap. 7, I suggest a new reading of racism and in particular anti-discrimination legislation building upon care ethics' deeper understanding of responsibility than the one a liberal ethic allows for. I argue that the main tenets of the concept of institutional racism are reinforced when anchored in a relational ontology. Such a paradigm shift leads to a critique of the shortcomings of anti-discrimination policies and illuminates potential transformations that care ethics can achieve within political theory. Again, this analysis is embedded in the concrete experiences of racism narrated by migrant and minority ethnic care workers.

The following chapter presents an overview of the main characteristics of the gender, migration, care and employment regimes in the UK, France and Spain in order to provide the necessary contextual elements to an intersectional analysis of participants' situated experiences.

3

Setting the Scene: A Gendered and Transnational Political Economy of Older-Age Care

This chapter provides an overview of the main characteristics of the gender, migration, care and employment regimes in the UK, France and Spain to provide the context to a gendered political economy of older-age. Before the following chapters explore how the intersections of these regimes produce specific structures of relations, experiences and contestations, this chapter presents defining features of these regimes and explores some of their similarities and differences cross-nationally.

Drawing on the transnational political economy of care framework developed by Fiona Williams, this chapter equally includes gender regimes (Lutz and Palenga-Möllenbeck 2011) in this multi-layered frame. The chapter starts out by outlining how the gender regime, and more specifically patriarchy, influences the place, understanding and meanings of care in society. It continues with the migration regime, here conceptualised as formed by three sets of norms and practices described as the immigration, minority and anti-discrimination regimes. The chapter moves then to a description of the different 'care mixes' that characterise the three countries and it analyses the growing role of private providers in older-age care in all three cases. Employment regimes, and the older-age care sector in particular, also display fundamental commonalities in spite

N. Sahraoui, *Racialised Workers and European Older-Age Care*, Thinking Gender in Transnational Times, https://doi.org/10.1007/978-3-030-14397-8_3

of the different industrial relations models in which they are inscribed. On a final note, this chapter zooms into the local political economy of migrant and minority ethnic care workers in London, Paris and Madrid presenting the capitals' context for racialised labour within the older-age care sector.

3.1   Gender Regimes: The Highly Determining Structure of Patriarchy

The gender regime, defined as the ways in which 'tasks and responsibilities are coded as either feminine or masculine' (Lutz and Palenga-Möllenbeck 2011, p. 350), assigns caring responsibilities primarily to women within the domestic sphere in all three countries studied here, relying on, and at the same time reinforcing, stereotypes around the caring skills of women. Care work remains associated in contemporary European societies with women's work and with a labour of love (Folbre 2012). Feminist sociologists have de-constructed the public/private divide, reflected upon its function in patriarchal and capitalist societies and uncovered its gendered implications (Delphy 2013; Federici 2012). Reproductive labour has been conceived of as women's responsibility in the bourgeois model of the family that emerged in the nineteenth century, and the feminisation of the labour market in the twentieth century left men's disengagement from household work and caring duties mostly unaffected. Rather, the burden was placed on other women as pointed out by the literature on global care chains (Hochschild 2000) or the international division of reproductive labour (Parreñas 2000). The emancipation of middle-class women is indeed indebted to the subordination of working-class, migrant and minority ethnic women. The cultural imaginaries attached to these inequalities were clearly transposed to the labour market. Empirical research in the UK has, for instance, demonstrated that within the care sector, the closer the roles are to direct care, the more the workforce is feminised (Shutes 2011). The labour market being embedded in society as a whole, gender inequalities are not only consubstantial with the labour market, but the workings of the labour market actually rely on these very inequalities. As argued by feminist sociologists since the 1970s (Delphy 2013), patriarchal capitalist societies hinge on women's work in the domestic sphere for the reproduction of the labour force. The feminisation of the care sector is thus the outcome of deeply rooted cultural norms: 84% in Ile-de-France (Pardini 2013); 87.9% in the UK[1]; and over 90% in Spain (León 2010).[2] Beyond slight differences in proportions, the extent of this feminisation reflects the social weight of gender roles and its implications in terms of labour market segmentation.

In addition, the construction of care work as feminised underpins the gendered bias on which the concept of 'skill' relies. The public/private divide has confined non-paid care to the private realm and associated it with feelings of love. Notions of 'skill' and 'profession' are fully embedded in the 'public' realm and have thus been constructed in opposition to the 'private' realm, which supposedly revolves around personalised relations and feelings. A structuring dynamic in professional hierarchies, this constructed binary is highly performative. The more a skill is seen as technical, a celebration of post-Enlightenment values of individuality and rationality, the higher it scores in the race to professionalism. In contrast, the more an occupation is associated with women's unpaid work, the less it deserves to be seen as skilled. Barbara Ehrenreich and Dreidre English have demonstrated how, in parallel to the progressive emergence of modern medical science, the knowledge of women who were involved in medicine was marginalised, notably through fierce legal battles, and women could only re-enter the healthcare professional hierarchy in the lowest positions (aides and nurses) where they were 'alienated from the scientific substance of their work, restricted to the "womanly" business of nurturing and housekeeping' (1973/2010, p. 27). The relegation of women at the bottom of medical professional hierarchies to occupations deemed more caring than technical (nurses and care workers vs. doctors and surgeons) unfolded in spite of the knowledge accumulated by women

---

[1] NMSD-SC database last accessed August 3rd, 2015: https://www.nmds-sc-online.org.uk/report-engine/GuestDashboard.aspx?type=Gender.

[2] The care sector includes for the British figure care assistants and senior care workers in domiciliary and residential care. The French figure is based on the share of women among healthcare assistants (aides-soignantes) in the Paris region. The Spanish figure concerns the domestic care sector.

in the medical sphere prior to its formalisation (Ehrenreich and English 1973/2010).

This section outlined broad trends produced by patriarchal gender regime in the UK, France and Spain, the following one breaks down the analysis per country and per sets of relations in relation to what concerns immigration histories and legislations, minority formations and 'models' of integration, and anti-discrimination discourses and practices. All of the three aspects—immigration, minority and anti-discrimination— form part of the migration regime and are relevant to the experiences of racialised care workers, including here migrant and minority ethnic workers.

3.2   Immigration, Minority and Anti-discrimination Regimes: Commonalities and Variations

Immigration Regimes: The Absence of Legal Routes into Care Employment for Non-EU Workers

Immigration regimes come to play an essential role in migrant workers' trajectories and individual decision-making. The notion of immigration regimes includes here national policies and discourses around multiculturalism. The UK, France and Spain are former colonial empires whose colonial history played a role in shaping their migration policies to date. The UK has a long immigration history that goes back, for the modern period, to the Irish and Russian Jewish workers who came in the nineteenth century. France has been an immigration country since the late nineteenth century. Already in the 1920s, foreigners represented 7% of the population (Noiriel 1988) and came mainly from Belgium, Italy, Spain and Poland. The economic crisis in the 1930s and the Second World War led to a decline before new migration waves resumed after 1945. In the post-war period migration patterns changed, European migration was mainly Portuguese and colonial and postcolonial migration corridors grew, with increasing migration from North Africa (mainly

Algeria and Morocco), South East Asia (Cambodia, Laos, Vietnam) and French overseas territories such as Guadeloupe and Martinique. Nowadays, one in four persons in France has an immigrant parent or grandparent (Tribalat 2004). Spain, in contrast, used to be an emigration country, and Latin and Caribbean countries, formerly under Spanish rule, represented a destination of migration for Spaniards since the sixteenth century (Anton José et al. 2010). After the Second World War Spanish workers migrated to Western Europe, to countries such as France, Germany and Switzerland. Only in the mid-1980s did migration flows to Spain begin to rise and they increased significantly throughout the 1990s (Solé and Parella 2003). Table 3.1 presents the share of migrants in the population of each of these countries as well as the four main countries of origin in each case.

Against this background, London, Paris and Madrid represent cosmopolitan cities with a significant share of migrants. The foreign-born population represented 37% of the Inner London population and 33% of the Outer London population in 2013.[3] In Paris and in Madrid, the share of those born abroad was, respectively, 15% and 15.5% in 2012.[4] Another point relevant to the comparison is the EU/non-EU line of division amongst migrants in the context of the European Schengen space of free movement. In the three countries under study here, there exist simultaneously at least two migration regimes, one designed for EU nationals

Table 3.1 Immigrant population in the UK, France and Spain

	UK	France	Spain
Immigrant population	5.2 million in 2014, that is, 8% of total population	5.6 million in 2011, that is, 9% of total population	5 million in 2013, that is, 11% of total population
Main countries of origin	India, Poland, Pakistan, Republic of Ireland[a]	Algeria, Morocco, Portugal, Italy	Romania, Morocco, the UK, Ecuador

Source: OECD (2015), own compilation
[a]http://www.ons.gov.uk/ons/dcp171776_414724.pdf. Last accessed February 2016

---

[3] http://www.migrationobservatory.ox.ac.uk/briefings/migrants-uk-overview, last accessed February 2016.

[4] http://ec.europa.eu/eurostat/statistics-explained/index.php/Migration_and_migrant_population_statistics, last accessed February 2016.

and another for the third country nationals according to EU terminology. This supposes two very different sets of rights and entitlements with differentiated implications for migrant workers according to their country of origin. In spite of the overarching European framework, these migration regimes specific to 'third nationals' present national specificities, notably in that they coincide with various degrees of capitalist utilitarianism and different forms of postcolonial racialisation. National migration policies implemented by individual European countries facilitate non-EU migration for the 'highly skilled' with paths to permanent migration, whereas 'low-skilled' migration is strictly limited, sector-specific and temporary (Stasiulis 2008). This outlook reproduces a gendered understanding of what constitutes a 'skill' in that it labels as unskilled all social reproduction-related work, notably care and paid household activities. If all European migration regimes rely to a certain extent on a categorisation of migrants according to their skills and the potential use of these skills in the national economy, it is certainly the British immigration points-based system that has pushed this logic the furthest. As a consequence, it is very difficult to migrate to the UK for work purposes from outside the EU unless one holds a qualification mentioned in the occupation shortage list, is highly skilled (according to the government's classification) or plans to invest in the British economy. Illustrative of this logic is the introduction of a £35,000 salary threshold for non-EU migrant workers that came into effect in April 2016.[5] The Royal College of Nursing has warned against the threat this created to the possibility of thousands of non-EU migrant nurses being able to remain in the UK.[6] Not surprisingly, non-EU migrant care workers' wages do not reach this threshold either. Deemed unskilled, care work is not on the shortage list. As a consequence, while the sector hinges on migrant labour as detailed below, there exists no legal route for non-EU migrant workers to migrate to the UK in order to work in residential older-age care.

The scarcity of legal routes available to non-EU migrants for work-related purposes is equally reflected in the distribution of entry catego-

---

[5] https://www.gov.uk/government/uploads/system/uploads/attachment_data/file/420536/20150406_immigration_rules_appendix_i_final.pdf, last accessed February 2016.

[6] http://www.bbc.com/news/health-33201189, last accessed February 2016.

Table 3.2 Migration inflow by category of entry in 2013

	UK	France	Spain
Work	29.7%	10.3%	20.4%
Family	22.2%	40.3%	21.1%
Humanitarian	7.1%	4.5%	0.2%
Free movement	33.8%	36.9%	53.8%
Others	7.1%	8.1%	4.5%

Source: OECD (2015), own compilation

ries, as illustrated by Table 3.2 for countries included in the analysis. Family reunification constitutes a more frequent category of entry to France and Spain than work-related visas, in the case of France the proportion being four to one. This point should not, however, conceal the fact that the type of entry is only indicative of administrative categories created by migration policies: non-EU migrants who are in employment might have come through a variety of routes. Those who came through family reunification or as asylum seekers are likely to be employed in 'low-skilled' sectors of the economy. In his study of the migrant labour force in the care sector throughout Europe, Alessio Cangiano observes: 'a second recruitment pool is the migrant population already residing in the country, admitted via so-called non-economic immigration channels such as family reunification, asylum and study' (Cangiano 2014, p. 140). Needs for 'low-skilled' labour are however continuously played down (Kofman 2008), and the trend is to further restrict legal routes of entry to the European Union other than those targeting the 'highly skilled'. These restrictive policies produce vulnerable workers due to the limitation of rights they engender. Illustrative of this trend is the tightening of family reunification possibilities (Kofman 2008). In France, in the 2000s under Nicolas Sarkozy, first in the Home Office and later as President, additional requirements for family reunification were introduced (notably a longer stay required to be entitled to submit an application, shorter residence permit granted to the spouse, language tests and resource thresholds). In Spain, the *Ley de Extranjería* enacted in 2000 regulated family reunification for the first time, as the 1985 immigration law did not address this right. Since then, it has been amended four times and the conditions for family reunification were restricted each time as to the requirements for the person applying in Spain and his or her family members (Montiel Perez-Nievas and Vintila Daniela 2011). In the UK, the Home Office's £18,600 minimum income threshold for family reunification (only for a spouse, the threshold increases with children) was confirmed in the Court of Appeal in July 2015.[7]

EU governments equally use employment related rights as a means to bargain temporariness for 'low-skilled' workers. Georg Menz and Alexander Caviedes (2010) have argued that migration policies came to be increasingly shaped by non-state actors and notably employers' organisations. There exists indeed a business case for more migration to answer labour shortages, but acknowledging these needs conflicts with populist and xenophobic electoral strategies. In this context, reiterating post-war projections over migration, governments aspire to 'import labour but not people' (Castles 2006, p. 742). This pattern of migration is viewed as a response to sector-specific shortages (Fargues 2008) that minimises the social impact of immigration (McLoughlin and Münz 2011). To ensure that workers only come for pre-established periods of time, the rights of temporary workers are limited. Rights to reside and work depend strictly on employment, and employer-sponsored visa schemes limit the possibility for workers to change employers. According to Stasiulis, 'eligibility to change status to permanent residence and the right to family reunification are the two rights that most clearly bleed particular temporary worker schemes into long-term resident migration' (2008, p. 107).

Citizenship laws also present significant differences, between countries and between various groups within one country. In Spain, the general rule requires ten years of legal residence before one is allowed to apply for Spanish citizenship. Some countries are nevertheless exempted from this rule and the required period of time is reduced to two years for people from Latin American countries, Andorra, the Philippines, Equatorial Guinea, Portugal, and for people of Sephardi origin.[8] Reflecting Spanish colonial (and Reconquista) history, this exemption enshrines in law racialised constructions of migrants' deservingness; Moroccans for

---

[7] http://www.bbc.com/news/uk-28267305, last accessed February 2016.

[8] http://www.mjusticia.gob.es/cs/Satellite/es/1215198282620/Estructura_P/1215198291413/Detalle.html, last accessed February 2016.

instance, even when coming from regions formerly colonised by Spain, are not included in this policy. In France and in the UK no official distinction is drawn between nationalities and the minimum duration of legal residency required prior to a citizenship application is five years.

Minority Regimes: From Postcolonial Continuities to Converging 'Models'?

The colonial history of the three countries under study also contributed to shaping past patterns of immigration that resulted in the presence of minorities, diversely defined in terms of ethnicity, religion or nationality according to different societal contexts. This research includes minority ethnic care workers in the case of London and Paris, reflecting the profile of the workforce present on site during fieldwork. While in Spain minorities are also present, for instance communities of Chinese and Moroccans born in Spain, their presence in the older-age care industry seems limited. The absence of analysis in terms of minority ethnic workers in Madrid thus results from the empirical characteristics of the sector; it should however not conceal the presence of such minorities in society at large.

In contrast, the presence of minority ethnic workers in Paris and in London harks back, at least partially, to state policies aiming at providing labour to the metropolitan health and care systems. For instance, the volume of migrants from French overseas departments to metropolitan France increased rapidly from the 1950s to the 1970s (Marie and Temporal 2011, p. 487). Many of the women who migrated during this period started working in public healthcare facilities, notably hospitals. Women from Guadeloupe were for instance overwhelmingly employed in the care sector: in 1962, 57.4% were healthcare assistants and 11.5% childcare assistants (Condon 2000). Overall, it is estimated that about 9% of the French population either came from French overseas departments or were born to parents from these departments, according to a recent study of the French Institute of Demographic Studies.[9]

---

[9] http://www.lemonde.fr/societe/article/2016/01/08/les-enfants-d-immigres-s-integrent-mais-restent-victimes-du-chomage-et-de-la-discrimination_4843872_3224.html, last accessed February 2016.

In the UK, postcolonial migration that took place mainly after the Second World War from South Asia and the Caribbean contributed to the formation of ethnic minorities. Black Caribbeans were for instance directly recruited to fill vacancies for nurses in the NHS (Heath and Cheung 2007, p. 510). In 1948 the British Nationality Act gave access to the UK to all residents of British colonies past and present by creating the citizenship of the United Kingdom and Colonies and the citizenship of Independent Commonwealth Countries. From 1962 onwards, starting with the British Commonwealth Act, the legislation became more restrictive with each amendment. First, a voucher system was put into place and then a yearly entry limit. In 1971, the Immigration Act introduced the concept of 'patriality' according to which the right to migrate was conditional on the fact that at least one parent or grandparent was born in Britain. Ten years later, in 1981, the privileges given to Commonwealth citizens were once more cut down by the introduction of the 'British Nationality Act' which distinguishes British Overseas Citizenship and Dependent Territories Citizenship, none giving the right to enter the UK. In today's Britain, one in five persons identifies with an ethnic group other than White British (Jivraj 2013). The largest groups are Indians (2.5%) and Pakistanis (2%), followed by Black Caribbean, Black Africans and Bangladeshis.

Scholarly traditions used to oppose France and Great Britain as illustrating two very different 'models'. From this perspective, France represents a 'republican model' that rejects any form of distinction based on ethno-racial elements because it presumably contradicts the French conception of civic citizenship. The British model is based, in contrast, on a 'plural' form of liberalism in which minority groups are fully recognised and benefit from programmes of equal opportunity (Bertossi 2007, p. 4). Christophe Bertossi notes however that researchers have moved away in recent years from this fixed opposition to acknowledge that in practice both countries deviate from the 'model'; he identifies several ruptures in the so-called 'models', notably a shift from ethnicity to religion that can be observed in the labelling of certain minorities across these spaces. It appears that both countries have to some extent reviewed their narratives and policies, which do not always fit the excessively rigid divide between a republican vs. a multicultural 'model'. For instance, in 2003, the French government established the French Council of the Muslim Faith (Conseil Français du Culte Musulman) in order to have a formal interlocutor on religious issues; while in Britain, the introduction of 'community cohesion' has assimilationist overtones through its emphasis on 'shared values, national identity and civic virtue' (Bertossi 2007).

In Spain, given the relatively recent history of immigration in the country, some authors speak of the Spanish 'non-model of integration' to describe the absence of an ideology fuelling the design of integration policies (Carrera 2009, p. 432). Corkill notes, 'there has been little synchronization between the growing need for foreign workers and the social integration of an expanding immigrant population' (2001, p. 830). Succeeding Spanish governments tended thus to draw on European policies in the field and to look at other European countries in search of best practices (Carrera 2009). Furthermore, the design and implementation of the 'Strategic Plan of Citizenship and Integration' (first one: 2007–2010, second one: 2011–2014) fall partly under the prerogatives of Autonomous Communities, in particular in relation to education, employment, housing and health (Cachon Rodriguez 2008; Hemerijck et al. 2013). Consequently, some authors speak of the 'patchwork model' (De Lizarrondo Artola 2009) to highlight differences between policies implemented in different autonomous communities.

Anti-discrimination Legislation: Between an EU-Driven Homogenisation and Implementation Gaps

The UK was the first country in Europe to implement anti-discrimination legislation with the 1965 Race Relations Act that made discrimination in public places unlawful (Heath and Cheung 2007). Labour market related discrimination was also soon to be outlawed through the 1968 Race Relations Act that forbade employers to 'discriminate on grounds of colour, race, or ethnic or national origins in recruitment, training, promotion, dismissals, and terms and conditions of employment'. The 1976 Race Relations Act extended the definition of discrimination to include indirect discrimination and established the Commission for Racial Equality. The Race Relations (Amendment) Act passed in 2000 extended further the 1976 Act in relation to public authorities, particularly to the police, and assigned to public authorities 'a "general duty" to prevent discrimination, promote equality of opportunity [...] as well as a "specific duty" to draw up a race equality scheme' (Cantle 2008). Finally, the 2010 Equality Act brought together several regulations and added, in relation to discrimination, 'harassment by a third party' to the existing categories of 'direct discrimination', 'discrimination by association', 'discrimination by perception', 'indirect discrimination', 'harassment' and 'victimisation' (ACAS 2011). Underpinning these legislative developments, government-commissioned reports influenced the way racism was thought about in public spheres. After the arrival to power of a Labour government in 1997, the 1999 Macpherson Report blamed institutional racism for the flawed investigation in the case of the Stephen Lawrence murder that took place in 1993. Racist practices within the London Metropolitan Police were suddenly exposed to the public (Rattansi 2011). William Macpherson underlined that 'there must be an unequivocal acceptance of institutional racism and its nature before it can be addressed' (Macpherson 1999). This ground-breaking change in the narrative engendered what Jenny Bourne calls a 'watershed in British race relations' (Bourne 2001, p. 8). The early implementation of anti-discrimination policies and the identification of institutional racism, a concept unheard of in continental Europe, did not however eliminate widespread discrimination. In spite of the tremendous change that it brought about discursively, Macpherson's definition of 'institutional racism' did not include explicitly the need to tackle 'state racism' since the government might well try to ensure equality of opportunity with one hand and introduce new forms of institutional racism with the other (Bourne 2001). The full implications of the concept as first theorised in Stokely Carmichael's writings are yet to be acknowledged (Carmichael and Hamilton 1967/1992). Furthermore, the paradigm shift that followed the 2001 Oldham riots with the Cantle report and its discourse of 'community cohesion' and 'parallel lives' (Cantle 2001) reversed this trend and arguably represented a backlash against the prominence of the concept of 'institutional racism'.

Unlike the UK, France's 'republican model' has historically imposed colour-blind assumptions in public policies. The past two decades witnessed however the progressive articulation of social and 'racial'/ 'ethnic' themes, as argued by Éric Fassin and Didier Fassin in a collective volume (2006), *From a Social Issue to a Racial Issue?*.[10] A debate emerged indeed in the 1990s around racial discrimination. In 1998, the High Council for Integration,[11] a governmental advisory body, recommended setting up an institution similar to the British Commission for Racial Equality to tackle cases of racial discrimination (Rattansi 2011). For this purpose, the 'Group for the study and fight against racial discriminations'[12] was established in 1999. The legislation started to evolve in the 2000s, admittedly against the background of these debates, but mainly as a consequence of EU regulations, notably the Employment Equality Framework Directive and the Racial Equality Directive adopted in 2000. A French law adopted in 2001 extended the definition of discrimination to indirect discrimination and reversed the burden of proof from the victim to the perpetrator (Fassin and Fassin 2006).

In Spain, EU directives constituted a major impetus for anti-discrimination regulations and legislation. One of the first academic studies on racial discrimination in the labour market was published in the early 1990s (Solé and Parella 2003), but nothing was achieved at the policy level before the entry into force of the European directives. The Colectivo Ioé, a significant network of sociologists in Spain, published in 2002 a report on the discrimination experienced by migrants. The authors did not recognise the existence of indirect discrimination, as they considered the intention to be necessarily part of an act of discrimination (Colectivo Ioé 2003, p. 10). With the same logic, they dismissed the concept of 'institutional discrimination' in order to focus on discrimination as a phenomenon that arises between individuals. Until recently, racial discrimination tended thus to be strictly understood as an interpersonal phenomenon caused by racist motives, while institutional racism as a concept was absent from mainstream academic literature and policy debates. The introduction of the European vocabulary of indirect and other forms of discrimination therefore brought significant changes at

---

[10] Original title: De la question sociale à la question raciale?
[11] In French:Haut Conseil à l'Intégration.
[12] Groupe d'Etude et de Lutte contre les Discriminations Raciales.

the policy level. In June 2007, Spain received a formal notice for not implementing the Directive correctly and for failing to publish the required data. A Council for the Promotion of Equal Opportunities and Non-discrimination on the Ground of Ethnic and Racial Origin was created the same year, and in 2011 a 'Comprehensive Strategy against Racism, Racial Discrimination, Xenophobia and Related Forms of Intolerance' was adopted by the Council of Ministers (ENAR 2013).

The comparative overview presented in the following paragraphs provides insights into the institutional practices deriving from anti-discrimination legislations in the three countries.

In the UK, 3064 racial discrimination claims were lodged with employment tribunals in 2013–2014.[13] Remarkably, this figure is lower for 2009–2010 with 5700 claims[14] after the government introduced claim and hearing fees in 2013. Discrimination cases are the most expensive, claim and hearing fees reaching £1200 as compared for instance with £410 for unpaid wages cases (Department for Business Innovation and Skills 2014). To add to this, only a minority of employment tribunal cases progress to full hearings: most cases are either settled by the Advisory, Conciliation and Arbitration Service (33% in 2010–2011), withdrawn (27%) or struck out (13%) (Ministry of Justice 2012). Once at the hearing stage, cases of racial discrimination have the poorest chances with an average of 16% success in 2010–2011.[15] In an online article published by the Institute of Race Relations,[16] David Renton questions why racial discrimination cases are so unlikely to be successful, not only in comparison with unfair dismissal or wage deduction cases, but also in comparison with other discrimination cases, such as sex discrimination (37%) or sexual orientation discrimination (26%). The argument he puts forward on the basis of several case studies points out that the understanding of racial discrimination is often conflated with racist intentions by judges. It is therefore not enough for the concept of institutional racism to be

---

[13] Source: http://www.bbc.com/news/uk-31856147, last accessed February 2016.

[14] https://www.gov.uk/government/uploads/system/uploads/attachment_data/file/218497/employment-trib-stats-april-march-2011-12.pdf, last accessed February 2016.

[15] http://www.irr.org.uk/news/culture-of-disbelief-why-race-discrimination-claims-fail-in-the-employment-tribunal/, last accessed February 2016.

[16] Op. cit.

discussed within the field of anti-discrimination policies for the judiciary system to take into account its implications for individual cases. Racial discrimination remains often equated with racist intentions of the perpetrator and cases tend to revolve around proving or dismissing the racist intentions instead of establishing the existence or nonexistence of discrimination.

In France, figures published by the High Authority for the Fight Against Discrimination and for Equality (HALDE),[17] an institution created in 2005 to comply with EU requirements, show that the number of complaints increased from 1410 in 2005 to 12,467 in 2010. The purpose of this state-funded body was to assist victims of discrimination by supporting their legal fights when the Authority had reviewed the case and established that discrimination took place. Around half of these complaints concerned employment, and overall, between 2005 and 2009, 28.5% of complaints mentioned 'discrimination based upon ethnic origin (real or hypothetical)'.[18] Ali Rattansi (2011) notes, however, that far fewer resources were attributed to this new agency than were provided to the former British Commission for Racial Equality. Moreover, the HALDE existed for only a few years, having since been integrated into a broader institution, 'Défenseur des Droits', chaired by an 'Ombudsman' in 2011. The disappearance of the HALDE and its merger into a broader agency has been vigorously criticised by grassroots organisations. Further to this merger, the Ombudsman and the corresponding agency are also in charge of children's rights, public service users' rights and security ethics. Moreover, the information accessible by victims of discrimination is limited and legal cases are no longer published online, contrary to the practice put in place by the HALDE. Success rates of discrimination cases are not publicly available either.

In Spain, similarly to the situation described for the UK and France, there exists an immense gap between the extent of discrimination, as subsequent studies have demonstrated (Colectivo Ioé 2003), and actual legal cases. Anti-discrimination legislation was introduced only a couple of years ago, and the economic crisis affected the state's capacity to

---

[17] Haute Autorité de lutte contre les discriminations et pour l'égalité, HALDE.
[18] Op. Cit.

implement its programmes. For instance, the Council for the Promotion of Equal Opportunities and Non-Discrimination on the Ground of Ethnic and Racial Origin, created in 2007, only registered 167 individual cases of discrimination in 2010[19] and soon started to lack funding, according to a 2013 report by the European Network Against Racism (ENAR 2013). This NGO also highlighted that Spain failed to publish a transparent database of all discrimination cases, so that an assessment of the efficiency of the legislation is hardly possible (ENAR 2013).

The following section studies the differences between the care regimes of the UK, France and Spain and highlights some shared trends such as the limited professionalisation of the sector and the growing marketisation of care provision.

3.3   Older-Age Care Regimes: Different 'Care Mixes', a Growing Marketisation

As outlined in Introduction, the ageing of the population, combined with societal changes (such as increasing employment rates for women, greater geographical mobility and work patterns) makes care for older adults a major challenge for the future well-being of European societies. Table 3.3 presents a series of indicators that illustrate this challenge. It shows that in the case of the three countries under study, the share of the population over 65 is of comparable proportion, as is the older-age dependency ratio ('population 65+' divided by 'population 15–64'), with France situated slightly above the EU average of 26.7% and Spain and the UK a little below. The three countries present, however, different profiles as to the relative importance of migration in population change. In Spain demographic growth was mainly due to net migration, while in the UK and in France it accounted respectively for half and for a third of population change between 2002 and 2011. Finally, in all three countries, women's participation rates in the formal labour market are above the EU average. If the UK presents the highest rate amongst these three

---

[19] http://www.msssi.gob.es/ssi/igualdadOportunidades/docs/2010_Informe_Anual_Consejoigualdad_Accesible.pdf, last accessed February 2016.

Table 3.3 Population ageing, net migration and female labour force participation indicators

	Population 65+ (%)	Older-age dependency ratio in 2012	Net migration (% of total population change) 2002–2011	Female labour force participation rate in 2011 in %	Change in female labour participation rate 2001–2010
EU-27	17.8	26.7	75.0	64.8	+4.6
France	17.3	26.9	32.2	66.2	+3.9
Spain	17.4	25.8	82.3	67.0	+16.6
UK	16.9	25.7	53.9	69.7	+2.0

Source: Eurostat (Cangiano 2014, p. 133, own selection of countries)

countries, the growth in labour force participation for Spanish women is particularly high: it increased by 16.6 percentage points within a decade.

Projections of the older-age dependency ratio furthermore suggest a rapidly growing challenge to the current care regimes and the associated care provision 'mixes'. According to Eurostat,[20] the projected trajectories of these three countries vary in terms of speed of change and demographic profile of the population at different points in time. Spain is ageing the fastest in this regard with a 125% increase in the older-age dependency ratio between 2015 and 2050, as compared to a 48% and 50% rise for the UK and France, respectively.

These three countries also present different levels of long-term care expenditure for health and social care. In 2015, France spent 1.7% of its GDP on long-term care, the UK 1.5% and Spain 0.8% (OECD 2017). Data compiled by Cangiano (2014, p. 135) offer further insights into how care for older people is provided in different European countries and the relative weight of each form of care provision. It captures first a fundamental difference as to the weight of informal care in the 'care mix' of each care regime. In Spain as many as 66.7% of older persons receive care only from family caregivers vs. 20.2% in France. The level of formalisation of care services affects the relative size of the care workforce: representing 8.8% of the total workforce in France, this proportion is situated

---

[20] http://appsso.eurostat.ec.europa.eu/nui/submitViewTableAction.do, last accessed December 30, 2015.

slightly above the EU average of 5.6% in the UK (6.2%) and in Spain (6.4%). While home care providers represent the most common employer in the UK, care institutions still employ 44.4% of the care workforce. In contrast, the high share of households acting as employers in Spain (59%) reveals a preference for this particular form of care provision and suggests the existence of a significant informal sector. In this country, care institutions employ 22% of the care workforce. France presents yet another 'care mix'. If care institutions employ 26.8% of the care workforce, a preference for home care services is visible (47.5%) along with an above-average share of household employers (25.6%). In spite of these major differences, Annamaria Simonazzi identifies common trends in the social care policies implemented in Europe. This shared orientation is to be found in a triple shift towards home care, private provision and monetary transfers (Simonazzi 2009). The latter corresponds to the transfer of cash for the purchase of care services (Ungerson 2003).

These 'care mixes' rely on different financing systems and degrees of privatisation. A study by Simonazzi shows that residential care is privatised to a significant extent in England and in Spain, respectively, to the levels of 76% and 60%. In France, the share of private residential care represents 40% of existing facilities, with the majority of care homes being state-funded (Simonazzi 2009, p. 217). While Simonazzi's study mentions a market share of 14%, more recent data situate this share at the level of 25%.[21] The capital that funds this residential care is increasingly transnational due to mergers aiming at economies of scale. Several for-profit private care providers share most of the market in the UK, France and Spain, with some of these companies deploying commercial services in several countries.

The UK represents a case of extended privatisation through the contracting out of services and the implementation of cash allowances, the share of the public sector being significantly reduced since the 1980s. Residential care, historically the responsibility of local councils, which used to provide these care services, has been progressively outsourced to private providers, following plans to implement a 'mixed economy'

---

[21] http://www.alternatives-economiques.fr/le-marche-des-maisons-de-retraite_fr_art_1094_54438.html, last accessed February 10, 2016.

(Glendinning 2013). Choice is at the heart of the consumerist agenda applied to care provision and justifies cash-for-care schemes. This form of care financing bears nevertheless social consequences for the workforce in terms of earnings, qualifications and working conditions, while approximately one in 16 workers in the UK is employed in the social care sector (around 1.8 million individuals).[22] The marketisation of care services 'has put pressure on costs, encouraging the development of a low paid and casualised workforce' (Simonazzi 2009, p. 227). A survey conducted by a major trade union found that 41% of homecare workers were on zero hours contracts (UNISON 2013). In the context of privatisation of public services, home and social care represents the sector where the highest increase in the use of zero hours contracts took place.

In France, cash-for-care schemes were introduced in the late 1990s with the Dependency allowance (*Prestation spécifique dépendance*) in 1997 and the Personal autonomy allowance (*Allocation personnalisée à l'autonomie*) in 2002, which can fund both domiciliary and residential care. Furthermore, the 'Borloo Law', named after the Minister who drafted it, and passed in 2003, serves the purpose of developing 'personal services' which group together domiciliary care and domestic work but also private lessons, gardening, home improvement small jobs and so on; in other words, all services related to the 'domestic sphere' (Aldeghi and Loones 2010). As noted by Simonazzi: 'in France, the policy on care allowances has been distinctive by explicitly linking the provision of services to the elderly (and other family services) with the creation of jobs, the specific intention being to reduce long-term unemployment and to drain the informal market' (2009, p. 217). When the Borloo Law was passed, the government publicised the fact that 'personal services' represented the sector with the biggest growth in employment: 5.5% per year since 1990 (Aldeghi and Loones 2010). Korczyk warns, however, that 'private contracts tend to pay less than formal jobs offered by private or government agencies, and they do not offer a career ladder' (2004, p. 14). The cash allowance can be transferred to older people living at home or in institutions and its amount depends on the assessed level of dependency.

---

[22] http://www.theguardian.com/social-care-network/2013/sep/30/where-social-care-jobs-future, last accessed February 10, 2016.

The distinctive feature of this scheme is that the purchase of the care package is determined by healthcare professionals and the use of the benefit is monitored (Le Bihan and Martin 2010). In terms of residential care, since 2002, all institutions were grouped under the same name, EHPAD or Residential facility for the accommodation of elderly dependant persons[23] (Le Bihan and Martin 2010). The for-profit private sector is growing significantly: between 2005 and 2008, 70% of new places available were created by for-profit private providers.[24] The industry shows growing revenues[25] and increasing concentration through mergers (Ernst and Young Advisory 2008).

The Spanish care regime is shaped by weak welfare and a strong reliance on the family (Romero 2012). In 2007, the Dependency Law entered into force implementing the SAAD (*Sistema de Autonomía y Atención a la Dependencia*): System of Autonomy and Dependency Care (Rodríguez Cabrero and Marbán Gallego 2013). The main contribution of this reform has been to turn the 'system of residual social assistance and social security' into a system with a universal approach (Rodríguez Cabrero and Marbán Gallego 2013, p. 203). However, autonomous regions have some leverage in implementing the law and this has created significant inequalities in terms of coverage (Rodríguez Cabrero and Marbán Gallego 2013). It relies upon a system of joint financing within which the cost of care is shared between public funds and the care recipient, but the respective shares can vary significantly from one autonomous region to another (Romero 2012). The law has further been criticised by feminist sociologists who pointed out that the focus on professionalisation and 'de-familiarisation' in the framework of this law was based upon a gendered understanding of autonomy, skills and care and, thus, instead of reducing the feminisation of the care sector, ended up adapting it to the market so created (Serrano et al. 2013). Central to the way care regimes work is indeed the question of skills recognition and the professional hierarchies attached to these skills. In the autonomous region of

---

[23] In French: Établissement d'hébergement pour personnes âgées dépendantes, EHPAD.

[24] Source: http://www.alternatives-economiques.fr/le-marche-des-maisons-de-retraite_fr_art_1094_54438.html, last accessed February 2016.

[25] http://www.lefigaro.fr/retraite/2010/01/12/05004-20100112ARTFIG00349-le-boom-des-maisons-de-retraite-medicalisees-.php, last accessed February 2016.

Madrid, official figures indicate that the most common form of care provision is residential care, which attends to 3.7% of the elderly population, mostly in private facilities (74%) (IMSERSO 2005). While these data reflect certain trends within the formal economy, qualitative research on the importance of the informal sector suggests that homecare remains more common than institutional care (IMSERSO 2005). There are various reasons why institutional care has not been more extensively developed in the region of Madrid in spite of the ageing population. On the one hand, there is a strong preference among families for care services provided at home: the dominant discourse of what constitutes appropriate care, that is, the 'care culture' (Williams 2012) constitutes one factor of explanation. On the other hand, the number of places in care homes is scarce. Publicly financed care homes (mostly managed by private companies through outsourcing) are unable to meet existing needs and long waiting lists are the norm. Furthermore, prices of private care homes make these services inaccessible to most families (IMSERSO 2005).

In parallel, in all three countries, the low level of qualifications required in older-age care—despite existing differences between countries—is related to the gendered understanding of care as innate and natural, rather than taught and acquired (see Chap. 6 for further discussion). The gendered inequalities that underpin care work also impact negatively the level of income and professional advancement opportunities. Yet, beyond the general devaluation of older-age care, key differences exist in terms of the professionalisation of this occupation between the three countries under study here. In the UK, there is no formal training requirement for care workers to start in the position of 'care assistant' in a care home or in domiciliary care. There exists only a duty of employers to ensure that at least 50% of their workforce attain National Vocational Qualification level 2 (Smith and Mackintosh 2007), a work-based professional certificate (replaced by the Regulated Qualifications Framework in 2015). However, as observed by Pam Smith and Maureen Mackintosh, 'by early 2004, only 48% of homes met even these minimum levels of qualifications and less than half were doing any staff training (Dalley et al. 2004)' (Smith and Mackintosh 2007, p. 2218). In France, three different statuses correspond to the work of care assistants in terms of daily tasks performed. These are Life assistant (*Auxiliaire de vie*), Medical/psychological assistant (*Aide médico-psychologique*) and Healthcare assistant (*Aide-soignant*). Training required for these positions ranges from 9 to 12 months.

In Spain, no formal requirement existed until 2015, yet after this date workers were expected to have obtained a formal qualification. As a consequence, employers started recruiting workers with formal qualifications before 2015 in order to comply with the law when the time came. The length of the training required varied. If completed at a state university it consists of a year of studies and a three-month work placement. Before this law was passed, most migrant workers in care home settings completed training through migrant associations or local authorities, as it often offered a way out of live-in employment arrangements, which however does not always qualify as sufficient training under the new reform. Table 3.4, on the next page, provides a comparative overview of the different degrees of professionalisation and regulations in the three countries.

To complement this contextual overview, the following section sketches out the main characteristics of the employment regimes of the three countries presenting indicators of part-time employment, employment protection and union density.

3.4   Employment Regimes: Diverse Models of Industrial Relations, Foreign-Born Women at Most Disadvantage

Table 3.5 provides an overview of the share of temporary and part-time employment in France, the UK and Spain. Each of the three countries presents a different profile in relation to these two indicators, but similar trends proportion-wise in terms of gender inequality. These indicators are commonly used to measure the share of non-standard employment (other than permanent and full-time). The meaning of these categories is however less straightforward than quantitative data tend to suggest. Employment regimes also entail national variations in terms of employment legislation and practice, and it has been long established that if the dismissal of permanent workers presents few constraints, there is little difference with tem-

Table 3.4 Qualifications and training for entry-level care, a comparative overview

	France		Spain		UK
Original name	Auxiliaire de vie	Aide medico-psychologique	Gerocultor	Auxiliar de enfermeria	Care assistant/Senior care assistant
Translation	Life assistant	Medical/psychological assistant	Geriatric care provider	Healthcare assistant	
Length of training	9 months	12 months	No formal requirements until 2015	1400 hours, translated in state universities into 1 year of studies and 3 months of work placement.	No formal requirements. On the job training online and NVQ levels.
			Aide-soignante		
			Healthcare assistant		
			10 months		

Source: Own elaboration

Table 3.5 Temporary and part-time employment, comparative perspectives

Employment regimes characteristics	EU 28 (2014)		UK (2014)		France (2014)		Spain (2014)	
Temporary Employment	14%		6.4%		15.8%		24%	
Women Men	14.4%	13.6%	6.9%	6%	16.8%	14.9%	24.5%	23.5%
Part-time employment	20.4%		26.8%		18.9%		15.9%	
Women Men	32.8%	9.9%	42.5%	13.1%	30.8%	7.8%	25.6%	7.8%

Source: Eurostat, own compilation

porary contracts (Rodgers and Rodgers 1989). Thus, the lower level of temporary employment in the UK, as compared with the EU average or France and Spain in this case, does not mean that workers enjoy greater employment stability and employment protection.

This point is demonstrated by OECD indicators on employment protection legislation.[26] These indicators take into account variables such as protection against individual and collective dismissals, regulations on temporary work, extent of social and welfare provision and collective bargaining coverage (McKay et al. 2012). On a scale of 0 (least restrictions) to 6 (most restrictions), the UK presents the least regulated labour market, with low protection against individual and collective dismissals (1.62) and almost no regulation as to temporary forms of employment (0.54). France in turn has one of the most regulated labour markets (with an indicator of 2.82 for collective and individual dismissals and of 3.75 for temporary forms of employment). Spain is situated close to the OECD average with an indicator of 2.28 for an average of 2.29 regarding individual and collective dismissals.

Migrant women face multiple inequalities and are thus at greater risk of being trapped in segments of the labour market characterised by precarious employment terms and working conditions. Table 3.6 presents the unemployment rates of foreign-born women as compared to native-born women. A smaller gap is to be observed in the UK than in France and in Spain, where the inequality is the widest.

---

[26] Source: http://www.oecd.org/els/emp/oecdindicatorsofemploymentprotection.htm.

Table 3.6 Unemployment rates of native- and foreign-born women

	UK	France	Spain
Unemployment rate of native-born women	6.7%	8.9%	25.2%
Unemployment rate of foreign-born women	9.8%	16.4%	34.1%

Source: OECD (2015), own compilation

The older-age care sector drives up labour needs in ageing societies and channels women, and in particular migrant and minority ethnic women, into these jobs. Indeed, Alessio Cangiano observes that 'in all European countries migrants account for a larger proportion of the care workforce than of the workforce in the rest of the economy' (Cangiano 2014, p. 138). Given these increasing labour needs, the current reliance on migrant labour is likely to expand and the number of migrant care workers to grow. For instance, it is estimated in the UK that the social care workforce caring for older people needs to increase by 79% by 2032 (Wittenburg et al. 2010, p. 15 in Shutes 2011).[27] Between 2008 and 2012, residential care as an industry experienced the biggest rise in employment and the highest rate of growth of foreign-born workers, with an increase of 44.5% in European OECD countries (OECD 2013, p. 82).

The same caution needs to be applied to the analysis of union density indicators and their correlation with unions' bargaining power for workers. Union density was in 2012 according to the OECD online database of 25.8% in the UK, 7.7% in France and of 17.5% in Spain, with an OECD average of 17.1%. The meaning of this indicator might vary according to different models of industrial relations. Comparing regimes of industrial relations raises many challenges due to national differences and concepts that are not transposable from one context to another (Hyman 2001). Union membership, collective bargaining coverage and political clout are all elements that shape unions' power differently according to each model of industrial relations. In the UK, union membership is, for instance, a significant indicator of unions' position within industrial relations, and the decline in unions' bargaining power was

---

[27] The report is available at: http://www.migrationobservatory.ox.ac.uk/sites/files/migobs/Social%20Care%20Policy%20Primer_0.pdf, last accessed February 2016.

accompanied by a decline in union membership during the 1980s and 1990s (Machin 2000). In Spain, in spite of low affiliation, unions have high mobilisation capacity, and collective bargaining offers high coverage due to the automatic extension of collective agreements (Köhler and Calleja Jiménez 2012). In France, where union density is particularly low, union membership also experienced a significant decline in past decades (Mouriaux 2013); however, it is unions' mobilisation capacity and institutional role within collective bargaining processes that shape their actual power (Andolfatto and Labbé 2006). What is more, unions have considered migrant workers in different ways across Europe, as a result of both diverging models of industrial relations and different understandings of migrant workers' position within the working class. Research into the reluctance of trade unions to include racialised workers into their ranks (Virdee 2000) or their hesitancy to acknowledge and fight racism in workplaces (Jefferys and Ouali 2007) demonstrated the historical ambivalence of trade unions in the face of racist discriminations. Even in the context of inclusive trade union organising, domestic and care labour represent one of the least accessible sectors. Domestic care workers are in this regard most isolated from trade union activities due to the fragmentation of the workforce employed in private households. Yet, trade unions struggle to be present in the care sector at large and in particular within private and not-for-profit provision (Lethbridge 2011). Growing privatisation and the reduction of the market share of the public sector in the UK has posed a challenge to union organising (Hardy et al. 2012). Union membership tends to be least frequent the more recent migrants are (Jayaweera and Anderson 2008) and the lower their professional status within the care institution (Stevens et al. 2012). In Spain, trade unions' presence in the care sector is very fragile, with only about 3% of union members according to one Spanish report (IMSERSO 2005). The same challenges characterise the French context, where trade unions remain absent from the domestic care sector (Avril 2009; Devetter and Messaoudi 2013) but have a limited presence within institutional care settings (Puissant 2011).

Finally, the last section narrows down the focus and presents the role of racialised care workers in older-age care at the national or city levels according to the available data.

3.5   Racialised Workers in Older-Age Care: Country and City Contexts

In London, there is a particularly strong concentration of Black, Asian and Minority Ethnic (BAME) care workers (including migrant workers), constituting two-thirds of the workforce (Cangiano et al. 2009). Most importantly, the share of migrant care workers in the sector is growing significantly with an increase of 112% between 2003 and 2008 compared to a 16% growth of UK-born carers (Cangiano et al. 2009). In terms of countries of origin, recent migrants (those who have resided in the UK for less than ten years according to the authors' definition) working as care workers came mostly from Poland, Zimbabwe, the Philippines and Nigeria[28] (Cangiano et al. 2009). In addition, the National Minimum Data Set for Social Care (NMDS-SC)[29] provides an interesting insight into adult social care in the London Region: 25% of the workforce hold a non-EEA (European Economic Area) passport and 8% hold an EEA non-British passport. Included within the category of those with British citizenship, who make up 36% of the workforce in London, are migrants who have gained British citizenship.

In France, it is not easy to obtain figures on migrant workers in the care sector for two main reasons. First, national statistics do not gather figures for the care workforce as such and care workers are counted in different categories according to the type of employment they are in (e.g. public hospital vs. domiciliary care), and then grouped with other occupations. Within employment statistics, the closest category is that of *services aux particuliers*, corresponding to a section of the service industry in which are grouped together jobs providing services to individuals such as domiciliary care, doing household chores or gardening. The over-representation of migrant workers within this category can serve as a proxy for the care sector. In 2010, 22% of workers in this sector were migrants while migrant workers represented only 5% of the total workforce (Alberola et al. 2011). Second, a database like the NMDS-SC in the UK is not available in France given that data on migration statuses are

---

[28] These results rely on a sample of 175 non-recent migrants and 285 recent migrants.

[29] Database last accessed on June 10th, 2015.

not collected within a publicly available database filled out by employers, and statistics on ethnicity are forbidden (except for limited collection and use by the National Institute of Statistics under special regulatory provisions). The government noted nevertheless the need to tackle the over-representation of migrant women in these services, in spite of the absence of data for the 'care sector' as defined in Anglo-Saxon literature (Garner and Lainé 2013). Their subordinated position within the sector was furthermore demonstrated by qualitative research (Lada 2011).

In Spain a significant share of older-age care is provided by the informal economy; according to Simonazzi, 'the underground economy covers one-third of the market in Spain' (2009, p. 226). Thus, the reliance on a migrant workforce for care provision can be apprehended only partially through statistical data. Residential care provides for a minority of older people and the 'migrant in the family' model of care mushroomed to replace women within the family who formerly provided that care (Bettio et al. 2006, p. 272). Amongst these migrants, some of them work legally and can contribute to social security; others are not given any contract by the family that employs them. Such figures, as they are available for those working legally, nevertheless reveal the central role of migrant workers: in 2008, in Madrid, 71% of domestic workers and 94% of live-in carers were migrants (Rodríguez Rodríguez 2012).

3.6 Conclusion

This chapter emphasised the growing challenge that meeting older-age care needs constitutes against the background of similar societal changes in all of the three countries and capital cities more specifically. Among the shared underpinning trends are the increasing participation of women in formal labour markets and the growing marketisation of care provision. Racialised care workers fulfil in this context a key function within the labour force employed to care for older persons in the three capital cities. OECD data demonstrate that migrant workers play a crucial role in meeting these labour shortages. Empirical evidence also hints at the significant role of minority ethnic workers in London (quantitative studies) and in Paris (qualitative studies).

The three migration regimes, in spite of national differences, concord in producing precarious legal statuses that contribute to channelling foreign workers to the most segmented sections of the labour market. The chapter highlighted in this regard the absence of legal routes for non-EU persons to come to the EU for work purposes, a determining feature of migrant care workers legal trajectories. Colonial continuities were emphasised in that they produce similar racialisation processes against the background of different 'integration models'. The adoption of anti-discrimination legislations, most developed in the UK, was driven in France and in Spain by the homogenising push of the European directives of the 2000s. Yet, practices continue to vary and countries present overall divergent institutional contexts in the field of anti-discrimination policies.

The expanding role of private providers in older-age care constitutes a remarkable feature of changing care regimes across these countries, though levels of spending and distribution of types of care provision still differ from one country to another. Such marketisation processes take place against the background of patriarchal gender regimes that transpose the subaltern position of care work from the domestic sphere to market relations. Owing to this, the overall level of professionalisation appears to be weak, yet at the same time, the three care regimes present crucial differences in terms of length of training.

The cross-national comparison of employment regimes contextualised the different sets of employment relations produced by specific models of industrial relations affecting the meanings of formal indicators such as permanent vs. temporary employment or union density. Overall, foreign-born women are at most risk of precarious employment in all three countries, reflecting the subpar employment conditions in older-age care as well as the gendered and racialised processes fragmenting the labour force.

The presentation of selected elements characterising the gender, migration, care and employment regimes highlighted some of the historical continuities as well as points of disruption. While patriarchy, neoliberal capitalism and colonial histories intersect in the production of these regimes, significant national and local differences persist and need to be explored to account for differentiated experiences of participants in this book. The following chapters initiate this task starting with participants' entry into the older-age care sector.

4

Entering the Older-Age Care Sector

What I like … you know we say it's a vocation, often we say I have a heart, I'm humane, I'm affectionate … all of this is false. It's extremely false because in cover letters it is often what is mentioned, I like older people, I like affection, closeness, I have a heart, all of this is very false. Everyone has a heart and no one has the monopoly of the heart. You have a heart, I have a heart … However you don't do this job … everyone has a heart, everyone is humane. (Bacar, 35, Senegal, Paris)

When I interviewed Bacar in the empty dining hall of a Parisian private care home, and asked him what he liked or enjoyed in his job, he seemed to turn the question around, as if asking me: 'Why don't you do this job?' As the interview went on, Bacar told me more about his life story. After finishing school in Senegal, he moved to France for his studies. He successfully completed a bachelor's degree in 'Economic and Social Administration' and a master's in History at Parisian universities. However, he never found a job related to his fields of study. He thought of becoming a teacher, which is a common employment opportunity for social science graduates, and started preparing for the secondary-school teaching diploma, a nation-wide examination organised annually in France. His plans, however, were cut short, as he did not meet the eligi-

© The Author(s) 2019
N. Sahraoui, *Racialised Workers and European Older-Age Care*, Thinking Gender in Transnational Times, https://doi.org/10.1007/978-3-030-14397-8_4

bility criteria established by the state. Successful applicants usually become civil servants in permanent positions after a probationary period, a status available only to French nationals since the early twentieth century. The exam is now restricted to French and EU nationals and as a consequence Bacar gave up his preparation. At the time of the interview, Bacar had been living in France for 15 years. He did apply for French citizenship once, but his application was rejected. After many years in France, bitter, resentful and needing to sustain himself, Bacar completed the one-year training required for care workers in France to be able to work in the care sector, known for its chronic labour needs.

Bacar encountered on his way many of the institutional barriers that result from the intersection of migration and employment policies, imbued with institutional racism. As outlined in Chap. 3, the three contexts present significant differences as to how care, migration and employment policies intersect, and thus impact racialised workers' trajectories into, within and out of private older-age care in London, Paris and Madrid. This first empirical chapter sketches out how and why non-EU migrant and minority ethnic care workers started working in older-age care in these capitals. In order to comprehend qualitatively the over-representation of migrant and minority ethnic workers in the sector and to analyse their work, it is crucial to first understand how these jobs came about in participants' lives. Shedding light on the routes of racialised care workers into older-age care, this chapter questions the implications of the workings of migration and care regimes for participants' trajectories. Attentive to their educational and professional profiles as well as employment preferences, the chapter demonstrates how a structural channelling of migrant and minority ethnic workers into this sector operates on the ground.

I intend here to combine the theoretical assumptions of a gendered political economy of care—as presented in Chap. 2—with labour market segmentation approaches to account for migrant and minority ethnic workers' routes into and within the care sector. Labour market segmentation theory posits that labour markets are socially regulated (Peck 1996) through socially constructed lines of division so that an individual's position within it depends on many more factors than human capital (Becker and Tomes 1994). The latter theory suggests that individuals' investments in education and skills acquisition translate into positive labour market outcomes, notably in terms of earnings. As illustrated by Bacar's story, this assumption proves to be of limited analytical relevance to the study of migrant and minority ethnic workers' positions and mobility within the labour market. The segmentation approach explored in this chapter offers theoretical tools to account for complex employment trajectories beyond the human capital theory that relies on the assumptions of classical economics. The segmentation approach serves here to explore how intersecting regimes both reflect and enact multiple inequalities. As Leontaridi (1998, p. 64) sums up: 'What emerges as the crux of the SLM (Segmented Labour Markets) approach is the idea that the labour market segmentation that exists does not correspond to skill differentials in the labour market, but rather institutional rules are substituted for market processes'. Developments within the human capital theory have progressively considered gender, ethnicity, nationality and other social categories as variables. The main difference remains, however, that whereas human capital theory conceptualises discrimination as an exception in the model, segmentation approaches construe discriminatory outcomes as structural to labour markets since they are the symptom of broader inequalities within society (Samers 2008, p. 131). The latter reflects the marginalisation of certain groups of individuals according to social markers and processes such as the ascription of gender roles and racialisation, which result in the existence of socially constructed barriers between segments of the labour market. Labour market segmentation approaches originally draw on the dual labour market theory elaborated by Peter Doeringer and Michael Piore (1971). These authors establish a distinction between the primary labour market, where workers generally have relatively high pay and status, job security, good working conditions and opportunities for promotion, and the secondary labour market, where jobs are low-status and poorly paid, with poor working conditions, little job security and little chance for advancement. Going a step further, migrant workers' trajectories call for a theoretical approach that is able to account for intertwining national and international dynamics at work in the production of various forms of segmentation. Michael Samers (2008, p. 131) developed in this regard the concept of 'international labour market segmentation'. He defines it as 'the "sorting" of labour on a global scale by national or macro-regional immigration policies according to a set of desirable characteristics'. In agreement with Samers, I view the segmentation observed empirically in the older-age care sector of most large European cities as the result of such processes of sorting workers according to desirable characteristics.

The role of intermediaries in the job search is described in the first section. The second part of the chapter presents the typology that emerged from the study of participants' employment trajectories from a cross-national perspective. It examines processes of deskilling that characterise the 'overqualified'; it looks into the reasons for entering the care sector for those labelled here as the 'channelled into care'; and it describes the profile of those who have positively chosen the care sector. Non-EU migrant and minority ethnic workers constitute two different groups in the analysis and several sections below focus on migrant workers for the purpose of a cross-national analysis that illuminates the differentiated implications of migration policies for these trajectories as examined in the final section. The routes taken by non-migrant minority ethnic participants in Paris[1] are analysed separately and contrasted with the findings that characterise migrant workers' trajectories.

4.1 Entering the Care Sector: The Role of Intermediaries at the Start of the Journey

Against the background of a structural reliance on migrant and minority ethnic workers, the routes that lead into the care sector differed to a certain extent among the three cities. Table 4.1 sums up the different types of intermediaries encountered along the way by migrant and minority ethnic workers.

Relying on networks of friends and family was very common, and participants' narratives illustrate how these networks are driven by existing labour needs in this sector. In the first quote Rebecca, who came to

---

[1] The choice to focus on Paris is based on the higher number of non-migrant minority ethnic participants in this case study.

Table 4.1 Intermediaries on the journey to the care sector

Site	London	Paris	Madrid
Shared characteristics	Family relatives and friends		
	Direct applications (walk in, via post)		
Distinctive features	Overseas recruitment	French Employment agency (*ANPE/Pôle Emploi*)	Migrant associations Churches Overseas recruitment

Source: Own data and elaboration

Spain from Peru, was convinced to emigrate by her sister who knew of a job vacancy. In the second quote, Julie, who came to the UK 14 years ago from Ghana where she worked as a teacher, explained that her cousin, who had resided in the UK longer than she had, introduced her to the idea of working in the care sector. And finally Jade, in Paris, found the care job through a friend of the relative she was staying with:

Rebecca: I had the opportunity, because there was this job offer and they called me if I wanted to come to Spain because there was a good job for me, expecting me. "Think about it". So I agreed, "Yes I want to come", I want to get to know Spain, at least for two years, so I came, I liked it and I stayed.
NS: And who called you?
Rebecca: My sister. (Rebecca, 46, Peru, Madrid)

> I was looking for a job but I didn't know anything about care but I was reading the newspaper as I told you and one of my cousin was talking about this and she is here for a long time so she explained it to me. (Julie, 45, Ghana, London)

> So, when I arrived, I thought, at worst I go back to studies. And when I arrived, one month, two months, I saw that financially it was difficult because I lived with a cousin of mine who did childcare so financially the situation became difficult. She told me "Listen, we'll try to find a job for you." (…) That acquaintance asked me to care for the elderly woman she was caring for because she went on vacation. And that's how it started. And since I'm here, thank God, I've never been unemployed. (Jade, 46, Ivory Coast, Paris)

In Spain, because of the importance of live-in caring arrangements, migrant associations and churches played an important role, as they were able to act as trustworthy intermediaries between employers and applicants. Adriana benefitted from the services of a migrant association:

> Through the women's association in which I'm a member ... I turned to them because I was interested in the workshops about older-age care. I registered with them and we did some activities, I did the training and later they gave me the phone number of this lady and I went there. (Adriana, 29, Ecuador, Madrid)

In France, over one-third of participants entered the care sector as a result of their contacts with the national employment agency, *Pôle Emploi*, previously named *ANPE*. This state agency dedicated to labour market integration played a significant role in channelling migrants looking for employment into the care sector. Several participants were 'guided' into the care sector when they found themselves unemployed. Aimée wanted to work as a social worker, but was convinced by the counsellor at the agency that care work represented a similar occupation.

> When I went to the job centre,[2] to ask ... to say what I wanted, they guided me, they told me about the sector ... domiciliary care, a lot about domiciliary care, "you'll help people, that's the same thing", so I thought why not to try and I started with the Red Cross as care worker in domiciliary care. (Aimée, 44, Guinea, Paris)

Whatever the intermediary, whether a friend, a cousin, the employment agency or an association, a care job often appeared to be one of the most readily available employment opportunities for participants I have met, especially migrant workers. In Spain, where the economic crisis provoked a spectacular rise in unemployment rates, the care sector represents a rare employment possibility, even though the crisis affected the level of wages, working conditions and the extent of the informal economy. Care work, a devalued, low-paid and physically demanding occupation, is unattractive to workers with full citizenship and without transnational

---

[2] Translation of ANPE, National Employment Agency in France.

commitments and responsibilities. Intermediaries, whether state-promoted or self-organised by migrants themselves, enter into play to respond to the needs created by the intersection of employment, care and migration regimes. Who these intermediaries are and how they operate differ from one capital city to the other, but their function is ultimately the result of a structural reliance on migrant labour, and to different degrees on minority ethnic workers as well. Looking into this segmentation requires therefore going beyond the front desk role of intermediaries for an analysis of migrant and minority ethnic care workers' profiles and trajectories.

4.2   A Typology of the Routes into Older-Age Care

Table 4.2 presents the four categories that emerged from the narratives as to participants' motives for entering the care sector. The first group is composed of nurses who obtained their qualifications back home and who cannot work as nurses in the destination country because their degree is not recognised. The second group of participants comprises those who possess a degree in a field unrelated to care. Some of them obtained these degrees back home; others completed their studies in the destination country. A challenge they share is that they do not work in their profession and face significant barriers to accessing segments of the labour market for which they are theoretically trained. In the third group, participants do not possess any other qualification and started working in

Table 4.2 Non-EU migrant care workers' motives for entering the care sector

	London (n = 21)	Paris (n = 20)	Madrid (n = 27)
Overseas qualified nurses	7	2	1
Overqualified in different sector	10	7	7
'Channelled' into care work (no overqualification)	2	7	16
Professional aspirations in care	2	4	3

Source: Own data and elaboration

the care sector without having positively chosen this occupation. Their stories often converge in that the care job came up unexpectedly. In the fourth group, participants chose to work in the care sector either before they migrated or before they entered the care sector. They took the decision to work in the care sector and their narratives are in that sense different from those of all three other groups.

First, it appears that the non-EU migrant workforce in the care sector is overwhelmingly overqualified. In London, in addition to half of the participants being overqualified in a sector different from care (and healthcare), a third are overseas graduated nurses. The workforce in Paris tends to be qualified in different sectors (one-third of participants), even if to a lesser extent than in London. The specificity of the workforce profile in Paris lies in the highest proportion in relative terms of those who chose to work in the care sector prior to migration or before entering the sector (one-fifth of participants as compared to one-tenth in London and Madrid). In addition to the non-EU migrant workers interviewed, ten and three minority ethnic care workers were interviewed in Paris and in London, respectively. While both these groups are relatively small, the motives of minority ethnic care workers in Paris were strikingly homogeneous: nine out of ten can be placed in the category 'Professional aspirations in care' and one in the category 'Overqualified in different sector'. This illustrates the significantly different position of non-migrant racialised workers in Paris as compared to migrant workers. Most minority ethnic workers chose to work in the care sector, while this is the case for only one-fifth of participants amongst non-EU migrants, their trajectories are thus analysed separately. Finally, it is striking that, in Madrid, among migrant care workers coming from outside the EU, almost three-fifths were 'compelled' into care work, that is, they neither chose it nor were they qualified in a different sector. Clearly, the situation in terms of workforce profile varies greatly from one European capital city to another, beyond the shared reliance on migrant and/or racialised labour. Why is the share of the deskilled nurses and overqualified workers so different? What does the analysis of the motivations of those who chose care work reveal? And, why do significant differences appear between the proportions of those 'channelled' into care work?

Processes of Deskilling

Among those holding a degree or diploma, two broad categories emerged: care workers with a nursing degree on the one hand, and care workers with qualifications in very different fields on the other, such as accounting, engineering, business administration or law, to mention only a few examples. This phenomenon is clearly observable among non-EU migrant care workers in all three cities: it concerned one-third of participants in Madrid, near half in Paris and eight out of ten in London. This section looks into the profile of overqualified care workers, that is, those holding a degree, and points to some of the major barriers that explain this mismatch. The next sub-section analyses the specific situation observed amongst participants in London, where overqualification appeared to be the norm, in order to shed light on the specific case of nurses working as care assistants.

The most common and obvious barrier to labour market integration is the non-recognition of qualifications acquired back home by a migrant person. The absence of recognition is the norm for non-EU migrants, while recognition tends to be facilitated for EU migrants in the framework of EU regulations through a general regime of recognition with sectorial limitations. More often than not, participants in this study hoped for a job in their profession and expected to obtain recognition of their qualifications. They became disillusioned after confronting multiple barriers while seeking to enter the labour market. Camille's quote below illustrates a phase many went through upon arrival:

> I had no idea. I even didn't know the profession existed. Because back home I went to university, I obtained a Bachelor in Law, private Law. I worked with bailiffs, lawyers. So, I would have liked to be a secretary in an office, continue in my profession here. But it's also a time issue. When I arrived I thought I have a big family, they're waiting for me. I can't go back to studies, even the nursing exam, I didn't do it, because I thought three years that's a lot. (Camille, 45, Cameroun, Paris)

Facing barriers that prevented them from continuing on the professional path participants had embarked on back home, the care job in many cases emerged as an opportunity because they needed to find a job as soon as possible and had limited options as to where to search for one. Victoria, in Madrid, explained that she didn't know what a live-in care worker was, until this appeared as the only employment she could easily obtain as a recently arrived migrant from Ecuador.

> So … I came with different … How do I put it? … with a different idea. I had a different life, a different situation. In Ecuador I worked as secretary in a ministry, my job was about informatics and things like this. So when I arrived here, it has been difficult for me because they told me I needed to get my qualification acknowledged first, and then to look for a job, to pass exams and so on. So you feel like doors are being closed in front of you, so what do you do? So the worse option for me was this, I asked around in what I could work and I've been told: "You have to work as live-in carer, there's no other options." And I said: "What's live-in?" I didn't know what it was. (Victoria, 54, Ecuador, Madrid)

The lack of recognition of the qualifications acquired back home requires migrants to complete additional studies, at times starting from scratch, in order to obtain equivalent qualifications. Many issues enter into play when deciding whether additional studies are conceivable. Studies are costly as they usually entail time off work and the payment of fees. Most importantly, workers' caring responsibilities, both in the country where they reside and back home, played a crucial role in their decision as to whether or not to complete additional studies for the purpose of recognition. The need to send remittances back home prevented Camille from taking the time she needed to study for her career again in France, a pressure many others were confronted with. The concept of international labour market segmentation (Samers 2008) is here illuminating: taking into account elements such as international agreements or remittance flows can explain the different position of migrant workers according to intersecting social and legal markers, such as nationality, 'ethnicity' and gender. The pressing need to send remittances creates in that sense a particular vulnerability and disempowers migrant workers by diminishing their bargaining power. The 'institutional insecurity' (Anderson 2010) in which denizens, that is, persons with limited rights

(Standing 2011; De Genova 2013), find themselves because of their migration statuses is connected to global inequalities and shaped by international relations imbued with post- and neo-colonial power relationships.

Among those holding a qualification in a different field, some decided to make the sacrifices required of them to obtain recognition of their qualifications. My focus on care workers did not allow me to explore the trajectories of those who effectively worked in a different sector after obtaining recognition. Participants I have met, still employed in the care sector, were unable to improve their labour market opportunities in spite of having either studied in the country they migrated to, or completed additional studies for the purpose of recognition. Fadila, who had arrived to the UK from Bangladesh four years before I interviewed her, completed a master's degree in Business Law, but could not find a job in her field because of the limitations imposed by her student visa:

> I tried different jobs but I couldn't find anything, they told me if you want to work it has to be full-time but I was not allowed to do full-time because that time I was student. So one of my friend, he used to work in (care home name), he told me you cannot find any job but if you are interested you can work in the care sector, there are some vacancies for part-time workers. (Fadila, 30, Bangladesh, London)

As for Claudia, she worked for several years in Peru as a child psychologist before migrating to Spain with her children to join her husband. When she arrived she was hoping to find a similar job in Madrid, but this proved impossible to obtain, even after she had studied for two years towards the recognition of her degree at the Complutense, a prestigious state-funded university in the Spanish capital. She felt deeply frustrated by this situation:

> My degree was in psychology, it has been difficult to get it, because to obtain the recognition it took me two years of studies at the Complutense, and there's nothing. Maybe there is but I would need some specialisation. (Claudia, 53, Peru, Madrid)

Clearly, the non-recognition of qualifications relates to broader inequalities, and qualifications by themselves do not necessarily translate into better labour market outcomes, contrary to what human capital theory would suggest. More helpful in this regard is the bourdieusian concept of cultural capital and the attached distinctions between embodied, objectified and institutionalised cultural capital (Bourdieu 1979). Embodied cultural capital is possession transformed into being: it is a person's habitus acquired with time and intrinsically linked to the person's body. In the last form of cultural capital described by Bourdieu, the process of institutionalisation through collective recognition owing to conventional values establishes cultural capital (Bourdieu 1979). Umut Erel (2010) argues that the notion of institutionalised cultural capital helps to 'explain how educational and professional institutions exercise nationally-based protectionism by not recognising qualifications acquired abroad' (p. 648). Furthermore, institutionalised cultural capital is intrinsically related to embodied cultural capital. Racialisation processes precisely deny migrants' ability to embody the dominant cultural capital, attached to criteria of nationality and physical appearance in latent and manifest forms. Pervasive labour market discrimination thus prevents some of those who obtained recognition from making use of their qualifications.

Employers have a vested interest in employing migrant nurses as care assistants from among the overqualified who completed nursing degrees but have to accept a lower position because they do not fulfil institutional requirements for recognition. Rita for instance had been a midwife in Ecuador; she did nightshifts as a nurse in a care home in Madrid and worked as a care assistant during the day in domiciliary care:

> In domiciliary care my contract is not as a nurse, no. But because they see in my curriculum that I'm qualified and that I have experience with elderly people, they give me work that is related, that requires trained staff. Because the company does more shopping, cleaning, cooking but they also have people who need nursing care. So taking advantage of my professional knowledge and my experience luckily they allocated me persons more in my field. (Rita, 54, Ecuador, Madrid)

While Rita was happy that she was not given cooking or cleaning tasks to do as part of her job in domiciliary care, the company was making use of her skills without compensating her with a corresponding level of earnings. If the share of nurses working as care assistants was on the whole limited in Paris and in Madrid, nurses represented one-third of the 21 migrant participants in London, which points to a structural pattern of professional deskilling. The following section identifies the encountered barriers.

Producing Overqualification Through the Points-Based Immigration System?

Overqualification emerged as the rule rather than an exception amongst care workers in London who came from outside the European Union. Eight in ten were overqualified and one-third of participants held nursing degrees obtained in the country of origin, not only, but most frequently, in the Philippines. Among the reasons why qualified nurses did not work in the corresponding positions is a combination of institutional barriers at the intersection of migration and sectorial employment policies. Formal requirements, and the costs they implied, appeared to be increasingly discouraging for migrant workers. These constraints were strong enough to deter overseas registered nurses from engaging in the process and kept them in positions in which their salary was the lowest in the professional hierarchy. According to Pam Smith and Maureen Mackintosh, 'many of the migrant nurses working as care assistants in the UK residential nursing and care home sector are among the 37,000 estimated in 2005 to be waiting for adaptation programme' (2007, p. 2218).[3] Among the participants in this study, some gave up on the idea of completing the adaptation programme someday. This was, for instance, Marissa's case: she referred to the changing opportunity structure in relation to the adaptation programmes required for recognition, and to her age. At the time of the interview she had been working in the UK for 11 years:

---

[3] An adaptation programme consists of a mix of required professional experience and formal education completed in the UK for the purpose of recognition of the nursing degree completed overseas.

Before it's easy to do adaptation now it's very hard because there were so many changes in the policy that you should do before doing your practising nursing here. Before there were loads of nursing homes and hospitals having adaptation but now it's very rare it's very hard so I said … because I'm already 60, I don't want to practice anymore as a nurse that's it. (Marissa, 60, the Philippines, London)

As noted by Eleonore Kofman and Parvati Raghuram: 'After 2005 a number of measures were brought in by the National Health Service (NHS), the Nursing and Midwifery Council (NMC) and the UK Border Agency, all working together to produce a downward trend in the registration of overseas nurses' (2015, p. 146). Restrictions on entering the National Health Service for non-EEA (European Economic Area) workers and reforms in the nursing adaptation programmes, with increased registration fees and fewer places, limited the possibility of working in the NHS (Shutes 2014; Kofman and Raghuram 2015). In the private sector, the lack of company-sponsored schemes requires workers to go through this process externally, which represents a financial cost and requires time off work, a concession that many could not make in the face of pressing financial needs. In the first quote below, Karen explained that she could not afford any income reduction, which would have happened had she decided to work towards recognition of her qualification. Family responsibilities often added to these difficulties given the unequal distribution of care responsibilities and domestic chores at home. For migrant women, these inequalities were exacerbated by the absence of support networks, as in the case of Alma.

At the moment I'm not doing it yet because I'm helping my family back home. Because they explained it to me if you are doing that they just give you small money that's my worry that's why I am not doing it. But in the future I want to do it as well. (Karen, estimated 20–30, the Philippines, London)

In the Philippines I'm a nursing graduate. But I can't work as a nurse because I need to do adaptation and everything and I don't have time for that yet with the children and all. (Alma, 41, the Philippines, London)

Caring responsibilities, whether in the country of residence or back home, had a notable impact on labour market opportunities because of the constraints they created. In his analysis of international labour market segmentation, Michael Samers pointed out that 'the degree of financial stress of the family in the country of origin may affect the migrants' acceptance of certain kinds of working conditions, including pay and hours' (Samers 2008, p. 138). Rosa, who came from China, found herself in such a situation. She came to the UK with an agency, through which she and her friends began English classes. In her case most of her entourage continued studying to achieve recognition of qualifications, but she was unable to do so because of the urgent need to send money home:

> Because before I came here I have English class, the English class through agency they send you to university. But for me I have family I have children, just to work I don't want to spend that money I need to make money for my family. So I chose to work and not go to university. If you can go it's okay, most of my classmates chose to go to Uni to study two years, three years and then pass the IELTS examination and register as a nurse but I gave up. (Rosa, 44, China, London)

The IELTS (International English Language Testing System) exam was considered a significant barrier to overcome, especially since the required level rose from 6.5 to 7 in 2007. Sitting such a written exam was therefore perceived as very time consuming due to the preparation it required, something that migrant care workers with caring responsibilities in the domestic sphere could not cope with. Joyce, mother of an 18-month-old son, saw the IELTS exam as the main barrier to the recognition of her diploma:

> A problem in UK if you want to work as a nurse, you have to do the IELTS exam, that's quite difficult and until now I didn't give my exam, for if I pass that exam I can work as a staff nurse here. I didn't try really, I don't get time to go for the school or training you know. (Joyce, 30, India, London)

Given that this requirement applies only to non-EU nurses, migrant nurses from the Central and Eastern European countries that joined the EU in 2004 did not have to pass this test. This further divided the workforce and was perceived as deeply discriminatory. It was interpreted as particularly unfair by some of the migrant workers I have interviewed, given that they were working with East European care workers and observed that their level of English varied greatly, with many having what they considered to be a rather weak command of the language. These institutional barriers provide an example of how migration policies create, on the one hand, inequalities between citizens and non-citizens and, on the other hand, between various categories of non-citizens, in this case between EU and non-EU migrants. The trajectories of these women further reveal how borders materially impact on their lives long after non-EU migrants enter the EU. The notion of 'proliferation of borders' highlights the temporal impact of a multiplication of borders: 'The control of international borders involved in such efforts also has marked effects on establishing internal administrative borders and categories that divide labor markets, separate migrant groups beyond and within the boundaries of ethnicity, and provide parameters within which individual migrants negotiate their biographies' (Mezzadra and Neilson 2013, p. 138). The lengthening of the time required to obtain recognition of a nursing degree, through the tightening of opportunities and increase in costs, creates a significant temporal border which keeps skilled care labour outside the labour market that corresponds to their level of skills and experience.

On the whole, overseas graduated nurses, who work as care assistants or senior carers, are caught up in a series of constraints embedded in privatisation processes, migration policies as well as gender roles. The externalisation of the cost of adaptation programmes by private companies constitutes a critical barrier; however, its implications need to be understood in articulation with additional elements such as the IELTS exam that is required for non-EU workers or criteria for accessing residency and work permits, pointing ultimately at British migration policies. Gender roles cannot be overlooked either, as they impose a set of responsibilities and duties upon women in the domestic sphere that shape patterns of labour market participation and often increase their vulnerability.

In comparative terms, the prevalence of overqualification within the care sector in London derives from the British points-based immigration system that denies the existence of labour needs for occupations deemed low skilled. This system, introduced in 2008, defines migrants' rights according to their alleged economic utility based upon labour needs identified at a given time. As a consequence of this policy, non-EU migrants can only qualify for skilled and highly skilled jobs whose definition depends on the 'shortage occupation list' elaborated by the Migration Advisory Committee. Care assistants are not on the list for the abovementioned reasons, in spite of the labour needs demonstrated by previous research (Cangiano et al. 2009). The introduction in the UK of a £35,000 salary threshold for migrant workers as of April 2016 further threatens non-EU migrant workers, and in particular care workers, and puts them at risk of being deported. The cost of these policies is mostly borne by non-EU migrant workers themselves, given that a pool of workers becomes available as a result of the institutional barriers that hamper their professional opportunities.

In the following section, I examine the trajectories of care workers who did not choose to be employed in older-age care but who, in contrast, were not overqualified. The comparison illuminates key differences between the three cities in terms of labour force profile in the sector, with this category of care workers representing the majority of participants in Madrid.

The 'Channelled' into Care Amongst Non-EU Migrants

The second most significant group of participants are those I have grouped under the category 'channelled into care work'. This category brings together all individuals that do not possess specific qualifications and for whom entering the care sector came as a surprise. They did not enter the labour market with the expectations held by those in the overqualified category, but at the same time they did not expect or choose to work in the care sector either. All individual stories within this group revolve around the idea that the care job somehow happened, was often conceived as temporary at first, but lasted in the long run.

To illustrate this argument, the following paragraphs describe the recruitment procedures as experienced by migrant care workers in London, Paris and Madrid. Workers' narratives converge in their description of care jobs as easily accessible and recruitment processes as particularly fast. Madrid is in this regard the only site where this perception of job availability needs to be nuanced because care jobs in residential care homes are considered relatively privileged employment opportunities in comparison with live-in caring arrangements, which are often informal and remunerated below the National Minimum Wage. Moreover, the extent of the 2008 economic crisis brought Spanish women back into the sector of residential care, as noted by migrant care workers I have interviewed. Migrant women who completed training in geriatric care, provided by an association, local authorities or an NGO, experienced nevertheless similar hiring processes to those undergone by their colleagues in London and Paris. In the three quotes below, Adam in London, Adèle in Paris and Imene in Madrid relate how they found their first job in the care sector:

> I saw a care home so I just came in and asked for it, can I have a job, like a vacancy. It was [the deputy manager] who was here, so she said—what job? I said 'any job, I don't mind doing any job'. (…) He [the manager] doesn't look up for person who has got a lot of experience or anything, he looks for people who have got good attitude towards work. (…) I was fortunate enough that I got the job and I couldn't even believe it. I came in 2009 December 16th, the 21st I started working here. (Adam, 29, India, London)

> So I passed the exam and I had many options. I had someone in the city, and I went to a care home, and I did domiciliary care, so I had three jobs. Three jobs at the same time. (Adèle, 56, Cameroun, Paris)

> The moment I received the certificate of studies from this company that provided it through local authorities, they said we could get a job in that company, that local authorities had a contract with the company, something like this. (…) Because I had completed the training and around where I live there are many care homes that are not from this company, I was about to drop off my curriculum but they called me so I accepted and I didn't have to look for long. (Imene, 31, Peru, Madrid)

The availability of jobs is here the decisive factor in shaping partici-pants' path into employment within the care sector. The recruitment phase can be described as a 'fast hiring process' (England and Dyck 2012), which partly explains why migrant workers are 'attracted' to the care sec-tor. Adèle and Imene, in Paris and Madrid, respectively, where training is required prior to recruitment, found a job even before they completed their training. Employers frequently offered jobs during work placements that were part of the training.

Moreover, the feminisation of the sector gave men an 'advantage' at the time of applying for care jobs. In London and in Paris, male workers had the impression that employers favour male workers, precisely because the majority of workers are women, so that men would be expected to be fit for the heavy bodily work that care work entails. The hardship of care work as bodily work that involves handling and lifting other bodies is part of what renders the profession unattractive (see Chap. 6). Migrant men's relative position in the labour market is defined both by gender and by migration, that is, the social marker of being a male migrant and the legal implications of being a denizen. Here, the intersection of gender and migration leads to a certain redefinition of gendered cultural norms. The NMSD-SC database[4] shows, for instance, that in London 14% of care workers are men whereas this figure drops to 10.9% on average in England (excluding London). Arguably, the higher participation of non-EEA migrants in London (25 vs. 7% in all of England but London) is the most significant variable explaining the higher proportion of men in the care workforce in London. Though the corresponding quantitative data are not available for Paris and Madrid, my qualitative insights suggest similar dynamics. Luc, employed in a private care home in Paris, explained that he could find a job anytime because as a male care worker his profile was very much sought after by employers:

NS: And to find the job was it easy?
Luc: Very easy, it's easy, very easy. I apply today, I drop off 5 CV, during the week I'll be called. Like now, I have maybe 6 messages on my phone. They're expecting me for interviews because I've sent my

---

[4] Database last accessed on June 10, 2015.

> CV and I receive messages, that's how it is. Being a man, it goes
> really fast. (Luc, 25, Cameroon, Paris)

In Spain, where many care workers are employed as live-in carers, gender comes to play an equally important role. After the economic crisis hit particularly hard in masculinised sectors like the construction industry, male migrant workers were massively laid off. While some decided to return, for example, return migration to Ecuador has been significant, a proportion of migrant men who remained in Spain entered the care sector. Illustrative of this trend is the case of Saul, a young migrant from El Salvador, who worked on construction sites and became a care worker after he lost his job. In the quote below, he explains how he had to leave a job where he cared for an elderly couple after the health of the woman deteriorated and the family who employed him did not want a male worker to attend to the elderly woman. In his next job, however, he was employed precisely because of being a male worker, as he was expected to care for a middle-aged man suffering from schizophrenia, who could behave aggressively.

> I was in charge of the man because the lady in spite of her age was very
> independent. But she had an accident, not really an accident but she had
> an illness related to her bones and she broke her hip (…) After this hap-
> pened her children took the decision to employ a woman instead of me,
> which was normal. (Saul, 27, El Salvador, Madrid)

Being easily accessible, care work was nevertheless quite unexpected, both for those who held higher qualifications and for those who did not. Importantly, participants described here as the 'channelled' (with or without overqualification) were not necessarily dissatisfied with their jobs (discourses around occupational identity are analysed in Chap. 7). I emphasise the distinction within the analysis between the study of participants' routes into employment in the care sector and the analysis of participants' discourses about their working experiences. That being said, for a great majority of participants, the care job constituted a new professional environment that they needed to accommodate and which they did not conceive of as positively chosen.

Participants thus often described the process they underwent to 'get used' to the daily tasks of care assistants and to overcome their apprehensions. Analyn, who came to the UK from the Philippines where she worked in the textile industry, and Beronica who came to Spain from Ecuador after having completed a degree in Administration, describe these early experiences:

NS: Did you think before that you will work in the care sector?
Analyn: No! Not in my dream! Because they said oh you gonna wipe a pooh, oh my God! But I tried. First time of course I cried. If you're not used to it, it feels really like a very small person looking ... you know ... wiping, cleaning the places first time I really looked like.... I'm crying I've never done this before isn't it? So I was crying before but now I don't care about that I'm just used to it. (Analyn, 50, the Philippines, London)

The next day I went to his place. I didn't know anything. (…) But I had to cook, I had no idea how to cook ... How I should care for an older person.... I was lost. I had a hard time getting used to it. (Beronica, 38, Ecuador, Madrid)

The large share of workers 'channelled' in one way or another into care raises the question of compelled care:

'Whereas in the past, caring was largely taken for granted as belonging in the private family sphere and as an activity natural to women, we see that the way in which it is organised and carried out is far from "natural" but rather is shaped by political and economic forces, social policy, and popular discourse. We can nonetheless see significant indications of continuity in the imposition of coercion, even if the outward appearance of the forms may have changed. Today, more women than ever before are being forced to care, in new and problematic ways'. (Nakano Glenn 2010, p. 182)

At the micro and meso levels, this theme is further explored in Chap. 6 in relation to the emotional labour performed by care workers. At the macro level, and from a political economy perspective, it raises the question of the distribution of care responsibilities within society and the underpinning global inequalities (Tronto 2013; Robinson, 2014, see also Chap. 9 in this book).

The fourth and last group of participants described in the following two sub-sections is different from the other three in one fundamental aspect: it comprises those who chose the care sector, either prior to migration or to their confrontation with the labour market in the country of destination (and who were not overqualified in care). The two sections below explore their trajectories and motivations and look into the specific case of minority ethnic workers in Paris who overwhelmingly belonged to this category.

Chosen Care Work: Workers' Agency in Building a Career

Amongst non-EU migrant workers in this study, few had professional aspirations in the care sector prior to migration or prior to their entry into the sector. Some participants developed such professional aspirations after having worked in the care industry for several years; the latter are not included here because this category attempts to capture the trajectories of those who wanted to work in the care sector, as opposed to those for whom it was not chosen and was unexpected at first. This distinction serves the purpose of better apprehending the impact of care, migration and employment policies on participants' trajectories.

The first group of workers within this category concerns those who considered their care job as a stepping-stone to obtaining a care-related degree, often within nursing. For instance, Selwa in Paris, a young woman from Morocco, started her career with the aim of becoming a nurse, which requires three years of study. Unable to support herself financially, she decided to interrupt her studies and work for one year as a care assistant in domiciliary care before resuming her career. In London, Aisha, a young woman who arrived four years earlier in the UK from Rwanda, was working as a care assistant in a care home and was studying at the same time to become a social worker. Her job helped her to finance her studies but she also believed it contributed to building up professional experience for her future career prospects:

NS: And how do you cope with your work and your studies?
Aisha: It's quite hard but I'm really glad because the kind of work that I do makes it so easy in my studies because I just apply it when

> I have the experience (...) because I'm doing it already it's easier for me to study and also because I study it comes back as well if I'm managing people or trying to help them with their personal care or emotional well-being it is easier for me (...) My studies help me do my job well. (Aisha, n.a., Rwanda, London)

Others had worked in the care sector prior to migration and resumed in the sector afterwards, at times directly through overseas recruitment schemes. Private companies in London and in Madrid used to resort to overseas recruitment, while this seems not to have been the case in Paris. Observing that one-third of participants in Paris were from French overseas departments, mainly from Guadeloupe and Martinique, reveals that private companies could indirectly rely on historic corridors of state-sponsored labour migration. Many of the care workers in Paris who came from overseas departments had worked in public hospitals before entering private older-age care. In the UK, in their study of the migration of nurses, Pam Smith and Maureen Mackintosh note that 'ambitious targets for increasing the NHS workforce were met through active recruitment of overseas nurses' (2007, p. 2217). In Spain, these practices seem to have come to a halt after the 2008 economic crisis. Naomi, who came from Colombia in 2007, gave the following account of her arrival in Madrid:

> I arrived through an agreement to bring people from abroad to work in this sector specifically. So (name of company) had an agreement or they were part of a group of companies that brought people from abroad and I applied being in my country, in Colombia. I'm a healthcare assistant, I applied and they selected staff there, I went to psychologists and I came. We arrived in groups, many of us, 200 people came and they spread us out in different workplaces in Madrid. (Naomi, 37, Colombia, Madrid)

Another group of participants who chose care work consists of individuals who worked in diverse 'small jobs' before they opted for care work. The reason most clearly articulated in these cases was a preference for a 'humane job' that contrasted with jobs in the retail or food industry. Often the level of pay would not vary greatly from one type of job to another so that the decision to enter and to stay within the care sector did not depend on the financial remuneration. Nabila, who worked in a private care home in Paris for six years at the time of the interview, explained her choice:

> I did a lot of casual work, but after that I turned to person-related work, older people, because I like to work with older people, so I changed occupation. Before that I worked in the food service industry, fast food, I worked in a McDonalds, I worked there for six years. (Nabila, 40, Senegal, Paris)

Several participants also referred to the choice of an occupation within the care sector as resulting from a personal trauma, an illness or death affecting one of their loved ones. Fouzia, who used to work in a bank, is one of them:

> I worked for two years at [bank name]. I didn't like it, because on the one hand there's stress, and on the other hand I've lost my parents, my mum, who was very dear to me. In the evening I call her over the phone, she was very well, and the next day she died. I couldn't … I didn't have time with the flight and everything … I couldn't go and see her. And I felt guilty because I didn't do many things for my mother, so I was depressed for one month. I told my husband I won't work at [bank name] anymore. Administration it's not my thing. So I resigned, I completed a small training and right away I found a job, I didn't even have a qualification. I found a job as life assistant. (Fouzia, 43, Algeria, Paris)

On the whole, those who presented their employment in the care sector as a choice constituted a minority (between one-tenth and one-fifth of participants) in all three cities. While this does not mean that it necessarily resulted in dissatisfaction with the job at the subjective level for most participants, it does however reflect the far-reaching implications of the channelling of migrant workers into care as a result of the articulation of various policy fields. Workers who chose care work did so for various reasons: as a stepping-stone, as a continuation of their occupation back home or as a professional vocation. The following paragraphs examine in greater detail the group of minority ethnic care workers in Paris, most of whom chose to work in the care sector and thus articulated different narratives than most of the non-EU migrant care workers.

The Case of Minority Ethnic Care Workers in Paris

Amongst the ten minority ethnic care workers interviewed in Paris, nine presented their employment in older-age care as a choice and the result of the career they envisaged in the sector. The individual trajectories of several women I met illustrated the French state's policies from the 1960s to the 1980s which supported the emigration of women from French overseas departments to metropolitan France, notably to fill jobs in public healthcare (Condon 2000), similarly to the role Caribbean women played in the British context to enable the National Health Service to be introduced and rolled out. Eloise, for instance, arrived in France in the midst of increasing migration to metropolitan France from Guadeloupe, Martinique and Reunion Island unfolding in the 1970s (Marie and Temporal 2011). She started her career at the bottom of the professional hierarchy in a public hospital but with civil servant status (a privilege that migrant workers could not access), as was common for many women from overseas departments at that time (Condon 2000). She chose to pursue a life-long career in the hospital and though older-age care was not her preference she started working in private residential care at retirement age.

> I came from Guadeloupe, I'm from Guadeloupe and there there were no jobs, but when I arrived here, in 1976, there were jobs here. I had the choice between public health, working in hospitals, or family allowances. I worked as cashier, I worked in a factory, I did small jobs before I started at the hospital. (…) I preferred working at the hospital, not with older persons, but when I started at the hospital it was fine. (Eloise, 59, Guadeloupe, Paris)

To the younger generations, care work was often conceived of as a step towards nursing, at times after a period of exploring various study and work opportunities. Four out of the ten participants in this group had either attempted to pass the nursing entry exam or were in the process of being trained as nurses. The case of Laëtitia illustrates these trajectories:

> The training as care assistant I did it in Guadeloupe. But in Guadeloupe I went on with my studies, I did the medico-social A-Level and after that I went to university for two years, I started a Bachelor in biology, I didn't like it, it was a bit to prove to myself how far I could get in school. After that I passed the nursing exam, I didn't pass the interview, so I told to myself, I start step by step, I start as care assistant and I'll see later for nursing school. (Laëtitia, 29, Guadeloupe, Paris)

The following section relates these insights to the workings of migration policies with a focus on the trajectories of non-EU migrant workers for comparative purposes.

4.3   Differentiated Shortcomings of Utilitarian Migration Policies

The presented typology of entry trajectories demonstrates (1) a significant mismatch between the aims assigned to utilitarian migration policies and the actual profile of the workforce in all the sites of fieldwork, and (2) crucial differences in the trajectories of non-EU migrant care workers in spite of a shared reliance on migrant labour for older-age care.

Cangiano argues that, besides EU migrants, another recruitment pool for the care sector is composed of individuals who entered via other categories than work, notably family reunification, studies and asylum (2014, p. 140). The insights of my research are in line with this statement and offer interpretations as to its meanings for migrant workers. The significant share of the 'overqualified' and the 'channelled' in the three sites hints at the long-lasting implications of migration and employment policies, beyond the role of intermediaries which only facilitates the working of broader processes.

With an overwhelming share of overqualified workers in London, those channelled into care work mostly possess high qualifications that would theoretically offer them opportunities in a less segmented section of the labour market. In this research, a group of migrant care workers were granted visas as students, and Cangiano notes that 'the UK stands out for the relatively large share of care workers entering via the student route', where this is the case for 15% of migrant care workers vs. 4% of the EU-15 average (2014, p. 141). The opposite can be observed in Madrid, where the majority of migrant care workers do not possess qualifications and where very few enter as students. Previous research (Rodríguez Rodríguez 2012), as well as this study, points out that many care workers come as tourists, start working in the care sector, overstay their visas and finally obtain documentation after varying periods of time. In Paris, among participants in this study, one in four migrated to France through family reunification and three obtained refugee status. This finding is confirmed by Cangiano's study: workers who came for family reunification play a crucial role in meeting labour needs in the care sector.

It appears therefore that migration policies, in all three cases, and in spite of the significant differences between the migration regimes, fail to achieve the goals they pretend to pursue. The British points-based immigration system selects migrants on the basis of their planned economic contribution. Arguably, there exists already a mismatch between the perceived needs and the actual needs, given that it is assumed that low-skilled labour needs will be filled by intra-European migration. Cangiano shows however that intra-EU migration in the care sector corresponds to around one-fourth of the migrant workforce, that is, three-quarters come from outside the EU. Furthermore, additional institutional rules, notably regarding qualification recognition, as well as pervasive labour market discrimination, intertwine with the long-lasting effects of migration policies so as to produce a great mismatch of skills. Highly skilled migrants cannot access the labour market opportunities they theoretically could aspire to, are effectively deskilled through institutional and social barriers, and are constrained to join the labour market at its lower ends as demonstrated by many of the trajectories described in this chapter.

While the Spanish migration regime combines utilitarian hypotheses with cultural assumptions, it similarly produces entrapment and discrimination for non-EU migrant workers. As mentioned in Chap. 3, the Spanish migration regime is strongly determined by postcolonial preferences that define rights according to the nationality of origin. Migrants from Latin America were able to travel to Spain on tourist visas, and consequently migrants from these countries present a more diverse profile (than for instance non-EU migrant workers in this sector in the UK). A significant share of participants did not complete studies in their country of origin, and either did not work prior to migration or worked in 'small jobs' or 'casual work'. From the perspective of the labour market, migration policies fail however to offer any consistent path into employment in this case too. Many participants from Latin America in this study have spent several years being undocumented after having entered the country as tourists. Given the weak welfare state, these migrants answer crucial needs in the labour market, filling in thousands of jobs: 71,194 domestic care workers were for instance registered in 2008 (Rodríguez Rodríguez 2012); and this figure would increase greatly if informal arrangements were included. This structural reliance is well researched (IMSERSO 2005; Rodríguez Rodríguez 2012); migrants need however to prove their utility to the Spanish economy on a case-by-case basis in order to obtain documentation and Spanish citizenship, often a lengthy and costly struggle, while the state benefits economically from letting them provide cheap care services.

These contradictions demonstrate that utilitarian migration policies, which define workers' rights according to their potential economic added value, are in fact detached from the actual needs of the labour market, while they do have a negative impact on migrant workers' employment trajectories because of the deskilling processes that they generate and the constraints they impose on workers' agency. This 'institutionalised uncertainty' (Anderson 2010) engendered by socially constructed barriers entraps workers into specific segments of the labour market. Subordinating workers' rights to their economic contribution, based on a manifest criterion of nationality and a latent criterion of gender, on the one hand serves employers' interests in that it sustains the figure of the 'good and disciplined' worker and on the other feeds into labour market segmentation and benefits those in more stable and privileged sectors of employment. This happens at the cost of hierarchising rights and turning workers into disposable units of labour on the pretext of ensuring they do not lay down roots in the EU. Given that for two decades the increase in total population in the EU is largely due to international migration[5] and that the demographic forecasts predict an increasing reliance, the economic justification of this temporariness mantra is questionable: 'can temporary worker programs meet the future labour needs of the EU, if these are not temporary in nature, but rather the result of long-term shifts in demographic and economic structures?' (Castles 2006, p. 759). Not only are these policies inadequate to answer the demographic and thus economic challenges of the EU, it is implemented by creating 'denizens' (Standing 2011; De Genova 2013) and fragmenting the workforce. Migrant workers' disproportionate participation in the older-age care sector is symptomatic of their exclusion and collective embodiment of the 'Other'.

> As the historical records show, if one wishes to exclude some people from participating in democratic life, then the problems of care are easily solved. One assigns the responsibilities for caring to non-citizens: women, slaves, "working-class foreigners" (More 1965 [1516]), or others who are so marked. But once a democratic society makes a commitment to the equality of all its members, then the ways in which the inequalities of care affect different citizens' capacities to be equal has to be a central part of the society's *political* tasks. (Tronto 2013, p. 10)

Molinier, in a similar vein, argues that 'the patriarchal dream can only hold by exploiting a silent and invisible workforce'[6] (2013, p. 36). Care provision through the market enacts this unequal distribution of care responsibilities along gendered and racialised divisions. The discourse of consumers' choice has played a major role in shaping the employment of migrant workers (Williams 2011c) but as argued by Tronto, the neoliberal ideology goes against the principles of democracy and equality entailed in a feminist democratic ethic of care in that choice isn't freedom, neither equality, nor justice (2013, pp. 40–41). In contrast, a commitment to care ethics requires that care workers have equal rights and equality of voice.

---

[5] Eurostats statistics: http://ec.europa.eu/eurostat/statistics-explained/index.php/File:Population_change_by_component_(annual_crude_rates),_EU-28,_1960–2014_(¹)_(per_1_000_persons)_YB15_II.png, last accessed February 2016.

[6] Original quote: 'le rêve patriarchal ne peut se maintenir qu'en exploitant une main d'œuvre silencieuse et invisible.'

4.4   Conclusion

The presented cross-national comparison analysed how specific dimensions of migration and care regimes influenced migrant and minority ethnic workers' employment trajectories in three European capital cities. The chapter highlighted the channelling of migrant and minority ethnic workers into older-age care and illustrated the social implications of labour market segmentation. The intersectional approach adopted here revealed how distinct migration and care regimes create differentiated outcomes for workers. First, looking into why and under what circumstances non-EU migrant and minority ethnic workers enter the care sector uncovered the distinct roles of intermediaries such as employment agencies, migrant associations, churches and informal networks against the background of various employment regimes. From workers' narratives, three main categories emerged: 'the overqualified', 'the channelled into care' without qualification and those with professional aspirations in care-related careers. Variations in the workforce profile between the three cities reveal the significant impact of migration policies on who these care workers are in terms of nationality, gender and qualifications.

Given the EU demographic scenario, being attentive to the trajectories of non-EU migrants in older-age care is crucial for the construction of inclusive European societies, and this chapter demonstrates that the articulation of migration, employment and care policies produces various degrees of segmentation in the UK, France and Spain. Looked at through the lenses of the care ethics paradigm, these inequalities raise the question of social justice (Williams 2011c; Tronto 2011b). The marginalisation of racialised care workers is detrimental to the very idea of a democratic society in that it excludes in many ways, notably legally and economically, individuals that play a major role in terms of society's caring responsibilities.

The focus of this chapter on the beginning of participants' trajectories within the care sector served to identify the meanings attached to care work in participants' narration of their lives, and to foreground the dynamics that underpin the channelling of certain categories of workers into a segmented section of the labour market. It sat the scene for the following chapters that focus on participants' employment terms and the content of their work.

5

Precarious Care Jobs in Neoliberal Times

So right now we don't know if in a year from now we'll still be employed or if we'll be laid off. Right now no job is stable, even if you have a contract. You know, I have a permanent contract but I don't know to what extent it's permanent, because we've seen ... we've seen cases of colleagues who were on permanent contracts and for one reason or another they were laid off. So, I tell you, right now no job is stable. (Victoria, 54, Ecuador, Madrid)

Victoria is an Ecuadorian woman who had been living in Spain for 26 years when I interviewed her. For most of these 26 years, she had been working two jobs: a couple of nights per week she took care of residents in a care home, and during the day she provided domiciliary care to several elderly persons. In spite of being on a full-time and permanent contract in the care home, Victoria considered it provided no employment security and thus no financial stability for her family. In the 'day-job' she had a written contract for the hours worked on Monday and Friday and she had no contract for the persons she visited during the rest of the week. In her eyes, nonetheless, she was far more likely to lose her job in the care home than one of these small jobs with older persons whom she had been visiting for years. Victoria's narrative reveals how the instability

© The Author(s) 2019
N. Sahraoui, *Racialised Workers and European Older-Age Care*, Thinking Gender in Transnational Times, https://doi.org/10.1007/978-3-030-14397-8_5

and low wages in both roles persuaded her to work multiple jobs simultaneously. In policy realms, the usual definition of precarious employment does not include full-time permanent contracts (ILO 2012), as these are deemed stable and secure. Focusing on workers' contracts in assessing the precariousness of a given employment relationship might, however, be misleading as to the actual security it offers to workers, as illustrated by Victoria's quote. The meaning of 'permanent' in a contract cannot be assumed and needs unpacking. If there is no significant difference in terms of employment protection between a permanent and a fixed-term contract in a given employment regime, then the boundary between temporary and permanent contracts is effectively blurred. The employment relationship is furthermore shaped by the characteristics of the employment sector, and the meaning of 'permanent' and 'temporary' for workers varies accordingly. This chapter revisits the concept of precarious employment by bringing in the subjective dimension contained in the meanings that participants attach to various indicators of employment precariousness.

As a matter of fact, employment conditions in older-age care are often described as 'vulnerable' or 'precarious' (Datta et al. 2006; Anderson 2010), reflecting material conditions which characterise marginalised and segmented sections of the labour market. I argue that the concept of 'vulnerability' does not allow for a thorough political economy analysis such as is enabled by the concept of 'precarious employment' (this argument is developed below). By drawing on the distinction put forward by Serge Paugam (2009) between employment precariousness and work precariousness (while insisting on their complementarity from the standpoint of workers' experiences), this chapter contributes to the development of theoretical bridges between a feminist moral philosophy and a sociological analysis of care labour. Chapters 5 and 6 argue that it is theoretically fruitful to conduct a care ethics-sensitive analysis of precarious employment and work. This chapter focuses on employment precariousness, while Chap. 6 looks into work precariousness. Employment precariousness concerns the employment status and rights attached to it, and work precariousness relates to the content of the work per se. Employment (in)stability relates for instance to the duration of contract, levels of pay and the prospects for future employment, whereas work precariousness entails aspects such as workload and health and safety issues. The conversation carried out in these two chapters between these strands of literature allows us to revisit both: on the one hand, calling for political recognition of the centrality of care ethics for life sustainability, as put forward by Tronto (2013), has implications for the status of care work within society and thus its material conditions; and on the other, the precariousness of life paradigm (explored in the following chapter) sheds light on dimensions of older-age care work that would have remained concealed within a narrow understanding of precarity.

The first section briefly situates precarious employment in relation to neoliberal capitalism and more specifically to current processes of marketisation within older-age care. Building upon the analytical framework presented in the first section, I then turn to the analysis of participants' perceptions of job stability and their lived experience of daily uncertainties. The third section of the chapter analyses cross-nationally participants' material precariousness resulting from low levels of earnings. In the final section I explore participants' perceptions of their entitlements to sick payments and annual leave as well as their involvement with unions.

5.1   Precarious Employment, Care Marketisation and Migration

Capitalism, Neoliberalism and Precarious Employment in Older-Age Care

There is no unique definition of precarious employment. According to Gerry Rodgers and Janine Rodgers (1989, p. 5) precarious employment involves instability, lack of protection, insecurity and social or economic vulnerability. They identify four dimensions of precarious employment: temporal, organisational, economic and social (Frade et al. 2004). In a more recent study, Leah Vosko (2006, pp. 3–4) builds on Rodgers and Rodgers' definition and defines precarious employment as 'involving limited social benefits and statutory entitlements, job insecurity, low wages, and high risks of ill-health'. Guy Standing (2011, p. 10) in *The Precariat: The New*

Dangerous Class identifies seven forms of security: labour market security (adequate income-earning opportunities); employment security (protection against arbitrary dismissal); job security (ability and opportunity to retain a niche in employment); work security (protection against accidents and illness); skill reproduction security (opportunity to gain skills); income security (assurance of an adequate stable income); and representation security (possessing a collective voice in the labour market). While all these aspects matter, Paugam's comprehensive approach offers a useful summary: a stable employment is defined as an employment that is stable enough for the worker to be able to plan his or her future and to be protected against the hazards of life (Paugam 2009, p. 7).

From a historical perspective, precarious employment is not a new reality, even though in most western European countries the concept emerged in public debates only in the last few decades, or even more recently, as in the UK. Bringing down the cost of labour (not only in terms of wages but also in terms of flexible employment relations) is a constant feature of capitalism inscribed in its core dynamic: capital accumulation. As David Harvey argues: 'struggles over status within the division of labour and the recognition of skills are in effect struggles over differential life chances for the worker and by extension—and here is the core of the problem—over profitability for the capitalist' (2014, p. 116). Before the emergence of various forms of welfare states throughout the twentieth century, and most significantly after the Second World War, labour was at the mercy of the conditions imposed by capital and more often than not wages barely ensured the survival of the workforce. Neoliberalism has thus not invented the precarious employment relationship, but the concept is embedded in a Western socio-historical context of labour market deregulation policies implemented from the 1970s onwards after a period of welfare state development. In the previous chapter, I exposed how labour market segmentation theories help to account for processes that lead to differentiated employment and working conditions, notably through an unequal distribution of securities and rights in the labour market. The concept of 'precarisation' goes somehow beyond an analysis in terms of labour market segmentation in that it conceptualises processes that disempower labour and thus enact the segmentation of the labour market through time.

In the following paragraphs, I situate the concept of precarious employment in academic and policy contexts relevant to the three field sites of London, Paris and Madrid.

The Concept of Precarious Employment in Comparative Perspective

The concept of precarious employment has undergone different fates in policy and scholarly debates in European countries, which needs to be unpacked. Though the use of the concept of precarious employment arguably increased after 2008 across these countries, the different historiographies of the notion still bear some relevance: 'the term "precarious employment" has been found to be commonly used in France, Spain and Italy, while in Germany it is mostly used in a rather restrictive way by social scientists but has not entered the public debate, and in the UK it is rarely used and has no relevance at all in the national debates' (Frade et al. 2004, p. 13).

In France, when the concept of 'précarité' emerged in the late 1970s, it was first associated with the notion of poverty, both concepts being used interchangeably. Precariousness was conceptualised as both a social condition and a process that could lead to poverty (Barbier 2002). This very close association between precariousness and poverty remains to some extent relevant today in mainstream public debates (Paugam et al. 2011); but the concept began to progressively characterise unstable forms of employment. French sociologists have significantly contributed to forging early understandings of the concept. The use of the concept of 'precarity' in academic and public debates paved the way for the incorporation of this term in French legislation in 1990 in order to regulate the use of temporary contracts, notably through the introduction of financial compensation for workers on temporary contracts amounting to 10% of gross income, with sectorial exceptions.[1]

In the UK, the concept is present in academic literature (Barbier 2005) but has been rarely discussed in public debates. A more common phrase

---

[1] https://www.service-public.fr/particuliers/vosdroits/F40, last accessed February 2016.

refers to 'vulnerable workers' as popularised by the TUC Commission on Vulnerable Employment set up in 2007. The TUC definition of vulnerable employment does not distinguish between 'vulnerability' and 'precariousness': 'we have come to define vulnerable employment as: Precarious work that places people at risk of continuing poverty and injustice resulting from an imbalance of power in the employer-worker relationship' (TUC 2007, p. 16). As mentioned in the Introduction, the concept of vulnerable employment presents however serious shortcomings. Anderson argues in this regard: 'the term "vulnerability" and "vulnerable worker" are more often used in the UK but these terms risk naturalising these conditions and confining those workers so affected to victimhood. Moreover, unlike "vulnerability" the notion of "precarity" captures both a typical and insecure employment and has implications beyond employment' (2010, p. 303). In spite of a weaker presence of the concept in mainstream discourse, the perception of a worsening of terms and conditions is nevertheless present in public discourse, notably in the aftermath of the 2008 crisis, as illustrated by debates in the run-up to the 2015 general election on the 'race to the bottom' or the use of zero hours contracts.

The conceptualisation of 'precarious employment' in the work of Spanish sociologists draws on Rodgers and Rodgers' four-dimensional approach (Cano 2004) and touches on issues also addressed by French sociologists, such as the diffuse nature of precariousness and its presence, to different extents, in various forms of employment (Cano 2004). Against the background of the dreadful social consequences of the financial and economic crisis in Spain, fighting 'precarity' has gained particular momentum in social movements such as the 'Indignados' of 2011. These massive demonstrations benefitted from the existence of a multitude of social initiatives in Madrid that articulated a politicised discourse, such as 'Precarias a la deriva', a militant network of academics and activists created at the turn of the century by feminist groups.[2] The interconnections between social movements and academia triggered a renewed interest in the study of the social implications of precarious employment (Rocha Sánchez 2012).

---

[2] For a presentation in English of the movement: http://eipcp.net/transversal/0704/precarias1/en, last accessed February 2016.

Beyond these contextual differences, processes of marketisation of care provision concern the care regimes of the three countries in a transnational fashion. The following section looks into the articulation of processes of marketisation with those of precarisation.

The Marketisation of Care Services Provision and Precarious Employment

Against the background of an ageing population, increasing employment of women and the retrenchment of the welfare state, the respective roles of states, markets and families for the provision of older-age care are transformed throughout Europe, as outlined in Chap. 3. In spite of fundamental national differences, certain dynamics underpin most of the on-going changes. In the European context Annamaria Simonazzi observes that in the pursuit of cost reduction all countries are moving towards more home-care, private provision and cash transfers (Simonazzi 2009). This shift towards more private provision takes predominantly two forms: the contracting-out of services previously run by national or local authorities and a preference for cash allowances instead of in-kind services, fostering a 'commodification' of care (Ungerson 2003). These trends are furthermore embedded in broader dynamics of capitalist economies, as noted by Harvey: 'there has been a long-standing trend within the history of capital for household labour to be supplanted by market-based transactions (everything from haircuts to takeaway or frozen meals, fast foods, to dry-cleaning, entertainment and child and older-age care)' (Harvey 2014, p. 192). Both marketisation, which refers to the increasing presence of markets in the care sector, and corporatisation (Farris and Marchetti 2017), more strictly related to the growth of for-profit actors, are related to the broader process of privatisation of care; care services being increasingly delivered by private actors, for-profit and not-for-profit. As noted by Anneli Antonnen and Liisa Häikiö, marketisation constructs 'both care as a commodity and the individual in need of care as a consumer' (2011, p. 71). How care is financed shapes to a significant extent the sector's employment conditions (Simonazzi 2009) as well as the type of care relationships to be found in a given care regime (Ungerson

2003). Simonazzi finds that levels of earnings as well as employment and work conditions tend to be worse within the for-profit private sector than for workers employed by public institutions, given that 'better public sector working conditions, which translates into higher labour costs' are actually what has 'encouraged the contracting-out of services to private providers' (2009, p. 220). Differentiated patterns emerge regarding employment terms and conditions along the private/public divide. Workers employed directly by local authorities tend to benefit from better terms and conditions than workers employed in the private or voluntary sector. Processes of precarisation of employment terms need thus to be analysed in conjunction with those of marketisation and privatisation.

In the market, the constant pressure on labour costs leads employers to recruit workers with the least bargaining power (Williams 2011a). I argue furthermore that this downward pressure affects the sector as a whole because not-for-profit organisations compete for funding in the market under the same conditions as for-profit companies (often competing for public subsidies) and because the 'new public management' has equally introduced continuous pressure to reduce costs in the public sector. Not-for-profit care organisations are increasingly adopting business management logics that resemble those of for-profit settings. The care industry is now largely composed of both types of organisations (i.e. for-profit and not-for-profit) often operating within the same markets and exposed to similar structural constraints, such as downward pressure on labour costs, which affects management policies throughout the sector.

In this context, precarious employment serves the purpose of transferring risks and socio-economic costs onto workers. The flexibility that precarious contracts offer facilitate the transfer from employers onto employees of the cost of uncertainty of the business environment (Cano 2004, p. 74) as well as the costs of social reproduction. Labour market deregulation is key from this perspective in that costless dismissals make workers bear the risk of economic downturn. Here, the expanding outsourcing of care provision erodes conditions in the care sector as a whole by reducing the number of workers directly employed by the public sector. 'The application of corporatized logics to the management of care services' (Farris and Marchetti 2017, p. 110) is relevant to the study of both for-profit and not-for-profit care-employment contexts, which are growing against the backdrop of a shrinking public sector.

Against this background, migrants are among the workers most at risk of precarious employment. The following section examines how legal exclusion and economic marginalisation are articulated.

Migrant Workers, Precarious Employment and Governmentality

Some groups of workers are particularly affected by precarious employment, notably migrants, racialised minorities and women. Migrant workers, and especially recent non-EU migrants (Sahraoui et al. 2018), tend to be more exposed to precarious employment than the rest of the working population. Migrants are disproportionately affected by pay below the National Minimum Wage, unpaid overtime, lack of contract and unfair dismissal (Jayaweera and Anderson 2008). The articulation of the migration and employment regimes produce unfavourable outcomes for migrant workers, in Anderson's words: 'through the creation of categories of entrant, the imposition of employment relations and the construction of institutionalised uncertainty, immigration controls work to form types of labour with particular relations to employers and to labour markets. They combine with less formalised migratory processes to help produce 'precarious workers' that cluster in particular jobs and segments of the labour market.' (2010, p. 301). Analyses in terms of precarisation have furthermore highlighted that the frontier between different segments of the labour market tends to become blurry as employment relationships are changing also for those traditionally belonging to the first labour market (Lewchuk and Clarke 2011). Arne Kalleberg makes a similar point when he states that precarious employment cannot be fully explained by dual labour market theory, given that it has spread to all sectors (Kalleberg 2009, p. 6), even though arguably to different extents in different segments of the labour market (Lewchuk and Clarke 2011). The concept of the 'destabilisation of the stable',[3] coined by Robert Castel, equally points to 'precarisation' as a central process in the evolution of contemporary capitalism (Castel 1995, p. 661).

---

[3] In French: la 'déstabilisation des stables'.

Precariousness appears from this perspective to constitute a form of governmentality (Foucault 1978/2002) in neoliberal capitalism. Bourdieu wrote about 'precariousness'[4] as a form of domination of a new kind, based on a state of permanent insecurity aimed at creating subordination, acceptance and exploitation. This oppression is all the more pervasive that not only those directly affected by precariousness suffer from it. Pierre Bourdieu observes that what he calls 'objective insecurity' creates a 'generalised subjective insecurity' that affects all workers (Bourdieu 1998). Isabell Lorey's development of the concept of precariousness brings Bourdieu's analysis a step further: 'Precarization has become an instrument of governing and, at the same time, a basis for capitalist accumulation that serves social regulation and control. Precarization means more than insecure jobs, more than the lack of security given by waged employment. By way of insecurity and danger it embraces the whole of existence, the body, modes of subjectivation' (Lorrey 2015, p. 1). Scrutinising employment conditions in older-age care from the standpoint of migrant and minority ethnic workers offers from that perspective a 'privileged' viewpoint (Smith 2005), shedding light not only on specific relations of oppression but also on the meanings of precarisation for society as a whole.

The following section analyses the lived experiences of migrant and minority ethnic care workers employed in the care industry. It scrutinises a central dimension for the study of precarious employment: perceptions of (in)stability.

5.2   Daily Uncertainties, the Transfer of Risks onto Workers

Relating Contracts, Job Tenure and Perceptions of (In) Stability

While 22, 21 and 18 participants were formally on indefinite contracts in London, Paris and Madrid respectively; in London and in Madrid only 10

---

[4] In French: 'précarité' and 'un mode de domination d'un type nouveau'.

and 11 perceived their job as stable. In Paris, 22 participants instead thought they were in a stable job. The juxtaposition of participants' answers on these two themes—contract type and perception of job stability—illustrates that while 'permanent contract' is widely used as an indicator of care workers' employment stability, this does not necessarily translate into perceptions of stability for workers, notably in the context of British and Spanish employment regimes. In London an equal number of participants perceived their jobs as stable vs. unstable; in Madrid a majority of participants had an overall sense of insecurity about their jobs; and a minority (one-fifth) of participants in Paris shared this feeling (Tables 5.1 and 5.2).

Beyond these apparent differences, looking into the lived experiences of workers questions these distinctions. For instance, the average job tenure shows that there is no obvious correlation between the type of contract (permanent or temporary) and the length of time participants were in their current job at the time of the interview (Table 5.3). There is equally no straightforward relationship between the type of contract and the average number of jobs held in the past five years: in spite of a much higher share of participants on temporary contracts in Madrid, participants in London and in Madrid had in both cases on average between one and two jobs over the period of five years prior to the interview.

Table 5.1 Participants' type of contract

	London	Paris	Madrid
Permanent	22	21	18
Temporary	3	9	7
No contract			2

Source: Own data and elaboration

Table 5.2 Participants' perception of stability

Feeling of employment stability	10	22	11
Feeling of instability	10	6	15
Feeling of security achieved through multiple jobs[a]	2	0	0
NA	4	2	1

Source: Own data and elaboration
[a]This category does not reflect the total proportion of participants who held multiple jobs, but rather those who explicitly linked multiple job-holding with the need to ensure stability

Table 5.3 Average job tenure and average number of jobs held in past five years

	London	Paris	Madrid
Job tenure in years	4.7	2.7	4.1
No. of jobs in past five years	1.9	3	1.2

Source: Own data and elaboration

The question thus arises: what makes an employment relationship precarious? The analysis of participants' perceptions uncovers the actual meaning of specific forms of employment precariousness for care workers. The perception of stability was only to a relative extent connected with the formal type of contract, and many other elements entered into play when participants assessed their employment stability. Some workers on permanent contracts felt that they were not in a stable job because they feared that they could be dismissed at any time; while, by contrast, some who were on temporary contracts at times considered their job as rather stable due to the chronic labour shortages in this sector. These perceptions had implications for how participants planned their lives and are thus relevant to a comprehensive analysis of when an employment relationship is to be considered precarious, in keeping with the above-mentioned argument by Paugam, who attached the notion of stability to that of being able to plan one's own life (Paugam 2009).

Mainly, two types of elements contributed positively to workers' sense of employment security: on the one hand the relationship developed with the employer over time, which created trust between employer and employee, and on the other hand a relative sense of security derived from the chronic labour shortages in the care sector in sizeable urban centres such as Paris, London and Madrid. In these cases, workers did not count on employment rights for their protection and were convinced that their stability hinged on the fact that their employers trusted and valued their work. Fadila in London believed her employment to be stable as a result of the trust her employer could have in the quality of her work.

> From the point of view of (name of the care home) I am confident that my performances are good and that they will not let me go. (Fadila, 30, Bangladesh, London)

This view was shared by a minority of participants and if employer-employee relationships certainly shaped the work environment, most participants who felt their employment was stable referred more generally to a sense of security derived from their knowledge of the sector's labour needs, drawing on their experience of recruitment procedures and sometimes on on-going job searches. This was the case for Luc, who knew he could find a similar job easily in Paris:

NS: Do you think you are in a stable employment?

Luc: Yes, yes, yes, of course because there's always work. As I told you, in this sector there are always jobs. I think it's one of the few sectors, where there's always demand. (Luc, 25, Cameroun, Paris)

In a similar way, chronic labour shortages were perceived as a form of employment protection in London, even though many insecurities remained when the sense of security was detached from a specific employment: while the possibility of finding a job was reassuring, the general precariousness of employment terms and working conditions in the care industry created apprehensions, notably as to the level of earnings, the working hours and the travel time that a new job would mean. Remarkably, amongst participants in London, those who derived a sense of job security based upon labour shortages in the sector all possessed British citizenship and consequently did not have to face the limitations imposed on migrant workers who at times needed the employer to sponsor their work permit. For instance, Analyn, a Filipina care assistant who had resided in the UK for 18 years at the time of the interview, felt confident about her ability to always secure a job:

NS: Do you consider the jobs you have as secure in the sense that you can stay in these jobs as long as you want to? [Analyn worked in two jobs.]

Analyn: Yes I think so because nursing home [jobs] is more around, isn't it, than other job? As long as you can do it properly and you're willing to do it I think you can do it for a long time. (Analyn, 50, the Philippines, London)

Migrant care workers in Madrid shared the idea that in the context of an ageing society carers will be needed, but this perception was nuanced by the difficult economic situation in general and the precarious employment terms and working conditions within older-age care in particular. Elena, in the quote below, believed that carers would always be sought after.

> In social care there will always be work, always, here or in another country because people get older and each day there will be more elderly persons, and they're getting older and their health is getting worse. (Elena, 42, Paraguay, Madrid)

If several participants shared Elena's point of view, most of them also shared some concerns. In the following quote Flor highlighted that having access to jobs is of no help if the level of earnings does not allow for the care worker's subsistence in decent conditions.

> I believe that to care for older persons there are many jobs. But the thing is if you work as live-in carer they want to pay you very little, very little. (Flor, 25, Peru, Madrid)

Claudia, who graduated as a psychologist, argued in turn that given the economic situation it wasn't easy to find a job even in the care sector, pointing out the entrapment that relative stability means if the working conditions and level of pay are precarious.

NS: Do you have the feeling of being in a stable employment?
Claudia: it's for stability that I put up with this place, for stability. Because if I wanted quality of life, I would have left it, but in this situation you can't say "I leave this job and tomorrow I'm going there, the day after that over there." We're not in this type of situation and that's why I stick to my job. I put up with it and everyone is telling me: "How come you stay there with the studies you have and you're still in that job?" But the situation isn't easy, if they're not taking in youth, they won't employ older workers either. (Claudia, 53, Peru, Madrid)

Asked if they feel secure about their job, another group of participants answered positively on the basis that they held several jobs and could still ensure some stability even if they would lose one. Holding multiple jobs might thus contribute to workers' well-being by enhancing their sense of security; it presents however the obvious downside of increased workload and raises the question of consequent health implications for care workers. Adam, a young worker from India employed in a care home in London recounts:

> When I first came I was a student so this was my only job. So 2011 I finished my course, I came in 2009 in December, November 2011 I finished my course. Then I changed my visa to work permit, but I still kept my job, like a backup you know and I am doing my management programme in Tesco. (Adam, 29, India, London)

While some hold several jobs in the care sector as a result of financial precarity (see next section), for Adam the care job provided a safety net to his main professional objective of achieving a managerial position further to his in-house training at Tesco. While his job remains precarious and the outcome of his training uncertain, his concomitant engagement in both provides him with a sense of stability. I now turn to examining perceptions of insecurity and accounting for observed similarities and variations in the three capitals.

Understanding Feelings of Employment Precariousness

Care workers' narratives revealed that employment protection legislation is experienced as weak within the care industry. The very nature of care work and the legitimate concern to protect elderly people affects the power relationships between employers and employees and tends to limit the effectiveness of employment protection. Interestingly enough, this perception was widely shared in Paris, London and Madrid, in spite of significantly different employment protection indicators at the national level as presented in Chap. 3. Aimée, who worked in Paris, illustrates this point with the following story:

> I knew a colleague who worked here … I identified with her … a couple of years ago when I arrived here I started on the 4th floor and that floor is tough. And this girl I saw her work, I found that she worked well and that she was very committed, very passionate, like myself … maybe that day she was a bit tired … A resident slapped her and she pulled the armchair of the

resident a bit too strongly and there was a psychologist who was there and who said 'No, you're not allowed to pull the armchair like this' She [the carer] said 'but you realize she slapped me'... She was affected by it because what we receive in the face it affects you, it hurts you. In no time her contract was terminated. So I was very affected by it. Because this young woman I saw her, her shift started at 9, I started at 8:30 but I would see her in the same train at 8:00. She started at 9 am and finished after 8 pm. She stayed extra hours to make sure all residents were safely in bed before she left. And you see ... the fact of pulling an armchair a bit too strongly ... and that's it. It saddened me a lot. (Aimée, 44, Guinea Conakry, Paris)

The weak bargaining position of care workers vis-à-vis employers, due amongst other things to low levels of unionisation and precarious employment terms, created a specific vulnerability because workers charged with professional mistakes were rarely able to formally contest the accusation. In the 2009 COMPAS report, the authors found that migrant care workers often described unfair treatment in relation to disciplinary and dismissal procedures (Cangiano et al. 2009, pp. 142–143). From being easily dismissible because of a professional mistake within care, it is only one step to finding oneself in a permanent state of fear of being dismissed due to such an accusation. Many care workers implied that it created a work environment in which they feared being laid off at any time. Martina in Madrid put these feelings into words:

You know now you can be on a permanent contract they can sack you in the same way. Before it gave you some security, 'oh I'm permanent' you were excited and you dreamt, and now no because you can be temporary, you can be permanent they sack you in the same way. If they want to they say look you committed that mistake and they sack you without any problem. (Martina, 51, Ecuador, Madrid)

These perceptions cannot be detached from the broader insecurity of the business environment fostered by the marketisation of care. The focus of this book on private providers of care services sheds light more specifically on how processes of precarisation are articulated with those of marketisation. The situations encountered in Paris, London and Madrid shared in this regard similar underpinning dynamics while at the same time presenting differences significant enough to affect perceptions of stability.

In London, I observed the process of a home closure that revealed how a collective redundancy was conducted by the company and dealt with by workers. The complete closure of the home was announced, as the facility was to be built anew. The care home belonged to a large care provider with several homes in the area. A union took part in the process as the care provider had recently opened its doors to several unions in the framework of a recognition agreement. The union was organising a recruitment campaign when the closure was announced to the staff. Union organisers accompanied their members throughout the process by informing them of their rights but no other action was undertaken. As all staff faced the risk of redundancy, the closure of the home uncovered the very fragile employment situation in which all care workers found themselves, regardless of their seniority. The re-opening of the home was planned to take place in a year's time, but all workers would have to re-apply for a job at that point if they were willing to come back to the same care home. Workers were 'welcomed' to apply to other homes of the same provider but needed to go through online applications that gave them no priority over external candidates for potential vacancies; consequently they had to go through the recruitment process again. Julie deplored the insecurity that this announcement had created and perceived the company's policies in this matter as profoundly unfair. She referred in this quote to a previous experience of home closure, in which the manager found her another job before the home closed:

> It's not understandable that I am here working for you and it is not my fault that they are closing the place, you have to give me a job so how are we going to apply for a job? If I go to a place and they interview me they might not like me. So how am I going to live? (…) I don't like the situation because normally when they are closing a home the lady pushed me to another door. She gave me to another company so I wasn't jobless so this one I didn't go for interview but this one we don't know. We will see what will happen. (Julie, 45, Ghana, London)

Confronted with an unavoidable dismissal and insufficient redundancy payments to provide security for a period of job search, some workers decided to look for a job and to resign before the date of closure, even if that meant they were no longer entitled to redundancy payments. The company offered payments equivalent to two weeks' salary per year of employment. Joyce, for instance, decided to look for another job as soon as she heard about the closure:

> They showed me how to apply for new job, how to fill in new application form for same company and how to go for interview. If they like me they take, otherwise I have to keep looking for another. (…) So that's why I decided to change my company, at the end of the day if they don't have this job for me, I will lose my job. So I decided to find a job before that (…) that's why I gave my resignation. (Joyce, 30, India, London)

In fact, Joyce had to accept a job offer with a lower salary. She needed to find an employer who would agree not to require overtime from her and who respected her needs in terms of schedule due to caring responsibilities at home which limited the number of hours she could work every week to 30.

Even though on the whole participants encountered in Paris tended to feel that they were in stable employment, feelings of insecurity were also present, partly derived from the risk embedded in the business environment. For instance, Doriane, who came from the French department of Guadeloupe, explained:

NS: Do you have the feeling that you are in a stable employment?
Doriane: No, you can never tell … at least in this sector, in care homes, no. I'll tell you why. I've been here for seven years and the care home has been open for seven years and almost every two years management changes, so it cannot be stable because of that. (Doriane, 59, Guadeloupe, Paris)

Management turnover meant that feelings of security based on relationships built over time, and the potential trust derived from it, were put at risk each time managers changed. Against the background of weak employment protection in the care sector due to the articulation of employment regimes with the specifics of care work, employer-employee relationships came to play a crucial role in ensuring a certain type of stability, and Doriane's example illustrates how the dynamics of successive privatisation and managers' turnover effectively weakens this resource.

The implications of privatisation in terms of job stability were probably most visible in Madrid, where the economic downturn increased the vulnerability of workers in many aspects. Beronica argued that the existence of a permanent threat of being dismissed completely annihilated in practice the difference between permanent and temporary employment:

> Yes, it's a permanent contract. But I can't tell you that contracts are permanent because from one day to another they can tell you "Good-bye and good riddance". Be it the company closing down, or being sold, I don't know, or a merger, or whatever. So it's not permanent, they can dismiss you straight away and that's it. Look, they told me: 'the difference between a permanent contract and a temporary contract is that the temporary contract has a date by which it will end, the permanent has no date." So the only difference is that you don't know the date with a permanent contract. But they can sack you, we can't be safe. (Beronica, 38, Ecuador, Madrid)

Most participants highlighted furthermore the worsening of employment terms that they observed over recent years. If Martina lamented the terms of the contracts to be found in the sector, Antonio considered himself lucky to be employed at all:

> Before they gave you a permanent contract, in the past. But now they only give you temporary or part-time, or for one month and they tell you we'll call you, then they call you, they give you three months, another time they just leave you like this. (Martina, 51, Ecuador, Madrid)

> In this country, to have a job is fortunate, in Spain right now given the situation. And then to have a permanent job or a full-time job is another success because sometimes we have part-time jobs or by the hour. (Antonio, 39, Cuba, Madrid)

A tangible aspect of this degradation was the extensive use of so-called replacement contracts, in principle aimed at filling needs arising from other workers' sick leaves. One-fifth of participants I met in Madrid were on this type of contract, which hints at its exaggerated use. Workers on these contracts could be asked to leave from one day to another and while they supposedly replaced another worker in fact a significant share of workers were maintained for longer on this type of contract, arguably to adjust easily to employers' needs at a given time. Workers on such contracts worked for varied periods of time; amongst participants I have met it ranged from a couple of months to four years. Imene was on such a 'replacement contract':

> They told me I'll be working until the other woman who's on sick leave comes back. When she's back they'll tell me: 'you know what? Your contract is finished, the care assistant is here.' And I don't know if they will give me a contract ... because here as you can see, the situation is really bad. Jobs are very much sought for so I don't know. It's gonna be until she's back. (...) I would like to have a normal contract, I mean a permanent contract to feel more secure, but in the meanwhile I have to wait. (Imene, 31, Peru, Madrid)

These examples, drawn from the three sites of fieldwork, illustrate different aspects of similar dynamics related to the privatisation of care provision. The latter exacerbated feelings of insecurity in all three contexts, according to workers' narratives. It is, however, important to account for the significantly higher perception of stability among participants in Paris, for which the figures of permanent and temporary contracts do not offer a straightforward interpretation. Several elements are relevant in that respect, notably employment legislation, professional qualifications and the choice of temporary work. While the permanent/temporary distinction appeared to be of little relevance in care workers' discourse in London and in Madrid, its significance, emphasised in mainstream public discourse in France, was equally foregrounded by care workers in Paris. Some of them identified tangible implications of a permanent contract for the planning of their lives. Camille, for instance, pointed out that being on a permanent contract had material consequences for her, allowing her to realise her projects by securing a loan:

> I told to myself I need to stop for more stability, also in relation to my family life, there are certain projects we want to achieve, and to be on a perma-

nent contract it can help. Otherwise, it would be only about earnings I would prefer to be on a temporary contract (laugh). But the problem of temping, it's the precarity of employment. (…) If I want to obtain a loan in the bank to do certain things I need to be on a permanent contract. (Camille, 45, Cameroun, Paris)

Camille's quote also refers to the above-mentioned financial advantage for workers on temporary contracts. French legislation rules that fixed-term contracts, known as CDD (*Contrats à Durée Determinée*) must include the payment of a 10% 'precarity bonus' (with the exception of seasonal jobs as defined by law). Given this specific regulation in France, several participants in Paris chose to work on temporary contracts in order to earn higher wages. Others chose temporary forms of employment for other reasons, such as being able to take care of their children during school holidays, as in the case of Saba who had five children in the first quote below, or when working after retirement as related by Eloise from Guadeloupe in the second quote. In these cases, with temporary employment being chosen for other than financial reasons, it did not negatively affect perceptions of stability.

I have children and since I'm a care assistant I've realised I wasn't enjoying life enough as I would like to, like to have holidays with my children from time to time. (Saba, 41, Cameroun, Paris)

I'm retired, because I worked before in the public sector and I'll be soon 60, and I don't see myself taking up a full-time job, as temporary worker I can stop when I want. (Eloise, 59, Guadeloupe, Paris)

On the whole, there exist many shades of perceived stability and the stable/unstable binary only serves the purpose of capturing global trends, while experiences are better described as parts of a continuum. Perceptions of stability are shaped by factors such as relationship with employer, labour market characteristics locally and sector-wise, type of contract and protections against dismissal but also caring responsibilities of the worker, age, qualifications or future professional prospects. In all three cities, the perception of instability was related, on the one hand, to the identifica-tion of the business-like environment of privatised care settings as less respectful of workers' rights; on the other hand, privatised care settings' levels of management and control of work performances created an atmosphere of continuous fear of unfair disciplinary procedures. Job instability constitutes one dimension of the transfer of socio-economic costs onto workers. By minimising the costs of the numerical flexibility of the workforce—that is, the costs attached to redundancies—private care providers limit the economic risks of their activities. This however implies that workers must themselves assume these risks through unstable jobs and weak employment protection. This section sought to account for participants' perceptions of (in)stability and lived experiences of employment precariousness beyond the usual indicators of precarious employment. The following paragraphs undertake a similar task from a different angle by looking into care workers' levels of earnings and their discourses on this theme.

5.3   Material Precariousness, the Transfer of Socio-Economic Costs onto Workers

Among the Lowest Levels of Pay in Society

The devaluation of care work and its historic invisibilisation in the domestic sphere translated into low levels of pay and precarious employment terms in the process of commodification and marketisation of care work. In the UK, care work remains one of the lowest-paid sectors of the labour market (Low Pay Commission 2014). Earnings can even fall below the National Minimum Wage (NMW) in domiciliary care when travelling times are not compensated for.[5] In my research, participants in full-time employment earned on average £854 net monthly; this represented 47% of the average income. Participants in Paris earned on average €1387 net, which corresponds to 64% of the average net monthly salary in France. In Spain, participants in this study earned €780 monthly on average, that is, 58% of the average net salary (Table 5.4).

---

[5] https://www.unison.org.uk/upload/sharepoint/On%20line%20Catalogue/21049.pdf, last accessed February 2016.

Table 5.4 Levels of earnings: a comparative perspective

	London	Paris	Madrid
Own research—average wage	854£ net monthly	1387 € net monthly	780 € net monthly
National statistics Average earnings whole of workforce (all sectors)	£27,200 gross income annually (ONS 2014)[a] Estimation of 1787£ net monthly income[b]	2154 € net monthly (INSEE 2012)[c]	1345 € net monthly (INE 2012)[d]
Average wage in this research/average earnings in the country	47%	64%	58%

Source: Own elaboration with national statistics and data from own research

[a] http://www.ons.gov.uk/ons/rel/ashe/annual-survey-of-hours-and-earnings/2014-provisional-results/stb-ashe-statistical-bulletin-2014.html, last accessed February 2016

[b] http://www.thesalarycalculator.co.uk/salary.php, last accessed February 2016

[c] http://www.insee.fr/fr/themes/document.asp?ref_id=ip1528, last accessed February 2016

[d] http://www.elperiodico.com/es/noticias/economia/sueldo-medio-1345-1982126, last accessed February 2016

On the whole, it appears that care workers are disadvantageously positioned in society and that their earnings are well below average earnings in all three countries. To add to this, the comparison presented above is based on full-time employment, while not all workers in this research were working full-time. In London and in Paris, the great majority of participants (nine in ten) were in full-time employment, but in Madrid less than two-thirds of participants were on full-time hours.

Coping with Insufficient and Unequal Earnings

Care workers I have interviewed voiced in many ways their dissatisfaction with the level of their earnings. Marissa, working in London and an overseas graduated nurse, explained that her earnings did not allow for independent living and Karen, also employed in London, explained how she had to combine day and night shifts:

I live together with my brother and my sister-in-law, we are renting a flat and sharing the payments. It's better to share than getting your own is very expensive, all your salary will go just for rent to get your own. (Marissa, 60, the Philippines, London)

I'm doing day and night otherwise how can you survive in this country? It's very expensive isn't? the food, the rent … you need to do something to survive. (Karen, n.a., the Philippines, London)

This feeling of having to struggle to make ends meet also relates to a perception of relative deprivation given the marginalisation of care work within society. Fouzia pointed out the devaluation of her work as compared to other care-related activities:

I sometimes work 230 hours a month. To earn a salary around 2,000-2,100 euros … it's not … you see if a doctor or a nurse would work 230 hours she would earn 4,000 or 3,000 euros. But I'm on Minimal Wage. It's 8.80 per hour, a woman, a home help, is paid 9.53 per hour (…) I don't know why there is this injustice. (Fouzia, 43, Algeria, Paris)

In Paris, the level of earnings furthermore depends on the type of contract. Camille had just started on a permanent contract in Paris after having worked for a couple of years on temporary contracts. Transferring onto a permanent contract had thus for Camille the consequence of lowering her salary due to the loss of the 10% financial compensation, mentioned above, attached to temporary contracts:

If I could be sure that I would have a job every month, I would have preferred temporary work, because it's better paid. After all, we seek to earn money, not that we do this profession for money but we also work for … the aim is to earn money, it's not because we work for money, we have feelings of love for our job, but in return we also would like to earn a good living, that's also the problem, we would like to earn a good living. (Camille, 45, Cameroun, Paris)

Earning a good living was also difficult for care workers in Madrid. If employed in residential care, their wages were low but the rate remained stable. In contrast, in the context of live-in care services, both formal and informal, wages could go down according to individual negotiations, as argued by Mayra:

> It's better to have a job than to be unemployed. So often they accept, so we got to a point where each time working conditions are more and more precarious. So if we accept that instead of paying me 800 you'll pay 600 and I say yes, to the next one he'll offer 500, and that's how it goes down and down. (Mayra, 52, Ecuador, Madrid)

The weak bargaining position in which care workers find themselves in negotiating their wages also means that they are vulnerable to various forms of malpractice or abuse by employers in relation to the payment of their salaries. In the UK, for instance, the Low Pay Commission (2014) indicated that NMW non-compliance in the social care sector was higher than average. An HM Revenue & Customs report published in 2013 found a 48% non-compliance rate after surveying 224 employers. 15% of employers presented average arrears of £1000 or more per worker. These arrears were due to various deductions of pay and amongst these the cost of uniforms provided to care staff constituted the most common type of deduction (HM Revenue and Customs 2013). In Paris, it appeared that malpractices in terms of wage payments were institutionalised in certain workplaces and contributed to a high turnover of staff. Hélène complained about such practices:

Hélène: Regarding pay it's always the same problem, some hours are not counted, so it needs to be fixed. That's why I go to them [the managers] mostly.
NS: And can it be resolved easily or is it problematic?
Hélène: No it's not resolved easily that's why I go to them on a regular basis, I'm not the only one who has this issue, it's almost all of my colleagues, they also have problems, so that's the way it is. (Hélène, 25, Guadeloupe, Paris)

Care workers in Paris were particularly vocal about perceived inequalities in terms of earnings. In the context of private for-profit care homes, it was up to the workers to negotiate their salaries if they could sense that they might obtain a little more than the minimal rate. This however created resentment amongst colleagues who might earn different wages but completed the same tasks, as explained by Amandine:

> I don't find it fair because for instance, someone starts here with 1,300, the basic salary, and another person that arrives a year later and who knew how to negotiate, the person can get 1,400 or 1,500. And the person who has been here for longer they don't raise her/his salary. And you know, amongst us we talk. (Amandine, 32, Ivory Coast, Paris)

One of the obvious consequences of insufficient earnings was that multiple job-holding became a common practice. In all three sites of fieldwork, a proportion of participants decided to take up several jobs simultaneously. As mentioned above, to some this provided a sense of relative employment security. Others pointed to the need for higher earnings. Martina, who worked in residential care in Madrid and held multiple jobs for many years, described her situation in an ironic tone:

NS: And how many hours do you work here?
Analyn: I do part time here Tuesday and Friday but I have another job as a full-time carer as well.
NS: In a different home?
Analyn: Mmh, different home. I work there four days a week, fixed days and this is fixed as well. So I must be enjoying it, six days a week, not bad! (Analyn, 50, the Philippines, London)

Holding multiple jobs was not without consequences when doing such physical work as caring for elderly persons. Sometimes workers would have full-time and part-time jobs with fixed hours, but in other cases they would work additional hours through an agency. In these cases, workers do not know how often the agency will call them, and each call sounds like an opportunity. Laetitia, for instance, combined two jobs as well as agency work paid by the hour. The day I interviewed her, she came straight from a night shift to do a day shift in another care home:

Laetitia: Like yesterday I worked a night shift because I wasn't here [during the day] I was sick. I wasn't feeling well so I didn't

| NS: | come. And later they called me for a night shift, I seized the opportunity. Night is better paid than day shift. |

NS: So they call you last minute sometimes?

Laetitia: If I'm already working I say no. But because I wasn't doing anything and I knew I was starting here at 9 so I accepted, I committed to that. I did my night shift, I did all the changes, it's fine. (Laetitia, 29, Guadeloupe, Paris)

Laetitia's story exemplifies the complexities of how precarious employment is lived with and acted upon. Exposing her body to health issues due to work overload, multiple job-holding was also what allowed Laetitia to present herself as an exceptional worker capable of earning relatively high wages (her total income amounted to over twice the average earnings of care workers in this research). Analyn and Laetitia, each in their own words and tone, uncover different ways of coping with financial precariousness in older-age care; Analyn with certain detachment and irony, Laetitia with the satisfaction of achieving higher earnings by taking on all possible shifts.

In these sections I explored two aspects associated with precarious employment: job stability and level of earnings. In both cases the analysis revealed how meanings attached to different elements of employment precariousness are key to understanding participants' lived experience. In what follows I interrogate participants' perceptions of their employment rights such as annual leave and sick pay.

5.4   Fragile Employment Rights, Uncertain Implementation

Perceptions Around Sick Pay and Annual Leave Entitlements

Participants' perceptions of their employment rights represent a further dimension of employment precariousness. Two variables are scrutinised here: perceived access to paid annual leave and perceived entitlement to sick pay. These elements are crucial to apprehending workers' well-being at work and their bargaining power in relation to employers. They reveal a dimension of employment precariousness that contributes, along with perceived job stability and level of earnings, to workers' overall understanding of security and stability. Figures presented in this section reflect whether participants thought they had access to paid annual leave and sick pay, not necessarily whether they actually did (Table 5.5).

While most workers interviewed in London were on permanent contracts (cf. Tables 5.1 and 5.2), the lower share of care workers who considered that they had access to paid annual leave in Paris and Madrid might be to some extent related to the higher share of temporary contracts. In Paris, as flagged above, the higher rate of payments for workers on temporary contracts is defined by law in order to compensate for the precarity of temporariness, and some employers present it as payments for 'annual leave' that workers would theoretically take in between contracts. While this might be the intention of some workers, as in the example of Saba who was able to take time off work in between contracts to spend time with her children during school holidays, many others take up one contract after another because they cannot afford unpaid periods of time. Fouzia felt that earning a minimum wage for her life came at too high a cost in terms of work-life balance:

> I need to work very very hard to earn a good salary. It means to be able to pay for my bills, my life, my leisure and to save some money for holidays. I never take a month of holiday. First because I can't leave the person for one month without her seeing me, second because I can't afford not earning money for one month. I can't. (…) I save some money to have 20 or 15 days holiday. That's my problem, to afford holidays. It's been two years that I didn't go on holiday. (Fouzia, 43, Algeria, Paris)

In Madrid, workers in residential care and live-in care workers were in very different situations as to their rights at work. While workers in resi-

Table 5.5 Participants' perceived access to paid annual leave

	London	Paris	Madrid
Yes	23	15	21
No	2	4	4
I don't know		1	2

Source: Own data and elaboration

dential care could take paid annual leave (even though the choice of dates was often perceived as unfair by migrant workers), workers in live-in caring arrangements had fewer rights by law and these rights were rarely respected. Flor accounted for her experience in her jobs as live-in carer:

Flor: Here the legislation says that those who work as live-in carers have the right to have a two hours rest every day and Saturday and Sunday free. That's the law. But here not everyone respects the law.

NS: And you did you have these two hours?

Flor: No I didn't have two hours. In one I did but in the others no. And I was only off on Sunday. And no pay, for Sundays, Christmas, nothing like this. Nor public holidays. (Flor, 25, Peru, Madrid)

Together with paid annual leave, sick pay entitlements are crucial for workers' perception of security and protection. What workers thought they were entitled to, or whether they knew or didn't know what they were entitled to, is here central to the analysis. For instance, in London if all workers had in principle access to statutory sick pay, Table 5.6 indicates that a third of participants considered that they did not have access to sick pay and a few did not know whether they did or not. This was due to various reasons: a lack of information, the fact that one is eligible for statutory sick pay only if off work for more than four days in a row, workplace practices around claiming these payments, or the perception that the level of payments was insufficient to sustain oneself.

Over half of participants in London either thought they would not receive any payment if they were sick or did not know whether they would. In terms of perceived precariousness this reveals that most work-

Table 5.6 Participants' perceptions regarding entitlement to sick pay

	London	Paris	Madrid
Entitled	12	14	18
Not entitled	9	4	6
I don't know	4	2	3

Source: Own data and elaboration

ers believed that getting sick would mean no earnings. This was the case for one-third of participants in Paris and in Madrid. A significant share of participants did not know what would happen if they got sick, and 'not knowing' fostered unequal power relationships between employers and employees. Others realised that they could not live on sick payments. Alma, who worked in London, explained how she continued working after an accident at work because sick payments were too low to enable her to sustain herself:

> Alma: Last year I had an accident with my finger it got caught in the door and I went to the A and E but … I asked my GP if I can have sick leave but you know it's a very small amount if you go on a sick leave so I asked if it's fine with them if they can give me lighter load for the meantime and they said it's fine so I just continued working. (Alma, 41, the Philippines, London)

Participants in Madrid also exposed how care workers were compelled to work following work-related accidents, this time not because of the low payments but because of institutionalised practices of non-acknowledgement of the implications of accidents at work. Many participants shared stories of how insurance companies called *mutuas*[6] did not acknowledge the injuries caused by accidents at work and considered care workers able to work in spite of the accident. As a consequence, these workers could not justify their sick leave and were compelled to work in the state they found themselves in. Claudia observed that many colleagues had to work after being injured at work because the *mutua* failed to recognise the injuries as work accidents and she considered that for Latino American women there was no chance to be covered in case of an accident:

> For Latinos, we wouldn't even go because for us you can be cut into two halves and you'll be able to work. If you're not able to work you go back to your country, that's what they tell you. And many complain about this, they feel they're being abandoned. "You don't like it? Go away, go back to your country" and that's it. So we have to bear this. (Claudia, 53, Peru, Madrid)

---

[6] Mutuas are funded through social security schemes, run by businesses under the administrative supervision of the Ministry of Employment and Social Security, and they are designed to cover work-related accidents and illnesses.

Limitations on sick pay implementation appeared particularly problematic and a recurrent cause for worry, suggesting a need for unions' support. Yet, the following section depicts a complex story as to how unions were perceived and as to their role.

Unions: A Battle on Two Fronts?

Three different types of attitudes towards unions emerged amongst participants: apprehension, indifference or a positive perception of trade union membership as individual insurance policy. Table 5.7 presents union membership rates among participants in this study (union density rates at the national level and qualitative insights into the sectoral level are presented in Chap. 3). In London several of the care homes visited for fieldwork were, during those weeks, going through a recruitment campaign by a union in the framework of a recently signed recognition agreement. This specific fieldwork context, though I also recruited participants in care homes that were not included in these organising activities, probably raised the share of unionised participants in this research.

On the whole, the majority of participants were not union members, but the rates presented here cannot be read without reference to the fundamentally different models of industrial relations in each of these countries, as argued in Chap. 3. Membership rates constitute one indicator of unions' presence that is not necessarily the most adequate reflection of unions' actual clout according to the specific socio-history of industrial relations in each national context. For instance, union membership is a precondition of advice and support in the UK while this is not always the case in France and Spain. The following quote by Marisol who worked in Madrid illustrates this point:

Table 5.7 Participants' union membership in this research

	London	Paris	Madrid
Yes	11	2	4
No	14	28	23

Source: Own data and elaboration

Marisol: If we have a problem we go directly to UGT [Workers' General Union] and they advise us, and if we have to we join, but as I didn't have any big problem up to now, I didn't have to. But if you want to join you pay 30 every three months or per year.

NS: And can they help you if you're not a member?

Marisol: Yes, they help you, they support you with lawyers they give you everything. (Marisol, 47, Ecuador, Madrid)

Amongst a first group of participants, a form of apprehension towards unions emerged from the narratives, and interestingly enough in similar terms in the three cities. In Paris, when asked about union membership, one answer was 'I'm not a trade unionist, not a rebel', on another occasion, 'I don't like this type of techniques'; in Madrid 'I don't like it because it's a commitment and you put yourself in trouble, I've always been neutral'; and in London 'I didn't join the union because of my personality, I am not going to argue for benefits I'm okay'. While these quotes are only representative of a share of participants in each of the cities, it is meaningful that these were heard everywhere. The story of Elodie, who was a union representative in her workplace, is transcribed at length and provides an insight into workers' fears and apprehensions about unions.

Elodie: They are scared because I joined CGT [French Union 'General Confederation of Labour'] to learn things and to know how to talk to management.

NS: Who is scared?

Elodie: My colleagues. In order to talk with management to make things progress, so that we're given more importance in the residence. (…)

NS: And why are they scared?

Elodie: They're scared because the union has always been scary for everyone. In my residence they think if they're unionized management will be upset. Management will get revenge… They didn't understand that being unionized it's a right if we want to, it's not an obligation it's a right. (…) It's not forbidden to be unionised. I'm unionized but I don't claim, I don't have flags, I don't prevent you from taking care of elderly persons.... It doesn't have anything to do with that. There are places where it's possible to go on strike but in hospitals and in care homes we can't, staff is already limited. But there are things to be said. Before there were things I couldn't tell her [the manager]... Before I told her "Did you notice that your employees are tired?" She would have said, what she did say before "I'm not a social worker, they're tired, the door is wide open." Recently I went to a CGT training, she didn't pay for that week but that's fine I went there to know things that's it. [Repeating a conversation she had with the manager] "Yes it was very good but I need to meet with you because I have things to tell you." "What is wrong?" "There are many things." "Elodie, we need to meet." (...) I put up things on the board and they would rip it.

NS: Management?

Elodie: No, no, colleagues. I said, listen, the day CGT comes, they have the right to come and see if rights are not being violated … if the board is empty … you know she [the manager] will be very upset because she will have to pay something. And she won't find it funny. So now they don't rip it anymore.'
(Elodie, 52, Guadeloupe, Paris)

If Elodie felt she was getting a voice through her status as union representative ('Elodie we have to meet'), clearly some of her colleagues saw in the presence of the union a danger for themselves. They finally agreed to let Elodie carry out her job because she used their fear of management as an argument against their resistance to the union's activities. This story exemplifies in many ways the hostility that unions can encounter in workplaces, even if it concerns a minority of workers. In Elodie's workplace, those who prevented her from putting up information on the board represented a group of five workers in a workplace of 49. This longer quote illustrates the opinions of a first group of participants, attitudes that ranged from apprehension to hostility with regard to unions' activities. Elodie, whose role was to represent workers, was perceived negatively by some of her co-workers: 'they think if they're unionised management will be upset'. In spite of their legal right to be members of a union, workers in this group shared the concern that union membership might come across as confrontational and would thus weaken their own sense of stability at work by endangering their relationship to management. Unions constitute a danger from this perspective, being perceived not as a source of mediation and support but rather as a source of conflict, which explains the hostility of some workers towards unions.

Amongst those with negative feelings towards unions, a bigger group of participants simply perceived unions as inefficient. The story below, told by Claudia, exemplifies the perceptions of this second group. Claudia's election by her colleagues as union representative resulted from the fact that she had been in charge of distributing the 'goodies' brought in by the union, 'pens, flyers and little things like this', as she said. The union's efforts to recruit members in the workplace were, however, not followed by involvement in workplace issues and with their members. Here it is revealing that these disillusioned views are those of the person who represents the link between the workers and the union.

NS: And were there situations in which you needed support from the union?

Claudia: The union … in the care homes they don't bring support. For example if we ask for the ratios: "We want to amend this convention, to extend the ratios [time] assigned to the persons", this they wouldn't even touch it. They say: "You already know that it has always been a problem, that the manager won't listen to that, that cuts were implemented" as if they were justifying it. Instead of defending, justifying the situation. So it's obvious that there is no support. The girls say it themselves: "What are the unions for if they don't do anything for us?" They don't do anything. (Claudia, 53, Peru, Madrid)

These attitudes towards unions were common and similar opinions were expressed in Paris and in London. For instance, Danièle conveyed in a tired tone:

NS: Are there unions that are present?
Danièle: Yes, they are of no use. Everyone seeks to save his/her skin.
             They can't defend us. Him for instance [pointing at some-
             one at the end of the corridor] he's part of it I think, union
             representative. No ... they are not up to the challenge.
             (Danièle, 53, Senegal, Paris)

To a third group of participants, unions fulfilled the role of an insurance
policy. For these workers, joining a union was often motivated by perceived
insecurity at work, notably in relation to their professional practice as care
workers and the specific risks it entailed in terms of disciplinary procedures.
Here again, these opinions were shared in the three capital cities in spite of
the differentiated roles unions play in each context of industrial relations.
These three participants, Joyce in London, Magdalena in Madrid and Sofia
in Paris, perceived union membership as a form of individual protection:

NS: And why did you join the union?
Joyce: Everybody joined the union, I think they support us if any
             incident happened, and we don't know what ... so maybe
             some people can put you in trouble without knowing.
             When I came here, many people are saying you should join
             the union and at the time I didn't think about this, then
             after lots of experience I think it's better to join the union
             if they do something wrong or something happens to me,
             they can support me. Maybe it's not your fault, you are in
             trouble it's not your fault, some people can put you in trou-
             ble. So that kind of situation maybe you can't fight so by
             the time you need help. (Joyce, 30, India, London)

NS: Since when are you a member?
Magdalena: For 4 years.
NS: And did the union bring you support?
Magdalena: I did not need it, I pay because of the insecurity that we
             have at work, that's why I pay for it, in case at some point
             I need to know and ask for something. (Magdalena, 51,
             Ecuador, Madrid)

NS: Are you member of a union?
Sofia: Yes I'm unionised with FO, *Force Ouvrière* [Workers' Force].
           (…)
NS: And did they bring you any form of support?
Sofia: Mmh … not personally because I didn't need it much, but if
           I need to I would call them. (Sofia, 36, French born to North
           African parents, Paris)

This understanding of union membership left little scope for collective action. This is not surprising given that none of the three groups presented could be characterised as motivated by the idea of collective action: workers were either hostile or indifferent to unions, and when they expressed positive views these reflected a conception of the union as an individual insurance policy. Elodie's understanding of union membership as commitment to collective representation constituted in this regard a minority opinion among research participants. At the individual level, unions thus played a significant role in attenuating the professional risks inherent to care work in cases of disciplinary procedures and unfair dismissals, but it seems that participants did not see in unions a tool to mitigate the insecurities and instability of their jobs.

5.5   Conclusion

This chapter undertook the task of examining employment precariousness through the usual indicators of job stability, earnings and rights at work but questioned the meanings of these indicators from the perspective of participants' perceptions and lived experiences. It demonstrated that a qualitative understanding of the concept of precarious employment requires reformulating the elements that serve as indicators in order to include the meanings workers assign to the latter, reflecting their subjective experiences. The analysis of racialised care workers' narratives has illustrated that 'job stability' was hardly measured by the type of contract but was better accounted for through a more comprehensive approach that considers the sector's specificities as well as employment practices. This chapter highlighted in this regard a process of precarisation at work in the care industry, dynamics that are not visible at first glance through indicators such as the share of permanent contracts or union density.

I equally argued in this chapter that the employment precariousness that characterises the care sector is exacerbated by the marketisation of older-age care provision. The intertwining of care, employment and migration policies shape the specific implications of these processes for care workers in the three countries. Stronger employment protection in France appeared to impact positively care workers' views on job stability as compared to their counterparts in London and Madrid. Beyond such significant contextual differences, participants' narratives strikingly revealed similar processes of precarisation in private older-age care across these European capitals. A shared feature of their employment settings is indeed the constant downward pressure on labour costs. These are the symptoms of a transfer of socio-economic costs onto workers, who assume the costs of numerical flexibility through precarious employment contracts. The disproportionate use of 'replacement contracts' in privately run care homes in Madrid is but one illustration of this dynamic. As a labour-intensive sector, productivity gains in the care industry are limited. In this context the intersection of care workers' uncertain migration and employment statuses provides essential leverage for reducing labour costs. For instance, migrant care workers in the UK who had obtained British citizenship perceived their employment situation as more stable than did those who had precarious migration statuses. In addition, dynamics of capital concentration pave the way to the corporatisation of the care sector (Farris and Marchetti 2017) that increases the occurrence of restructuring and transforms the management practices of care facilities. High management turnover weakens care workers' relationships with their managers and enhances their feeling of being disposable workers. The individualisation of wages equally contributes to maintaining low earnings levels in the context of the sector's weak unionisation rates. Participants' wages in the three sites were situated well below the respective countries' average earnings, with differences that arguably reflect broader patterns of inequalities in these societies. Looking into workers' perceptions of health coverage also demonstrated the vulnerable conditions in which a significant share of migrant and minority ethnic workers cared for older people, most strikingly in London where over half of participants considered that they were not entitled to sick pay or did not know if they were. Finally, beyond the variations observed between the three cities, the growth in the private provision of older-age care, and the structural reliance of corporate care providers on racialised workers, accompany the gradual emergence of intimate care as a site of capital accumulation.

In the following chapter, I analyse the notion of work precariousness from the perspective of participants everyday experiences in older-age care. Drawing on the theoretical contributions of care ethics, I reflect on the gendered bias of most acceptations of precarious work and set out to highlight dimensions of work that are key to the lived experience of precariousness, though silenced by dominant analytical frames.

6

Lived Precariousness Through Body and Mind

> They teach us that we need to learn to separate emotions and work, I'm against it. For me for example, that's my emotions that make me work with passion. That's what makes me love each person. (Saba, 41, Cameroon, Paris)

Saba eagerly emphasised the importance of emotional commitment to carry out her work in a for-profit residential care home in Paris. Employed as a care assistant, Saba could not conceive of caring for older persons in a detached manner. Building upon the literature on precariousness as a bodily and social ontology (Butler 2009/2016) inseparable from the very 'precariousness of life' (Perez Orozco 2014), this chapter aims at casting new light on the concept of 'work precariousness' (Paugam 2009). This chapter explores how the ground-breaking contributions of care ethics transform understandings of precarious work, through an empirical analysis of migrant and minority ethnic workers' experiences in private older-age care. Precariousness is substantial to life itself, it is thus a condition shared by all, albeit differently. Bodies that are racialised—as are migrant and minority ethnic care workers—are exposed to specific social, economic and political forms of precariousness. Isabell Lorey draws on Judith Butler when she writes 'an "ontology of individualism" is not capa-

© The Author(s) 2019
N. Sahraoui, *Racialised Workers and European Older-Age Care*, Thinking Gender in Transnational Times, https://doi.org/10.1007/978-3-030-14397-8_6

ble of recognizing the precariousness of life' (Lorey 2010). This, precisely, is the corner stone of the feminist ethic of care presented in Chap. 2. The assumption of autonomy and independence is symptomatic of the principles on which neoliberal capitalism relies producing the marginalisation of care as an invisible and taken-for-granted set of activities. By exposing the biased ideology that the invisibilisation of care produces, feminist moral philosophy and the care ethics literature in particular provide theoretical tools for uncovering dimensions of care work, and of care labour, that are overlooked by dominant worldviews, and thus silenced. While the literature on feminist moral philosophy and on the ethics of care rarely addresses care work at the empirical level, I argue that it offers unique theoretical insights into the meanings of care work and the challenges arising from processes of commodification, marketisation and neoliberal restructuring. In turn, building upon feminist moral philosophy uncovers the physical and emotional implications for workers' lives of finding themselves at the centre of the capital-care contradiction (Fraser 2016).

Engaging with racialised care workers' bodily and emotional experiences leads to discussing the concept of emotional labour. Arlie Hochschild first introduced this concept in 1983 in *The Managed Heart*, defining it as 'the management of feeling to create publicly observable facial and bodily display; emotional labour is sold for a wage and therefore has exchange value' (1983/2003, p. 7). Hochschild referred to the notion of 'emotional dissonance' to capture this separation between display and feeling (1983/2003, p. 90). And yet, Saba's views point in a different direction. Rather than a burden, Saba claims that emotions are her best tool for providing care. The airline company Hochschild studied taught flight attendants how to feel about customers and how to perceive them; workers were for instance encouraged to see them as children who need attention, so that their behaviour seems less irritating and flight attendants avoid getting angry or upset (1983/2003, p. 110). The care provider who employed Saba also indicated how employees should feel about residents and, most importantly, how they should not feel about them. Care workers are supposed to deliver professional care without getting attached to residents or coming to see them as members of their own family. The airline company had an interest in having flight attendants who would work as if the aeroplane cabins were their homes (1983/2003, p. 105) to enhance the service provided to customers. In contrast, care workers were not supposed to think of residents/service users/clients as their grandparents. However, Saba's words exemplify a widely shared discourse around attachment and feelings, present in participants' narratives in all three sites of fieldwork, that reveals some of the limitations that the concept of 'emotional labour' presents for the analysis of the role of emotions within care labour.

This chapter explores how care work is experienced through body and mind and interrogates notions of precariousness and emotional labour from this perspective. First, I emphasise care work's materiality and bodily dimensions, foregrounding the heavy physical labour that older-age care entails. Then, I scrutinise the role of emotions in participants' narratives, both as actively mobilised by care workers to carry out their work and as endured because of the affective implications of such emotional labour. Accounting for various dimensions that emotional labour involves, this chapter reconciles analytically participants' discourses of authenticity, attachment and love with the performance that emotional labour supposes. Finally, I turn to the analysis of another apparent contradiction: on the one hand the marketisation of emotional labour in a commercial setting and on the other its invisibilisation in the institutional practices of care homes and its marginalisation at the sectorial level. This leads me to elaborate a feminist perspective on the professionalisation of care, building upon care workers' own articulation of an ethic of care.

6.1 Care Work's Bodily Labour

Working Bodies Around the Clock

Providing care to elderly persons requires lifting, carrying and holding up, to mention only a few tasks that involve bodily work. Care work relies ironically on contradictory stereotypes. Feminised sectors of employment are often characterised as 'softer', 'lighter' and 'emotional', as the opposition between the construction and care sectors epitomises. Care work, however, is neither soft nor light; care workers' bodies are on the frontline of much lifting and carrying, arguably much more so than in the masculinised work of doctors and surgeons. Participants' narratives do not lack descriptions of this dimension of their daily labour; Amandine's words are in this regard representative of many other experiences:

> It's physically strenuous. (…) I think that in the long run it costs us our health. Our health is affected because I see women who retired as care assistants and they're not fine physically. They have pain, tendonitis, things like that, knees, the back … so it makes you think … (Amandine, 32, Ivory Coast, Paris)

This heavy physical work makes care work with elderly persons hardly viable as a lifetime occupation. From a feminist moral philosophy perspective for a democratic society, like the one outlined by Tronto, one would interrogate the distribution of care responsibilities: the exploitation of low-paid labour along gendered and racialised divisions constitutes probably the model most distant from one of justice and fair distribution. The question of the long-term sustainability of this occupation emerged in a similar manner in workers' narratives in the three cities. Naomi worked in Madrid and talked about a limit reached by her body. Her account echoes those of many other participants:

> At times we feel that our bodies don't cope anymore, not only me, my colleagues as well. All of us, because every day it's the same, it's lifting people because older people are heavy too, we have to lift them because they are bed-ridden, and we need to handle them completely. So there's a moment in which everything accumulates and it stays with us, the body also gets weaker. There are moments in which we say: 'No more'. (Naomi, 37, Colombia, Madrid)

Time is another key dimension of workers' bodily experience of care labour because of the 24-hour shift work that care-giving entails. While this book does not focus on night workers, a significant share of participants worked night shifts. Isabel, who was employed in a care home in London, worked night and day shifts but felt that the permanent changes in her work schedule did not allow her body to rest and thus put her and the residents at risk.

> Giving us shifts like that, you're working at night and the following day working late, health and safety is not there anymore because you're taking a risk you don't have enough sleep you will be dealing with the residents. What if you really feel weak because you don't have the energy, you don't have the sleep and then you are still working you are dealing with the residents so what if something happened while you are dealing with the resident because you're not really feeling okay, you are still tired. (Isabel, 37, the Philippines, London)

From worn-out bodies due to lifting and carrying, to bodies working around the clock, care labour is embodied, and it is embodied along gendered and racialised divisions of the labour force. The precariousness of life itself is determined by socially constructed forms of precariousness and the link between bodily and social precariousness needs emphasis. Judith Butler offers a way forward in this regard: 'To be a body is to be exposed to social crafting and form, and that is what makes the ontology of the body a social ontology. (…) The more or less existential conception of "precariousness" is thus linked with a more specifically political notion of "precarity"' (2009/2016, p. 3). In what follows, I examine how the political economy of care provision shapes the conditions of workers' bodily labour.

Work Intensification in the Industry

The division of care into separated tasks, or what Molinier calls the 'compartmentalisation of care' (2013), transforms care into a fragmented labour process. This labour process is under pressure in the context of the marketisation of care provision, all the more so as the public subsidies which partly fund the private sector tend to decrease (Simonazzi 2009). The intensification of work is an important dimension of its precarisation processes. A major outcome of this intensification is that it exacerbates negative implications for workers' health. Luc lamented the consequences of increased workloads and denounced a Fordist labour process:

It's assembly-line work. In normal circumstances we have to use the equipment, for instance the equipment to transfer the resident onto an armchair. The time to go get the equipment, to plug it out, install everything, it takes a lot of time, it's not possible. (…) For instance, we have half an hour we do 3 residents, half an hour. When we finish with one who weighs 200kg we have to be fast, we can break our back. It happens, it's like this. We're under pressure. Because we only have half an hour. At noon they need to be in that room and if at noon they're not, for the management we didn't do our job. That's how it works (…) Assembly-line work, like in factories. Unfortunately. (Luc, 25, Cameroon, Paris)

Tronto highlighted this tension in her critique of the neoliberal world-view: 'there is one important vector along which the spread of market thinking poses real problems from the standpoint of care, that is, time. (…) No greater time efficiencies can be achieved in intimate caring, where spending time itself is part of the activity' (Tronto 2013, p. 121). Another symptom of downward labour cost pressure was the insufficient number of workers in some of the care homes, which equally led to work intensification. Rosa in London pointed out the shortage of staff that resulted from a failure to replace workers on sick leave:

We used to, company used to, if short of staff, never short because we can call agency but now, it's private company, the top director they don't allow that we call agency (…) your company pay more money so they don't want. (Rosa, 44, China, London)

In older-age care, this intensification means a higher number of residents to be attended to by each care worker, and hence less time to dedicate to each one, often in a context where this time has already been squeezed in the usual working conditions. This intensification of work is thus detrimental to the quality of the care provided. These narratives demonstrate that workers' and residents' interests, at times presented as contradictory (see below in relation to care workers' sense of responsibility) actually converge within a comprehensive approach. If labour costs are at the heart of the labour process of care provision, and thus at the centre of the strategy to reduce the cost of older-age care, other expenses are also subject to cost-cutting policies. Equipment, food and all material objects purchased to provide care are scrutinised according to the same logic. In several care homes, workers lamented the multiplication of restrictions in place for the use of the daily goods needed to provide care, such as incontinence or shower products. Often, it was not only the inadequate stock, but also the quality of the products themselves, that prevented workers from providing good quality care. The replacement of incontinence products by cheaper ones can go unnoticed by visitors or relatives but it makes all the difference to care givers and care recipients. The permeability of the cheaper products was lamented by workers who were unable to ensure the well-being of residents when bed sheets constantly got wet. In the following quote, Luc illustrates how restrictions on the equipment necessary to provide care led to deterioration in the quality of care. Situations like the one described below also require emotional labour by care workers in that they face discrepancies between the reality of care and the 'ethic of care' on which they construct a positive occupational identity.

> Savings are one of the things, one of the things … I don't want to say that I dislike, but that's a pity because I think above everything else residents are human beings. Human beings. I take a simple example. For example, imagine you're given two protection pads, two for one resident. And during the day he gets wet three times. So there are not enough protection pads. Because if he gets wet three times each time you need to change because he's a human being. In addition to that they are older persons, it's like babies, they can get wet anytime. You need to change. And there are two protection pads for the day. If there is none left you need to call someone responsible for giving it away, it's complicated and you waste time. (Luc, 25, Cameroon, Paris)

Increasing cost restrictions on available products affect care workers' capacity to provide good quality care in pervasive ways. There is obviously the material dimension (lack of products, lack of time), but bringing into the analysis the physical and the emotional dimensions of care labour uncovers implications at additional levels of experience. The intensification of work and the precarisation of working conditions also affect workers' well-being by shattering the potentially rewarding self-representations of their occupational identity. The dignity and pride in providing care, the feelings of usefulness, all these aspects that participants shared and performed in an interview setting, are negatively affected by increasing precarisation. In the context of low earnings and precarious employment terms, participants' discourses around an ethic of care gave consistency to a positive occupational identity for themselves on the one hand, and enabled them to perform it in various social settings on the other. Fouzia's words illustrate the complexities inherent in care work, in how it intertwines feelings, bodily work, commitment and possibly harmful implications for workers.

> It hurts my back when I lift her, there's a way to lift her but it's my job it's like this. Sometimes I want so much to help her standing up to come to eat I don't even pay attention that my back hurts, you see that's love. I think it's love. It's pleasing someone, that's love. (Fouzia, 43, Algeria, Paris)

Fouzia took great pride in her work and was concerned with sharing with me the practices that she considered good care. If backs are hurt frequently and tendonitis suffered regularly, it is not enough to address this merely as a health and safety dimension of care labour. The analysis also needs to consider the 'I want so much to help' dimension of this emotional and bodily labour. Both aspects are intertwined and constitutive of a specific form of work precariousness. The following section seeks to address this dimension by examining the role of emotions in care workers' daily labour.

6.2   Shades of Emotional Labour

Contributions and Shortcomings of the Concept

In contrast to the concept of 'affective labour' (Hardt and Negri 2000), that replicates the idea of 'producing something in a passive object that is laboured upon' (Lanoix 2013, p. 93), the notion of 'emotional labour' seems better suited to incorporate a relational understanding of care work. The concept of 'emotional labour' originally developed by

Hochschild in her study of flight attendants, and since then applied to many other professions, made a breakthrough contribution to the sociology of work when it was first published in 1983. Hochschild raised a fundamental question: what happens when emotions are used by capital as its best-selling strategy? When prices were still regulated in the US airline industry, the competition was overwhelmingly concentrated on service quality and in this regard flight attendants' smiles became a strategic asset for airline companies. The marketisation and privatisation of care services in the neoliberal era created an industry with some similarities to Hochschild's case study. An overview of the websites of for-profit private care homes shows without exception pictures of smiling care workers and smiling older persons. Here, too, smiles are the centrepiece of the selling strategy.

By selling care services, residential care providers sell an idea of what constitutes proper care and what a good caring relationship is. Care workers' emotional labour consequently upholds the company's profits and this leads the company to impose on workers the emotions they are supposed to display. Emotions and feelings embodied by care workers are commodified, acquire exchange value, and are sold as a service. Smiles and attention become something one can buy and voice an opinion on when the service does not live up to expectations: 'ordinary niceness is no longer enough; after all, hasn't the passenger paid for extra civility?' (Hochschild 1983/2003, p. 95). The care industry's communication strategies similarly do not hesitate to marketise feelings and emotions, as the following slogans taken from care providers' websites suggest: 'We really care about people, looking after their health and understanding what makes them happy'; 'Our philosophy is centred on the provision of excellent care by an organisation based on family values'.[1]

In this chapter I build on Hochschild's work, notably in relation to how she problematised the role of emotions in an industry driven by profits on the one hand, and on the other in relation to the attention she dedicated to workers' narratives around it. However, from my own fieldwork with migrant and minority ethnic care workers, additional ques-

---

[1] First quote: http://www.fshc.co.uk, last accessed in April 2015. Second quote: http://www.caring-homes.org/what-we-offer/, last accessed in April 2015.

tions emerged which classical understandings of emotional labour do not entirely grasp within a theoretical perspective. Care workers referred repeatedly to feelings of love, attachment and friendship as well as sadness, anger and grief, to explain why they loved their job, why at times it was challenging or why they didn't want to stay in it any longer. While care work entails an enormous amount of emotion work to bring oneself to provide care no matter how one feels, I argue here that there is more to it than this dimension of emotional labour, and that emotions also play an essential role in constructing care workers' occupational identity, pride and, as argued by Rodriquez, dignity (2011). In the following pages, I scrutinise how emotions are both positively mobilised and endured by care workers.

Mobilising Emotions to Provide Care

The central role of emotions within care related activities might seem obvious. Because care is relational, it involves the interaction of two or more human beings which inevitably triggers emotions, and which in a commodified setting supposes emotional labour. Though my interview guide did not explicitly mention emotions at work, in the analysis of the 82 interviews I coded extracts from 70 interviews for a total of 269 citations related to various aspects of emotional labour. Thematically, emotional labour was part and parcel of significant sections of each interview. Mentioned as a tool, as hardship or as reward, it was definitely at the heart of participants' daily activities. While Hochschild evidenced how employers' expectations and guidance shape the emotional labour performed, the latter is also shaped to a great extent by workers themselves in a profession such as care work (Rodriquez 2011, p. 266). I argue here that descriptions of emotional labour in care workers' discourses demonstrate on the one hand that emotions are actively mobilised by workers to provide care, and on the other hand that providing care triggers emotions, both positive and negative, which lead workers to engage in continuous 'emotion work' to adjust their reactions to institutional expectations and, at times, to protect certain boundaries between their paid employment and their personal lives.

Participants unanimously emphasised verbal and non-verbal communication in the narration of their work. Any act of care is swathed in words, exchange and gestures. Talking to residents is what care workers do all day long. During my interview with Danièle, she pointed at a resident at the other end of the lounge where we sat and commented:

> The one who talks over there, it's been a week she's here, she likes me. (Laugh) She's very very nice, we like to have residents like this, they make us laugh, we make them laugh, they make us laugh ... we feel less the weariness when we laugh with them. If there is no communication ... it's not possible not to communicate. Laugh is like a therapy. (Danièle, 53, Senegal, Paris)

Communication serves to build relationships with residents and care could not be provided without it; care workers have to communicate so that the person receiving care accepts the care that the worker needs to provide. This is most obvious in daily caring activities that relate to residents' intimacy, as this often triggers resistance and confrontation. Communication is a skill that cannot be reduced to 'talking to the resident while providing care'. The accumulated experience of care workers plays a role in their ability to communicate with residents. Many participants spontaneously referred to the centrality of communication, as did Doriane, a care worker from the French overseas department of Guadeloupe, while describing her daily work:

> So we start bathing, during the bath we communicate, it's important to really facilitate communication a lot, a lot, a lot, it allows the person to be more relaxed, even if the person is tense at times because many are, so the bathing is more relaxed and it goes smoother instead of standing here as if in front of a subject that we just wash ... no that's not what we do it's really a communication. (Doriane, 59, Guadeloupe, Paris)

If this communication is so crucial, it is also because refusing care is quite common amongst residents and service users. Institutional caring practices might appear as highly intrusive or violent to elderly residents. As a matter of fact, care workers need to wake the residents up at a scheduled time and to make sure all residents on the floor are washed or show-ered before breakfast. Many residents do not want to be washed or showered and refuse the care that care workers are supposed to provide. The whole of the interaction in these cases revolves not around the act of bathing or showering itself; instead, the worker needs to focus on bring-ing the resident to accept being bathed or showered. This challenging task is difficult and time-consuming, and at times it exposes the care worker to aggressive reactions by residents when the conversation turns into a confrontation. Immense emotional labour is invested by care work-ers in such interactions in an attempt to provide care as smoothly as pos-sible. Fouzia described this challenge:

> They have a lot of sloppiness, they refuse life in general. So it's the case of this person, so I have to make jokes, or facilitate conversation and give him a bit of humour so that he does his personal hygiene. It's very very hard. The gesture of doing personal care is very simple but to convince a person to do it it's very hard. (Fouzia, 43, Algeria, Paris)

Participants shared many examples of such daily conversations, which often sounded like negotiations with the residents. Andrea, employed in a private care home in Madrid, described a situation most care workers shared in similar words, not only in Madrid but also in Paris and London:

> You arrive at eight in the morning, you wake them up, you call them and prepare to wash them, they don't like it … Because they probably are com-fortable and warm and you have to wake them up. 'I don't want to take a shower, I don't want you to wash my hair, I don't want this and that.' And you have to do everything possible to try to wash them, to clean their teeth, and to help them wash their hair. So you have to make it go smoothly … to divert their attention from what you're doing, to talk about something else and see if they can 'forget' what you're doing. (Andrea, 47, Cape Verde, Madrid)

Making use of a repertoire of communication techniques does not necessarily mean that care workers are always successful in gaining the resident's trust or merely acceptance. Confrontations are sometimes left unresolved. Nada, employed in a private care home in Paris, shared the following challenge:

> There is a lady who did not want to be washed and I'm not sure she will agree tomorrow to be washed. I will try again tomorrow but she's almost 100 years old and she considers that she doesn't need a shower. What do we do? I force her to take a shower? It's a woman who urinates in bed and I change her bed sheets but I don't know if she washes herself … (…) but I can't force her either. Tomorrow I will try, as I have written in the handover report, it doesn't mean I will succeed tomorrow. It doesn't mean I will succeed the day after tomorrow either. But it means that in a given moment we will have to wash her despite herself. We will have to wash her. (Nada, 31, French, North African parents, Paris)

In their attempt to make residents feel at ease and trust them for the delicate care they need to provide, care workers continuously engage in emotional labour. This emotional labour serves to build relationships with the elderly persons they care for, and in this interaction, they are both agents and receivers. Their actions do not simply have an impact on the feelings and well-being of the persons who are cared for, as the concept of 'affective labour' suggests, according to Hardt and Negri's understanding mentioned above. The care relationship cannot be described as one between an active and a passive agent, and in this regard the concepts of 'care-giver' and 'care-receiver' are misleading; rather the care relationship is created by a dynamic interaction. Care relationships are more adequately described as co-produced, what Paul Browne names the 'care effect' (2010), whereby the care-giver also receives and the care-receiver gives.

An obvious form of emotional labour, one that illustrates Hochschild's definition of 'the management of feeling to create publicly observable facial and bodily display', is found in care workers' description of the mental preparation they required to start the day and enter into contact with residents. Elena describes a state of mind many participants experienced:

> We all have personal problems, and these problems you can't bring it to the company, especially in a care home where you care for dependent people,

persons who are sick, who need affection, cuddling, attention, who need an example, a smile on your face. You have to be in your best mood. Problems, you leave them in the street, you have to come with very good energy to be with them because there's no reason why they would need to pay for all the problems of those working in this, they're innocent. (Elena, 42, Paraguay, Madrid)

Most situations that are narrated by care workers described, however, forms of emotional labour that do not fit so easily into Hochschild's definition. How to analyse feelings of fulfilment that workers share spontaneously with residents? Or a feeling of powerlessness and guilt when a resident's health deteriorates? Arguably, the concept of emotional labour—as defined by Hochschild—cannot fully account for the blurred boundary between the personal and the professional in long-term care settings. First, the idea of a two-way relationship, if not reciprocity, needs to be stressed. Residents trigger emotions for care workers when they display signs of appreciation and gratitude. Seeing it from this angle differs from the previous point: care workers not only perform emotion work to be in the right mood to provide care, they are also subject to emotions of their own that are created by this interaction. These can be very positive as in the idea of fulfilment, or devastating, as when workers feel unsafe because they are exposed to aggressive residents, or when they feel guilty. The strength and pervasiveness of these feelings often require additional emotional labour in an attempt to preserve their personal lives from the emotion-laden environment of care work.

Amongst aspects of the care relationship that do not follow from purposeful emotion work by the workers was the satisfaction that learning from older persons procured. Many shared the view that they were learning something every day. A typical quote on this theme is that of Eloise, employed in Paris:

We learn a lot from elderly persons. We learn a lot and I like the contact with … even if they have Alzheimer, I talk to them as if … (laugh) not like children, as we always have a tendency to infantilize a little. No, I like to hear their stories. We learn a lot. It's a human relationship. (Eloise, 59, Guadeloupe, Paris)

Feelings of reward and fulfilment constitute another positive example of the 'two-way relationship' that care work represents and of its importance for care workers, as illustrated by the following quote from Adriana, who worked in Madrid.

> What I like most is the gratitude of the persons, they are grateful. I have worked in different places and I don't know why generally speaking the work one does nobody acknowledges it or thanks you. But an elderly person will always appreciate, will be grateful … this affection that they give you or this gratitude because you're caring for them, it's something that has surprised me a lot and I enjoyed working with elderly persons. (Adriana, 29, Ecuador, Madrid)

I now turn to the dark side of care workers' emotional labour and explore feelings of fear, guilt and mourning, equally prevalent in participants' daily labour.

Enduring Challenging Emotions

From one end of the emotional spectrum to the other, feelings of fear, guilt and mourning pose a similar theoretical challenge to the concept of emotional labour. A story frequently narrated was one of helplessness over having to care for residents who never recover, who might preserve their health for a while, but who inevitably see their health deteriorate as time passes. Being continuously confronted with diseases from which residents could not recover triggered sadness and a sense of guilt. Elena was caring for an elderly man for several years as a live-in carer until she decided she would like to obtain a nursing degree to improve her professional opportunities. When the possibility arose for another carer to take her place, she decided the conditions were met for her to be able to leave. Her account shows however that such decisions might bear an emotional toll:

> When I left him, he died after a month … I left the house to start studying nursing. I left and a girl came that they had something like 5 or 6 years earlier, who got married and left for a different place. So this girl was about to come back, so I said: 'given that this person is here, I go'. And the man

told me that if I left he would die. I don't know, I was always saying that this … no, this can only God decide, that neither him nor me could know when. So it was how he saw things, so I left and he died after a month. (Elena, 42, Paraguay, Madrid)

These situations are difficult to manage emotionally and they reveal the fragility of the boundaries that workers are told to draw between their paid work and their personal lives. Confronted with terminal illness and death of residents for whom they provided care, sometimes for years, care assistants often experience difficulties in confining their emotions at work to the job. Patricia in Paris and Isabel in London shared feelings that are familiar to all care workers involved in older-age care.

We can always tell there need to be a barrier, it's true, but we can't, there are moments when we get attached. But we know that … We're human so it affects us when there's a death. It affects us, it has to. Because it's like a family in the end because we spend a lot of time here. Eleven hours per day, now we're working the whole week-end, three days, we're more here [than at home], when we get back home it's late already. When I get home it's after nine, so it's like a second family, I always say. And we get attached inevitably and when they die, it affects us. (Patricia, 34, Reunion Island, Paris)

It's hard if you are a carer and you've been dealing with them for quite a long time it's hard to be attached to them. That's why we have that … what do they call that … like limitation like that. Because to be attached to them is not really good, because when they are gone it's like your family member then you will mourn as well. Actually I got a very good relationship with all the service users, especially I have got one, but when I was on my maternity leave she died and then [a colleague] has just informed me about her death and I was lying in bed, I was really shocked because the death it's really abrupt so I was really crying and I realised you know it's hard to be attached to the residents. (Isabel, 37, the Philippines, London)

Another set of emotions derives from the harm that residents can cause to care workers by being aggressive. Residents with certain conditions such as Alzheimer's tend to be aggressive towards care assistants, whose only protection is often the emotional labour they perform in an attempt to keep the resident calm while they provide the care the person needs. Examples of violent gestures by residents are almost countless in carers' narratives. Workers in domestic settings are in this regard most exposed. Feeling at risk of physical harm was most emphasised by live-in care workers met in Madrid, like Gladys:

> To be with one person is a lot, you absorb everything from that person and even more when the person … because according to the pathology … there are persons … when you first start it's very difficult, because many are aggressive. And being at home you run the risk that they attack you. (Gladys, 37, Ecuador, Madrid)

Physical violence, though marks were sometimes visible on the hands and arms of the participants I have met, was not the only form of violence. In many ways, insults and comments could provoke emotional distress. Residents' insults were oftentimes racist comments, as explored more specifically in Chap. 7. In addition to the emotion work one does to 'leave personal problems outside' before starting the shift, after a difficult day, care workers need to do additional emotion work if they intend not to let these feelings impact on their private life. This point was often made by women with children who felt they needed to take up the role of mother as soon as they left the workplace, which required them to put aside emotions lived in the job. If emotions can be positively mobilised by care workers, or celebrated when they offer a sense of satisfaction at work; intense emotional labour is equally necessary to cope with the daily interactions that characterise care relationships.

Overall, these experiences were similar in care workers' narratives in London, Paris and Madrid in spite of institutional differences. The difference was that in some private care homes I visited in Paris a psychologist could meet with care workers to provide some support and help when workers went through the mourning process. Not employed full time, the psychologist would nevertheless come for a couple of hours per week and meet individually or in groups (varying from one home to another) both with workers and with residents. Being able to talk to the psychologist or being encouraged to do so by the nurse in charge, when a worker was affected by some events at work, represented a form of acknowledgement of the implications of emotional labour. Danièle recounts, for instance:

> With the psychologist, when we lose someone for instance, we talk about it. There is one who died, when? ... in December ... very nice lady. This one she affected me I had to talk to the psychologist because I was seeing her night and day, night and day. In the evening, it's me who put them to bed on the floor, my colleague leaves at 7 and I leave at 8. Every evening she would tell me 'Go and stay with your children', these are words that touch me, each time, every evening she would tell me this, as soon as I had put her to bed 'go home and get back to your children'. (Danièle, 53, Senegal, Paris)

Danièle clearly describes here a care relationship in which she's not the sole care-giver; the resident also *cares for* her. The resident might not be able to provide care, as in Tronto's use of 'caregiving', but she definitely 'cares about' and 'cares for'. Within this dynamic interaction of care, an emotional labour of a particular kind ensues from the responsibilities that care work supposes. In the following paragraphs I relate how participants experienced responsibility with understandings of this notion in the care ethics literature.

The Emotional Burden of Caring Responsibilities

Feelings of responsibility were part and parcel of the everyday experiences of interviewed care workers. This point is in line with the findings and analysis of Pascale Molinier, who conducted a participatory action research in a care home in Paris (Molinier 2013). Care provided to elderly persons depends on perceptions, emotions and feelings that are both person and context dependent, while marketisation relies on the interchangeability of workers. This tension feeds into work precariousness for workers in many ways. Workers' claims for improvement in their working conditions or lessening of their workload can appear to conflict with the interests of the care recipients. Stories told in the following paragraphs illustrate how these tensions emerge.

Responsibility is also an important theme of feminist moral philosophy: there cannot be a 'caring democracy' without responsibility (Tronto 2013). This ethic of care can be found in the daily caring practices of care workers, who feel responsible for the well-being of the persons they are taking care of. Fouzia's account explains this fundamental dimension of care work through a simple example:

> We can't cheat in this field, I could cheat when I worked in the bank, I could postpone chip files, I worked with cards' chips. I could leave a file from someone, it doesn't matter if he doesn't get the chip today, he'll get it tomorrow, that's not the end of the world. This is very serious, I think it's more serious with people. We can't leave lunch-time drugs for tomorrow. It's a disaster, we can't. Maybe it's possible not to wash these sheets today, but not the drugs. So I'm committed, that's for her health, for her well-being. The well-being of a person, it's not a machine. You really need to do it every day, day by day. There's no stop or pause, there's not such a thing. (Fouzia, 43, Algeria, Paris)

Feelings of responsibility are also intertwined with those of guilt. Amongst other aspects, death and grief, a constituent part of caring for elderly persons, unavoidably remind care assistants that they work every day with the very precariousness of life. Being confronted with this precariousness on a daily basis profoundly affects their work experiences. Affected by the death of a resident and experiencing a sense of guilt, in the following quote Doriane offers insights into how workers' emotions create certain vulnerabilities and bear implications beyond the context of work. Instructed to stop caring for a resident by the supervisory nurse, Doriane relates how she resented this managerial decision:

> It was against my will, I'm here and she liked that I spend time with her, that I took time to wash her, and she told me that, and when she started to become weaker, the care assistant told me that's not your role, you leave her to us. So I left her and she died soon thereafter. (Doriane, 59, Guadeloupe, Paris)

If there are as many specific stories and as great a range of feelings on this theme as the number of participants I met, they nevertheless all relate to the burden of responsibility placed on care workers' shoulders. Highlighting the weight of responsibility is crucial, as the gendered understanding of care labour effectively conceals the degree of responsibility borne by care workers. In a similar fashion to the invisibilisation of the heavy physical work, the vital responsibilities inherent in care labour are silenced. Acknowledging the existence and importance of these responsibilities would contradict the devaluation of care work and its characterisation as 'unskilled'. At the bottom of the professional hierarchy, care assistants see the importance of their work denied and the responsibility transferred onto professionals deemed highly skilled, such as doctors or care home managers. Foregrounding actual caring practices uncovers the gendered and racialised construction of care work that deskills the occupation and marginalises the workforce. Aimée shared an experience that affected her deeply and which epitomises this paradoxical combination of responsibility without voice:

> The resident I told you about had to run away for us to receive a couple of days later a training on the steps to be taken when someone runs away. (…) It affected me when she left, two or three days later we have the training, what we need to do, what steps to follow, and everything. But I realised that even the director didn't know all residents in the protected units [units for patients with illnesses such as dementia and Alzheimer's], she didn't know her … and when she ran away, after 30 minutes … I'm sorry [Aimée holds back her tears] after 30 minutes I looked for her, I told them she left, she is not here. That's what hurts, they didn't listen, I told them I know her she's not here anymore, not in the care home. It's after an hour that the director realised, she said why you didn't inform me earlier … I told her I tried to call many times through the switchboard to tell you that she is not here anymore, that we need to call the police station, start searching. They didn't listen to me. (Aimée, 44, Guinea, Paris)

Aimée in these extraordinary circumstances had no means to contact the director directly, a fact illustrating the weight of the professional hierarchies in place. At this moment in the interview she appeared to be deeply affected by what had happened, but amongst her feelings there also seemed to be anger: anger for not having been listened to, anger for becoming visible to management only when being blamed, anger for being voiceless when she needed to reach out to higher managerial levels.

I have so far attempted to uncover the complexity of what emotional labour entails and questioned from the empirical perspective of older-age care work the shortcomings of the concept of emotional labour as originally defined. The following pages expose that this emotional labour fails to be acknowledged by the industry practices. Furthermore, the professionalisation discourse does not provide a bridge to bring the two closer together as one might expect, but reproduces a biased understanding of care work overlooking participants' own articulation of an ethic of care.

6.3   Where's the Work in Care Work?

A Capitalist Miracle: Marketising Emotions While Making Emotional Labour Invisible

Selling care services brings private companies to depict emotions in their advertising materials. Happy workers and happy residents are portrayed in images of smiling faces, clasped hands or joyful group activities. These representations in text, pictures and videos, to be found on the companies' websites, serve to showcase the care provided in these facilities. Daily caring activities such as personal hygiene and continence care are implied but not explicitly mentioned and most communication materials revolve around ensuring the emotional well-being of residents. These representations convey the image of happy, well-attended residents, enjoying a better life quality than at home. There exists, however, a fundamental contradiction between how emotions are portrayed, and thus apparently valued, and how emotional labour by care workers is rendered invisible and is de facto devalued. This section unpacks the contradiction between the importance of emotional labour in care workers' narratives and the lack of recognition of its crucial role by companies through the procedures they implement and expectations they formulate towards workers. A contemporary consequence of the historic assignation of domestic and care work to women—and its consideration as unskilled—is the on-going invisibilisation of emotional labour within marketised care provision. While low earnings are undoubtedly a symptom of this marginalisation, I focus here on several instances of this invisibilisation related to the organisation of work at the workplace level.

Supervision procedures implemented in British care homes to ensure care quality constitute a case in point. The indicators chosen for reporting, presented as neutral and objective tools, reflect in fact a deeply gendered understanding of what work is. These indicators determine which aspects of care deserve to make it into written reports and which supposedly can be left out, and by the same token silenced. A report published by the Joseph Rowntree Foundation (Warmington et al. 2014) listed all paperwork in use in care homes according to who fills in the forms, whether doing so is a legal requirement, and how often the forms are used. The list comprises 101 items that correspond to different forms and reports. It includes items such as risk assessments for handling medication, checks for fridges' temperatures, and monitoring daily laundry services. Among these items, none actually addresses the relationships between care workers and residents, for instance none gives the worker the chance to value the time spent ensuring that the resident agrees to the care provided. Only three items—out of over 101 in total—remind the reader that the work assessed is care for older persons and not inanimate objects: 'Life story', 'Communication assessment' and 'Spiritual needs'. The rest is about risk assessments, medical charts and technical maintenance issues. All this leaves little room for the emotional labour performed to become visible within supervising mechanisms. Whatever is quantifiable and apparently 'objective' can more easily be turned into an indicator. For instance, counselling a depressed resident appears to be subjective and the 'outcome' of the time spent doing this is hardly measurable. In contrast, caring activities that are defined by a medical or technical criterion can be regarded as 'objectively' assessed, as, for example, monitoring a resident's fluid intake. Inevitably, the normative implications of this bureaucratised and Taylorism-inspired supervision of care come to undermine care workers' emotional labour. Care becomes a series of disembodied tasks in the paperwork and the subjectivity of the caring relationship gets lost in translation.

This attempt to standardise care by scheduling each task tends to be resisted by care workers when they perceive it as hampering or diminishing the quality of the care they provide. Claudia, who worked in a private care home in Madrid, felt rushed in the morning because of the number of residents she needed to attend in a limited time. Most participants employed in residential care facilities mentioned an exaggerated workload in the mornings:

> If the day starts at 7, in the morning at 9:30 at latest they need to be in the lounge. So you need to be there in 2.5 hours, you have to be fast, 'pin pan, pin pan'. And they have this protocol with a timetable but I think that this timetable harms residents because time that should be dedicated to a person is not respected. (…) Because they plan really little time and it is a constant struggle, what they call the 'ratio', it means how many persons we have to do each, and apparently they don't have budget for this 'ratio' that they call it. (Claudia, 53, Peru, Madrid)

The implementation of such a schedule implied a supervision that focused mostly on making sure the timetable was respected. Martina argued that such supervision missed the point:

> The nurse in charge is only looking if all are seated, are washed, are showered, if their hair is done, if they are dressed, and these things. So you see the difference, care in a private one (care home), and in spite of the fact that they pay double than in a home from the city of Madrid [care home run by the local authority] they aren't well cared for anyway. (Martina, 51, Ecuador, Paris)

Care workers were caught up between residents' needs and expectations on the one hand and institutionalised practices of care that imposed strict rules about when and how each task was to be carried out on the other. In spite of this institutional framework, care workers were creative in finding ways to make timetables slightly less rigid and better adapted to residents' needs. In a private care home in Paris, Saba, for instance, managed little adjustments:

There is Lady M, she doesn't like water, as she says. She wants wine and beer. She likes that we stay seated next to her, on the edge of the bed. So sometimes I stay with her and I listen to her. Or she only looks at me and we say "we're well here". Even if we don't talk … I rest as well. And it makes her feel better. She smiles. And I enjoy this smile and after that I can only give her five more minutes because after personal care there's lunch. (Saba, 41, Cameroon, Paris)

This tension between the time a care worker would like to spend with the resident and the time the carer is actually able to do so creates frequent distress. Time pressure shapes the way emotional labour is performed and triggers additional emotion work to deal with the consequences of stressful time management. Often, care workers voiced their disapproval and unease when confronted with such constant time pressure, as did Mayra:

To be honest, I don't like working in a residential care home because I'm very affected by how residents are treated. The truth is I worked because of necessity. I worked and tried to do the best way possible with the best consideration towards the persons, but the truth is that working in care homes is hard because they require a lot from you. You have to care for many persons in minimal amount of time and it makes you rush the persons, you understand? It's not the same when you care for one person at home, you take your time, you bathe the person slowly, you give the person time to dress up, to do his or her hair, or to put on some face cream. Whereas when you're in a care home, everything is running, running. Very fast, very fast … I tell you it is often as if we weren't dealing with persons. I tell you sincerely, it happened that I cried for the inhumane treatment of working in a care home. (Mayra, 52, Ecuador, Madrid)

When workers disapproved of caring practices in a given workplace, this state of mind had emotional implications for them as they needed to deal with the experience of doing something against their judgement and their will. Whereas Mayra could not leave her job because of financial constraints, Martina was able to find a job in a different setting when the situation became unbearable:

So in the private ones there are few care assistants on the floors. In the night, in a private one, we put to bed 50 residents, three girls, two ok and one for instance with a broken arm and they did not give her sick leave or with a lumbago and they wouldn't put her on sick leave. As she couldn't lift weight she was standing watching that they don't fall. So that the two of us who were ok we looked like machines, with the famous hoists … tititiit- tititi … lower the bed … it was like something automatic up to the point that you say it's not possible. Because if we go as if we weren't putting per- sons to bed, or I don't know as if they were things or as if you're abusing … I didn't like the private one at all. I stayed a very short time and left. (Martina, 51, Ecuador, Madrid)

The reduction of care to a series of technical acts, most obviously feed- ing and personal hygiene, is not confined to institutional practices. Rather, these reflect dominant norms and values within society at large. Care workers were highly aware of the relative devaluation of their work because of its association with 'dirty jobs' and the general view of it as unskilled. They confronted these representations in their social relations both at work and outside. Many in this study said they were hurt by com- ments and remarks that were demeaning and that could take different forms: a relative saying to the person caring for her mum, 'You could do better', meaning the person had the capabilities to pursue 'better' profes- sional aims; or an employer telling an applicant 'And the "wee and poo" is all you know?' in a condescending tone. The devaluation of care work could also take on more subtle forms. The story told by Saba illustrates the idea commonly shared that paid care is composed of tasks that visi- tors and relatives could not do, as if the similarity of paid and non-paid activities would render care workers' earnings less legitimate. In this case, it was making pancakes that was not considered part of 'proper care':

It was "What is this? You are here you're not doing anything!" But Madam, making pancakes it is an activity, an activity it is not only playing. Pancakes, talking to a resident, these are activities. Doing manicure, massaging hands, it is an activity. Everything we do is an activity. "Oh no, this is not normal, that's not possible." We were almost "good-for-nothing" and I found it quite hurtful. On top of that she did not want to listen to us, to hear us. Nothing at all. (Saba, 41, Cameroon, Paris)

The distinction between paid and non-paid care resides in the monetised relation that paid care establishes. Care activities, however, overlap and caring for someone's personal hygiene or psychological well-being is part of care in both paid and non-paid settings. Saba considered the reactions of family relatives in this instance, displaying the little consideration they had for activities deemed trivial and/or pleasant, to be demeaning.

The following section looks at the contradiction that emerges between, on the one hand, care workers' articulation of an 'ethic of care' and the ideas underpinning care professionalisation on the other. The commodification and commercialisation of care activities previously confined to the private sphere (where they were no more immune to exploitation) led to a certain professionalisation of older-age care. Yet, the boundary between what is strictly professional and what goes beyond the professional sphere is not always easy to draw. Emotional labour in long-term care often gives rise to strong and contradictory emotions that affect care workers.

Listening to Care Workers: The Case for a Feminist Professionalisation of Care

Care workers' narratives made systematic references to commitment, love and attachment. The starting point of the analysis in this section is the mobilisation by care workers of these discourses to account for their working experiences. The question I raise is: why does this ethic of care, as constructed by care workers themselves, differ from the dominant professional discourse? Workers who were too committed were considered unprofessional, but if workers would not care, as in Tronto's distinction between 'caring for' and 'care-giving', they would not be appreciated by their professional hierarchy either. Where should the line be drawn? And most importantly, can a boundary be set at all? This section contends that these questions remain open due to the unresolved broader question of the place of care in our societies. As long as the organisation of society won't address the fact that 'humans are not only creatures of the market, they are creatures of care' (Tronto 2013, p. 45), care will remain marginalised and devalued. The questions raised here do not contradict a certain potential for the improvement of working conditions through professionalisation (Moré 2018). Rather, the paradox studied here reveals the limitations that professionalisation processes entail under the current political economy of care. Existing contradictions between how paid care is institutionally defined and what care workers have to say about it are most relevant in this regard. The analysis of their discourses invites a thorough rethinking of the place of care in society.

First, what are the manifestations of such an ethic of care when discussing workers' professionalisation? Interestingly enough, and in contrast to the points analysed above, discourses vary here between London, Paris and Madrid. While love, commitment and attachment are mentioned, described and illustrated with numerous examples, care workers' narratives are to some extent shaped by the degree to which professionalisation has penetrated the institutional environment they work in. In this regard there are significant differences between the three countries (as detailed in Chap. 3). In Paris, all care workers interviewed completed at least six months of training, and often nine months. In Madrid, professionalisation was being implemented while I was doing fieldwork, given that a new regulation required a certificate from all care assistants as of 2015. Local authorities in Madrid, however, did not provide precise information until the end of 2014 and care home managers addressed this issue unevenly, with many care homes leaving it to the workers to look for private schools where they could complete this qualification. Before the reform, care workers in Madrid were often recruited on the basis of 200–300 hours of training provided by local authorities or certified associations. A lighter degree of professionalisation characterised care homes I visited in London. Care workers could be recruited with no previous training at all and consequently received 'on-the-job' training. Knowledge was transmitted through online training and an induction with more experienced colleagues. This form of training exposed workers less to a standardised professional discourse because the values and norms promoted depended for a large part on the colleagues who were doing the induction. In the following paragraphs, I look into the differentiated expressions of this tension between professionalism and workers' understanding of care.

In Paris, this contradiction was explicitly raised in the interviews, given that care workers completed a training that indicated detachment as prescribed norm. The introductory quote by Saba illustrates this point, and in the French context most participants expressed thoughts that foregrounded a tension between this norm and their lived experience. Danièle shared the following reflections:

> We get attached to them, me personally I'm a very sensitive person, during training they were telling us not to get attached to residents but it's not possible, it's inhumane, it's inhumane not to get attached to these persons. They need us, even us we need them. We also need to communicate with them. It's not only them. They need our presence, our help but we feel down sometimes too, we confide to some residents with whom … but during training they tell us no … but other persons told me that's not possible and that's true it's inhumane, every day … me for example it's been three years that I'm here, how can I not get attached to them, especially on this floor? It's not possible not to get attached to these persons, it's not possible. (Danièle, 53, Senegal, Paris)

This discourse, which echoes the fundamental interdependency stressed by an ethic of care, also emerged in the interviews with care workers in Madrid, although only a few pointed to the contradiction it supposed with teaching materials in the field. One of them was Saul, a young care assistant from El Salvador working in domiciliary care:

> It is a very humanizing work that makes you reflect, it's not simply as people think cleaning others' people dirt and that's it, no … You have to get involved … in classes about care they tell you quite the opposite, in the classes they tell not to get involved in things, that these are personal matters, that this shouldn't be carried out this way but I believe that we're human beings and that's very difficult to disconnect things. (Saul, 27, El Salvador, Madrid)

The important role of emotional attachment in performing intimate care that Saul emphasises here can be compared to Cinzia Solari's insights into Russian migrant domestic workers' experiences (2006). In her case study of Jewish and Christian Orthodox Russian care workers' narratives in San Francisco, she distinguished between two discursive practices she encountered amongst her respondents: care as a religious calling (saints) vs. care as a professional commitment (professionals) and noted that those who relied on a religious framing were more at ease with intimate care labour than those who understood their role strictly in professional terms. She accounted for these diverging framings by shedding light on the role of the settlement organisations and their more or less religious vs. professional discourses and practices (Solari 2006). In this research, participants' narratives in Madrid and in London implied that an opposition between emotional commitment and professionalism would emerge if more professional training were provided, because most described their attachment to residents in similar words to those employed by their counterparts in Paris.

What is more, emotional engagement with the residents often led care workers I interviewed to describe their relations with residents as similar in nature to those they had with their own parents or grandparents. Here the 'professional' discourse also had a differentiated impact on the narratives shared in Paris, Madrid and London. Further to the training they had received, workers in Paris showed they were aware that they were not expected to equate their relationships with residents to family-type relations. Amandine said for instance:

Actually I consider them a little bit like if they were, I don't know if I'm allowed to say that, but as if they were my grandparents actually, because back home, I'm from the Ivory Coast and back home we're very close, parents we're very close, generations mix. (Amandine, 32, Ivory Coast, Paris)

This tension was less clear in Madrid where care workers would positively mobilise the analogy with family relatives very often. The words of Naomi below echo many other statements of care workers in Madrid:

What I like is to be able to help them. They wait for someone ... because their relatives can't be with them, so we have to think that they are our relatives and care for them as one should. (Naomi, 37, Colombia, Madrid)

Job stability facilitated the emergence of such relationships in that it fostered attachment and provided meaning. Jacques, who was employed in residential care in Paris, explained his state of mind:

For me work is to feel at ease where we go to in the morning because during the interview I told them I preferred to stay here. On a temporary contract for one month, they can prolong or you can be told not to come anymore. When I'm in a permanent job I tell myself I go home, I go to see my grandmother, I go to see my grandparents, I have a moral obligation, a moral obligation that makes me stand up in the morning. I have a task to fulfil every day in my life, I go to work. Whereas if it were a temporary contract, I would always have this question, this interrogation ... we think what will happen if tomorrow they don't want me anymore, what should I do, I have to search. (Jacques, 31, Cameroon, Paris)

Given the absence of training or qualification requirements in the recruitment processes in London, care workers were more at ease than in Paris with depicting their relationships in terms of family-like relations. Less exposed to the 'professional discourse', they described their relationships with residents freely and did not hesitate to use the family analogy. Fadila, who came to the UK from Bangladesh, described how her mentor in the workplace, the care assistant in charge of her induction, encouraged her to think of residents as her grandparents:

When I joined I got really scared whether I can manage to have a very friendly relationship with them (the residents) but now I feel very comfortable I feel like I'm helping my own grandparents. (…) I thought it was not possible for me to do anything and they told me if you are coming to a person, they need your help, don't get scared just take it easy and think, use your brain, use your heart if she is your grandma or if he's your grandpa how you will deal with them and then slowly I got used to do all my work and I found that it's easy it's not hard. (Fadila, 30, Bangladesh, London)

Though the tension explored here between the expression of emotions and the detachment that professionalisation prescribes is less experienced by care assistants in London due to absent or limited training, the debate is nevertheless present in the care industry. For example, in September 2015, the Care Quality Commission (CQC) answered a polemic triggered by its alleged ban on the use of 'love' to address residents. They came to the following conclusion: 'the important issue is that people are called what they want to be called. Some will really appreciate affectionate terms of endearment, others will not'.[2] Again, this illustrates a different work culture as compared to the work environment observed in Paris, where care assistants would be expected to address residents formally instead of using 'terms of endearment', as the Care Quality Commission labelled them.

The chapter exposed so far the necessarily ambivalent role of emotions in care work and the tensions that the current organisation and professionalisation of care trigger. I now turn to the meanings carried by how these emotions are depicted. In what follows, I argue that workers' understandings of care work as relational and emotion-laden feeds into a positive construction of their occupational identity in which elements of an ethic of care are central.

Being Proud, Against All Odds: An Empowering Ethic of Care

From care workers' narratives there emerged a much more positive representation of care as paid occupation than the one conveyed in society's dominant discourses, as explored above. Participants actively constructed a positive perception of their occupational identity and valued the work they accomplished. Overwhelmingly, they stressed the importance of care work and underlined its essential function in society. This shared discursive practice between the different sites of fieldwork illustrates empirically the central argument of the care ethics literature that places care at the centre of society and emphasises 'what really matters' (Perez Orozco 2014). Not only did care workers value the work they accomplished they also experienced a sense of pride derived from the feeling that they were doing their job properly.

'Doing something useful' is a consideration that was stressed in most interviews, and rare were the persons who did not mention it. It does not matter much here if this was an artefact of discourse, an 'authentic' feeling, or a bit of both. What matters is that most workers relied on this idea to construct a positive representation of their occupation in their own

---

[2] http://www.cqc.org.uk/content/terms-endearment, last accessed February 2016.

eyes (through the interview performance), and thus within the profession. Amongst the countless possible quotes, I here share those of Mike, a care worker in London, and of Laetitia, a French care worker:

> And I got the job as a carer here because I feel with care job I will be able to deliver to the less privileged what I have, taking care of them, my objectives will be met. Because I like to contribute—I've been a member of the Red Cross Society for about 35 years back in my country, so what we do is like humanitarian activities. We take care of our people, but we are not being paid for it back home (…). Just to acknowledge your activities, the Government might just give some remunerations to encourage you. But here when I came into the UK, I discovered that what we are doing back home for free could be a source of livelihood. So I've got in that mentality taking care of people, it's my joy. (Mike, 55, Nigeria, London)

> I consider that their families place them in residential care, either because they didn't have time, or they don't feel capable of taking care of their father, of their mother, so I do it but I don't do it because they can't, but I do it out of love. I feel I'm making myself useful. (Laetitia, 29, Guadeloupe, Paris)

A sense of satisfaction was derived from the perception of contributing to the well-being of society by providing care to those who needed it. A sense of pride was implicit when participants made the point that not everyone can do this job, which most emphasised. Though care jobs are formally quite accessible (in London and Madrid, care assistants could be employed without prior qualifications; in France they need six months' training), these discourses argue exactly the opposite: not anyone could do this job, rather, a certain set of qualities are required to be a good carer. By describing their occupational identity in these terms, care workers effectively portrayed themselves as possessing these valuable qualities. Hawa said in this regard:

> It's an occupation one needs to like before doing it because there are many incidents. You need to clean the stool, to wash private parts … if you don't like the person you can't. When I say the person it's in general, it's not… One need to love humans, to like what we're doing otherwise it's not easy.

I know some people they got some jobs when they arrived, they saw the stool and they said they couldn't. So it's really not easy. It's really not easy. (Hawa, 34, Ivory Coast, Paris)

In a similar vein, Patricia spoke of her work as a calling:

As I told you this occupation you really need to like it, not to do it … we all work to provide for our needs but I mean it can't be only for that. One need really to have a calling for this occupation. Otherwise forget about it. And if one really likes what one does, generally everything goes well. And it's my case, it goes really well with residents. (Patricia, 34, Reunion Island, Paris)

Male care workers constructed their narratives in a similar way. These are the words of Antonio for instance, who came to Spain from Cuba thanks to the emigration possibility arising from the fact that his grand-parents were Spanish:

The persons who come to this world [the care sector], they need first of all to have a heart as a human being. Second, to see this person as a human being, a human being that could be you, your mum, your grandfather. And third, as professional staff, if you decided to enter this world, you need to see it from the perspective of the professional that you are. (Antonio, 39, Cuba, Madrid)

An idea closely related to the one that 'not everyone can do it' is that 'there's only one way to do it well'. Previous sections have already looked into the role of attachment in providing care, and to add to that, this aspect was at times articulated with a sense of occupational identity. Fouzia, for instance, advocated the introduction of recruitment tests to see if applicants are guided by their heart or by their brain. She introduced her proposal as follows:

Honestly if you don't work with your heart, you work only with your brain, you'll be like a machine. So you don't bring anything to that person. Nothing, what will you bring? Nothing. You take note of the time you arrived, what time you left, what drugs she took, what she ate, she doesn't need only this, it's very important but the most important, a little gesture, we touch the hand. (Fouzia, 38, Algeria, Paris)

Finally, a form of narrative that arguably constitutes the other side of the same coin is the claim that 'one doesn't do this job only for money'. This type of discourse suggests that it would not be right to do a care job just for the money, as already suggested in Patricia's quote mentioned above. This is also a way to highlight the specific skills that caring for someone requires and to derive a sense of pride from one's dedication. Nabila, employed in Paris, stressed this point:

I like my occupation, I like my job, this kind of occupations, you need to like it. So when you like, you do it easily. But if you don't like it, you can't look at the money only, you need to like it as well. So I like my occupation, I like elderly people. (Nabila, 40, Senegal, Paris)

The positive understanding of care work that these discourses convey play a crucial role in empowering care workers. Experiencing every day that their labour truly matters, participants I have met drew from this fact their energy, dignity and pride.

6.4   Conclusion

This chapter focused on chosen aspects of participants' everyday working experiences in older-age care with a view to exploring the theoretical venues opened up by the cognitive devices of feminist moral philosophy. Work precariousness in the older-age care sector presents specificities related to bodily and emotional labour that need to be accounted for, all the more that the latter tend to be concealed by usual indicators of precarious employment and work. Drawing upon feminist moral philosophy sheds light on the emotional and physical implications for workers' lives of having to deal daily with the very precariousness of life in a context of socially constructed employment and work precariousness. These multiple layers of precariousness render it substantially different from work precariousness experienced in sectors non-related to care and thus its specificities need to be highlighted. Work precariousness within older-age care tends to be concealed by the lack of indicators with which to measure it. The exposure of workers' bodies and their emotional endurance are key elements that are overlooked by narrow definitions of precarious employment and work.

In these settings care workers are active agents performing emotional labour, but emotions also serve to render the work itself bearable and workers sometimes are deeply affected by feelings that their interactions with residents trigger. The ethic of care mobilised at the discursive level, and theorised by feminist moral philosophy, contributes furthermore to building a positive occupational identity in spite of the devaluation of care work within society at large. The chapter argued for the need to revisit the concept of emotional labour in order to account for the contradictory role of emotions within care labour, where they are as much the result of workers' emotion work in the spirit of the concept of 'emotional dissonance' (Hochschild 1983/2003, p. 90), as they are fulfilling a supportive role when mobilised at work and narrated to others for the construction of a strong occupational identity.

The chapter equally argued that while emotions are marketised by private care providers, the emotional labour performed is structurally devalued by gender regimes and silenced within the industry's procedures and supervision mechanisms. The professional discourse that serves the purpose of detaching care work from the domestic, the familiar and the private, and introducing it into the public, the regulated and the professional, is problematic, as care workers' narratives have illustrated. It is crucial to reflect on why care workers' narratives around care ethics are not in line with the content of professionalisation. The paradox analysed here uncovers the limitations of professionalisation attempts in the absence of fundamental paradigm change. It appears that the argument for bringing care from the margins towards the centre of society's concerns is present, in many ways, in care workers' narratives. Care ethics allows us to go beyond 'emotional labour' and helps to explain workers' discourses around emotions in all their dimensions, that is, both as a powerful tool and as a source of suffering. This is theoretically possible thanks to the contributions of feminist moral philosophy: by shedding light on the gendered dimension of dominant understandings of morality (Tronto

2013) and professionalism (Molinier 2013), this literature effectively deconstructs these notions and the oppressive structures attached to them, and thus offers new spaces for workers' voices to be acknowledged through emerging conceptualisations that include all the complexities that these voices express. The care ethics paradigm highlights the importance of these voices at the centre of reflections on the place of care in society. The tensions uncovered in this chapter demonstrate that these voices are overlooked in institutional processes. Even when the purpose of policies is to professionalise care work, gendered understandings of what constitutes work underpin the ways in which it is conducted, replicating the marginalisation of emotional labour upon which the devaluation and segmentation of the occupation relied in the first place. An approach in terms of care ethics offers here a vehicle to empower those currently most involved in 'care-giving'.

Finally, two themes across the different sections of this chapter serve to discuss how the lenses of a shared ontological precariousness allow for exploring differently the precarious conditions of migrant and minority ethnic workers daily experiences in older-age care. When Fouzia says 'it hurts […] I want so much to help' she voices this complex dimension of care work that affects workers without however being formally acknowledged, neither at the workplace level nor within employment policies, as contributing to work precariousness. Thinking care as fundamentally relational and thus as a two-way relationship, as posited by care ethics, builds on the notion of an ontological precariousness—without care no life can be sustained—bringing to the fore that racialised care workers are currently exposed to this fundamental precariousness to a greater extent given the contemporary political economy of older-age care. The second point that these findings unlock is that acknowledging a shared ontological precariousness possesses an empowering potential. When Aimée stated in a saddened tone 'that's what hurts, they didn't listen' she pointed to another common characteristic of care workers' experiences, namely being in practice responsible for sustaining life while being formally voiceless due to hierarchies in place at the workplace level and to the devaluation of care work as unskilled within society. It is because a shared fundamental precariousness is not recognised that it cannot function as a starting point for politics (Lorey 2010) and that a caring democracy cannot be achieved (Tronto 2013). A central tenet of a feminist democratic ethic of care is in this regard to pursue equality of voice so that a meaningful democratic discussion on care responsibilities and justice can take place (Tronto 2013, p. 33).

Ultimately, a paradigm change is necessary to improve the precarious working conditions in older-age care in the long run; anything that falls short of that would only mitigate those conditions without addressing the root causes of this precariousness and would reproduce the structures of inequality upon which the current political economy of the sector relies. A care ethic sensitive analysis identifies how the capital-care contradiction translates into emotional, bodily and material tensions in racialised care workers' everyday lives and hints at new directions for a critical re-assessment of the place of care in Western societies.

7

Racism, the Industry's Blind Spot

If you see somebody oppressing someone, you have to speak up or if you can't do anything, in your mind you have to be against it. But if you just sit down and watch, this makes you also a sinner, you understand? If you bear oppression, and if you don't fight it, you also make a big sin, that's why we have always to fight, we have to. Wherever you are, life is not easy, it's always a challenge, always. This will make you stronger. What about you, are you a fighter? (Sameera, 32, Mauritius, London)

Sameera came from Mauritius 12 years ago. In Mauritius, she had been working in a pharmacy, and on arrival to the UK, she found employment in a pharmacy in London, though in a lower position. For four years she did not have a single day of annual leave. Exhausted, she left the job and looked for something else. She then found a job as a care assistant in residential care. In her new employment, she went through tough times once more; she was harassed by her colleagues and felt discriminated against by her managers. Immersed in these unpleasant memories during the interview, Sameera made the statement quoted here. From the perspective of individual experience, Sameera's narrative appears to be specific and personal. Analysed as part of an institutional context shaped

© The Author(s) 2019

N. Sahraoui, *Racialised Workers and European Older-Age Care*, Thinking Gender in Transnational Times, https://doi.org/10.1007/978-3-030-14397-8_7

by employment rights, migration policies and anti-discrimination legislation and practice, such narratives reveal differentiated forms of institutional racism.

Through care workers' narratives in London, Paris and Madrid, manifestations of racism can be analysed at different levels. The exploration of the dynamics of labour market segmentation in Chap. 4 outlined a form of systematic discrimination against racialised workers through migration and employment policies that produce deskilling and entrapment. While this constitutes a form of institutional racism due to the racialisation on which these dynamics rely, the focus here is on experiences of racism and discrimination as narrated by participants themselves. The chapter brings out how these experiences, on the one hand, and participants' ways of coping with them, on the other, inform the 'ruling relations' that characterise participants' work environments. I argue that participants' experiences reveal institutionalised forms of racism. On the basis of this demonstration, I reflect on what the main tenets of care ethics can contribute towards a more comprehensive understanding of racism and, *in fine*, towards more efficient ways to challenge it.

To scrutinise migrant and minority ethnic workers' experiences of racism and discrimination in the older-age care industry, this chapter looks into three types of experiences: racial prejudice by elderly residents, racist behaviour by colleagues and harassment/discrimination by managers (the distinction between racism and discrimination is clarified below). The first section situates the concepts of racism, racialisation and racist discrimination and examines how the anti-discrimination policies described in Chap. 3 are implemented in each of these three countries. The second section looks empirically at the three types of manifestations of racism and discrimination mentioned above. I focus first on the fact that the older-age care sector is characterised by recurrent exposure to racist comments, a phenomenon which can be exacerbated by the illnesses residents suffer from (e.g. dementia, Alzheimer's) when they lead to uninhibited behaviour. The following section is dedicated to how workers cope with this form of abuse and how managers and companies deal with; it allows identification of differentiated features of institutional racism and of differing interpretations mobilised to articulate these experiences from one capital city to another. Finally, situations of racist behaviour by colleagues and of harassment/discrimination by managers are scrutinised, and the last section explores the means available to workers to challenge these situations.

7.1 The Racist Subtext of Western European Societies

Racism, Neoliberal Capitalism and Care Ethics

The assumption that we live in post-racial societies de facto obscures the continuity of 'race' as an organising dynamic in European societies. The political economy of the Western world is increasingly shaped by neoliberal values. Under the umbrella of neoliberal governmentality, 'everyone is expected to have full personal responsibility' and as a consequence risks a 'loss of right for a life mismanaged' (Lentin and Titley 2011, p. 163). Everything in neoliberal societies is 'judged according to its profitability and "rationality"' (ibid.). While capitalist structures of production rely intrinsically on socially constructed divisions among people—including processes of racialisation—these stratifications are effectively covered up by a governmentality that constructs the illusion of neutrality. Neoliberalism is perceived not as a 'particular set of interests and political interventions, but as a kind of nonpolitics' (Duggan 2003, p. 10). This obscures power relationships at work and forms of oppression on which neoliberalism relies and which shape the everyday life experiences of women, racialised groups and other minorities.

From this perspective, the paradox of anti-discrimination policies implemented simultaneously with the continuation of institutional oppression of racialised groups is only superficial. The neoliberal system of values effectively organises the ignorance of those in privileged positions, notably by fostering these groups' perception of having deserved their privilege. Individualism and meritocracy assume the existence of equal opportunities and delegitimise policies of wealth redistribution to address social inequalities. Anti-discrimination legislation is conceptualised within this perspective as a means to achieve equal opportunities by merely granting individuals the same rights. While such regulations might be useful for challenging certain manifestations of racism, it also serves to legitimise inequalities within a society and allows for a naturalisation of these inequalities. If anti-discrimination legislation ensures that *anyone* can denounce discrimination, then *everyone* is held responsible for his/her individual position in the labour market and in society at large. One of the perverse results of focusing on individual rights to refine legal definitions of discrimination is the omission of the fact that this can only offer a very partial way of addressing deeply rooted inequalities which require social change beyond formal equality. Furthermore, anti-discrimination legislation has a differentiated impact following class and gender divisions, and the most privileged amongst racialised workers are in a better position to make use of it.

Mobilising the concept of racialisation raises the question: how does 'race' relate to racialisation? The construction of inferiority, as well as the discrimination and inequalities that ensue from it, might refer to 'race', 'ethnicity', culture, religion, nationality or any other socially constructed category. Robert Miles argued that the term racialisation, building on the notion of 'race' as a social construct, should be preferred to the use of 'race' (Miles 1993). This critique is here acknowledged and it is further argued that the concept of 'ethnicity' deserves similar deconstruction. The use of 'race' is often justified by the need to make visible the oppression created by racism or to acknowledge the activism that aims at combatting it (Gilroy 1987/2002), a vital commitment that arguably can also be led with the concept of racialisation. Ethnicity emerged as a concept in the twentieth century and started to be referred to in the Anglo-Saxon academic literature in the 1960s (Martiniello 2013), either in combination with 'race' or as a way of avoiding reference to 'race'. Colette Guillaumin wrote in this regard in 1972: 'The word "ethnic group" presents itself as a compromise between the unconscious belief in a biological determinism of cultural features and a distance voluntarily taken with the word "race"' (Guillaumin 1972/2002, p. 85, my translation). While the social construction of 'ethnicity' is not as self-evident as that of 'race', whose historical fate revealed its destructive power, 'ethnicity' equally implies a categorisation of individuals through a combination of cultural and blood-related filiation. For instance, in an OECD paper, Francesca Froy and Lucy Pyne (2011) referred to the following description by

Milton Yinger (1981): 'An ethnic group perceives itself and is perceived by others to be different in some combination of the following traits: language, religion, race and ancestral homeland with its related culture.' The use of the concept remains fuzzy and its shifting meanings are best demonstrated by critical enquiries into its changing signifiers. Olivier Roy illustrated this with historical examples of religious markers that became ethnic markers in different times and spaces and studies of multicultural policies that have at times constructed ethnicities (Roy 2008).

While I make a strategic use of the concept of 'minority ethnic' (Aspinall 2002) in the spirit of the 'intercategorical complexity' (McCall 2005) within intersectional studies as presented in Chap. 2, the concepts of 'racialisation' and 'racialised groups' are here preferred in an attempt to capture the social process at work without granting 'ethnicity' or 'race' a material existence, but acknowledging the sociological implications of the existence of both constructions as well as the role 'ethnicity' plays in struggles for recognition. It is important to highlight, however, that 'ethnicity' is systematically applied to minority groups while majority groups escape 'ethnicisation', given that they are seen to embody the universal versus the particular. The fundamental problem with this concept is thus that, while it is granted political correctness, it effectively reproduces racialisation by ethnicising those who were yesterday racialised by biological racism.

Overall, the denial of the continued relevance of racialisation processes in contemporary societies, and of their social implications for racialised individuals, amounts to a form of racism. The critique of the shortcomings of the rights framing invites a reflection on the different approach that a care ethic enables. The situated morality of care ethics (see Chap. 2) considers the lived situation in all its complexity. I argue that this starting point avoids the pitfalls of the liberal framing of rights that assumes fairness on the basis of equal rights. Treating unequal situations the same might well reproduce and widen existing inequalities. Admittedly, it is the recognition of these shortcomings that brought about corrective policies, for example, quotas for women's participation in political parties. These, in a liberal perspective, are however temporary exceptions, a compromise between ideological values sustaining the political organisation of society and the complexity of the social world. An approach in terms of care ethics, by incorporating contingency as the norm rather than the exception, is better equipped to acknowledge and address the far-reaching implications of racism. In this chapter, I hint at some of the ways in which care ethics can contribute to think about racism in different terms.

Institutional Racism and Racist Discrimination

A focus on racialisation as process is crucial given that the definition of what constitutes racism cannot be static either. Racism is best apprehended in plural: 'racism [is] not a permanent human or social deposit which is simply waiting there to be triggered off when the circumstances are right. (…) There have been many significantly different racisms—each historically specific and articulated in a different way with the societies in which they appear' (Hall 1978, p. 26). Paul Gilroy warns in an analogous way that racism 'exists in plural form' emphasising that 'it can change assuming different shapes and articulating different political relations. Racist ideologies and practices have distinct meanings bounded by historical circumstances and determined in struggle' (Gilroy 1987/2002, p. 42). The notion of 'total social phenomenon' forged by Etienne Balibar highlights furthermore that racism is to be found in everyday practices, discourses and imaginaries (Balibar 1988/2012). To clarify, racist discrimination implies a practice and thus differs from the concept of racism, which entails a broad range of possible manifestations, racist discrimination constituting one of these.

In this regard, the relationship between ideology and practice, in other words the question of intentionality, needs also to be raised. The 'race relations' model of British sociology tended for instance to focus on personal prejudice up to the mid-1970s. Similarly, philosophical accounts of racism tend to put the issue of intentionality at the heart of the definition of racism, referring for instance to 'motivational racism' (Headley 2000). In contrast to this approach, I here subscribe to Floya Anthias and Nira Yuval-Davis' argument that 'racist practices do not require the racist intentionality of structures (…). Practices may be racist in terms of their effects' (1992, p. 13). In a nutshell, racist discrimination can result from policies and practices, which might or might not be imbued with explicit racist ideology. In that sense, the concept of 'institutional racism'—developed to a much greater extent in the Anglo-Saxon literature than in French and Spanish studies of racism—proves to be crucial for conceptualising racist outcomes without necessarily systematic racist intentionality. The early conceptualisations of institutional racism are to be found in the Black Power movement and notably in Stokely Carmichael's writings (Carmichael and Hamilton 1967/1992). Later on, Ambalavaner Sivanandan (1985) distinguished between what he named 'racialism', defined as prejudice displayed by individuals, and racism understood as structural racism. Power relationships are at the heart of this oppression, as stated by Polycarp Ikuenobe (2010, p. 162): 'not all forms of racial discrimination or prejudice may be characterized as racism. In order for racial discrimination or prejudice to be characterized as racism, it must involve social-political power.' Experiences lived by racialised workers are here analysed as racist in the sense that they are embedded in power relationships that produce racist collective outcomes as well as individual experiences of racism.

This first section of the chapter has presented the key concepts mobilised in the analysis of the empirical data, notably racism, racist discrimination and institutional racism. In the following section, I scrutinise the different manifestations of racism in migrant and minority ethnic workers' daily experiences in older-age care.

7.2   Everyday Racism in Care Interactions

Across the three capital cities studied here, a little less than half of the participants recounted experiences of racism and discrimination in relation to either residents, colleagues or management in older-age care (11 in London, 14 in Paris and 12 in Madrid). Participants had to deal with overt and covert forms of racism and their experiences varied greatly. Systematically exposed to racist comments by residents, some of them were also discriminated against or harassed by colleagues and managers. Individual stories also revealed how exposure to different manifestations of racism sometimes happened simultaneously.

Facing Daily (Some) Residents' Racist Prejudice

The older-age care sector is highly segmented in London, Paris and Madrid and racialised workers (migrants and non-migrants), who make up a significant share of the workforce, are very often exposed to racist prejudice by residents in the form of insults and refusal of care. In her ethnography of Black domestic workers in the Netherlands, Sabrina Marchetti characterises these encounters within home care as a 'scenario of racism' (2014, p. 151). The description of participants' experiences in this research reveals an extensive and general phenomenon and implies that most probably it affected the majority of racialised workers; the more residents they took care of, the more likely it was that they would encounter racist attitudes. If a respondent did not share such experiences during the interview, it does not necessarily mean that the person was not confronted with them. The question systematically asked during interviews referred to experiences of discrimination and fairness in general and not specifically in relation to residents. It appears overall that these experiences were common and not specific to one place of fieldwork.

First, patterns of racialisation are multiple, and socio-historic distinctions emerged in participants' narratives. Amongst non-migrant participants in Paris, most were French nationals from French overseas departments (Guadeloupe, Reunion Island and Martinique). As explored in Chap. 3, the channelling of these workers into the healthcare sector constitutes a historic practice that developed in the 1950s and 1960s. Those workers are exposed to racist prejudice by residents as are non-EU racialised migrants, but at the same time, they are in a different position because they hold French nationality, and also, arguably, because they are the object of different collective imaginaries about their lesser 'distance' from the majority group. Elodie, from Guadeloupe, shared the following story:

> It's with residents in the care home because these persons they've never travelled, it's difficult for them to accept … and me it's not that bad, I'm not too dark but I see with my African colleagues, African immigrants, it's hard for them. They're being despised all day long, they (the residents) don't even want to be touched by them. And the proof that there was a

barrier between the Africans and me: I plaited my hair and they [the residents] told me, don't plait your hair, you're not African, they even gave me a nickname, "you're the colour of biscuits". (Elodie, 52, Guadeloupe, Paris)

Spanish colonial history also shapes racialisation processes that affect migrants in Madrid. Those designated as 'Latino Americans' find themselves in a different position than other non-EU migrants. These stratifications rooted in colonial hierarchies are apparent in legal terms and have implications for migrant communities in Spain. Citizens of South American countries who can demonstrate their Spanish ancestry can apply for Spanish citizenship and benefit from financial support on their arrival in Spain, as positive incentives for them to migrate. At the other end of this hierarchy, Saul, who came to Spain from El Salvador, migrated because of the extensive discrimination he faced as an indigenous person. Unable to finance his studies, his job applications in El Salvador were often rejected on the ground that the company wanted to 'preserve an international image' which he explained as meaning 'we employ only Whites here'. He thus rejected the designation 'Latino American' that obscured the oppression of indigenous people, and he felt that this hierarchy was very much alive in Madrid:

It's very divided, it's very difficult, here it's very difficult, you're frowned upon by all, you're like an outcast, like a leper, like the indigenous. It's not the same treatment, for example a Salvadorian who's white, a latinoamerican, because they're latins, descendants of the Europeans for me, because that's the word latino. These people here are relatively well, they have these links. On the contrary, us who are natives … there's a lot of racism, there and even more here. (Saul, 27, El Salvador, Madrid)

Dynamics that reproduce racist hierarchies forged over centuries of European colonisation remain powerful today in shaping processes of racialisation. Differentiated racialisations have in turn material implications for workers' lives. Martina, who came from Ecuador and considered herself Latino American, observed the differential treatment of Black workers in the care home where she had been employed for seven years at the time of the interview:

> For example in the residence, they recruited Black people, with Black skin, Brown as they say, colleagues. They always sent them to the fourth floor, where there are bed-ridden residents, where they don't see, they don't speak, they don't say anything. They never put them in the first floor, never. I've realized it. They work all their lives in the fourth floor where residents don't speak, they hear something but they don't answer. And others didn't take turns (…) Why? If we're all equal… (Martina, 51, Ecuador, Madrid)

In the UK, the racialisation operated by the dominant group also follows differentiated paths according to various forms of essentialisation and the socio-history of the British Empire. The presence of settled Black and Asian communities, their own and their ancestors' struggles for rights and against discrimination, as well as their status as nationals versus the more precarious legal statuses of migrants, results in significantly different positionalities. In this perspective, racialisation based solely on social markers attached to physical appearance does not produce the same set of relations as the combination of racialisation and migration. Sameera, who came to the UK from Mauritius and worked in a care home, perceived her migrant status as making her particularly vulnerable and was of the opinion that Black British workers were in a better position to defend themselves in the face of the abusive White English management she encountered. A telling anecdote, this does not mean however, that racialised UK-born individuals are necessarily *less* discriminated against than migrants since other factors enter into play such as gender, class and age.

In spite of existing differences between these racialisation processes, being exposed to racist prejudice by residents often manifests itself in similar incidents: refusal of care, comments or insults. Quotes by Doriane in Paris, Mary in London and Marisol in Madrid, all suggest that exposure to racist comments is nothing less than frequent and that it constitutes an important aspect of their daily work:

> In France, people who are in this sector, care homes and hospitals, you see who does the job? Mmh, who does the job? It's Blacks and Arabs who do these jobs and in spite of this, it's been years that care homes exist, residents see only Blacks and Arabs and they're still racists! (laugh). (Doriane, 59, Guadeloupe, Paris)

Well, you know not everyone is the same. You have some nice service users and you have some really nasty ones when I say nasty I mean racists and all of that sort, with the nice ones it's really good you can communicate with them one-to-one they reply back to you calmly everything is perfect but with the majority, which is not a few, that are really nasty, really racist as well, they get really picky about your colour and your skin, your accent, anything that does not sound or look English to them they don't like. (Mary, 20, Black UK, London)

First the reaction is "You Black, you foreigner, go back to your country, what are you doing here?" That's how they react. From the residents there is this rejection towards us foreigners, immigrants. (Marisol, 47, Ecuador, Madrid)

Facing residents' refusal to be touched, or being exposed to racist insults, requires workers' emotional labour if they are to overcome these difficulties and carry on with their jobs. Eloise in Paris and Mayra in Madrid described in those terms the contexts and ways in which they were confronted with racist insults:

Older persons, some of them they show us bluntly that they don't like Blacks. So what can you answer to this? You do your job…. Once I even cried, the nurse in charge told no, don't cry, because I couldn't answer, because I couldn't tell this resident all what I thought. I preferred to hold back everything and I started to cry, because it affects you, when you're told, about slavery, they tell you about slavery that we used to keep our mouth shut and that now we have big mouths. It's tough to hear. (Eloise, 59, Guadeloupe, Paris)

One man especially, he lived only with his wife who was elderly as well. So I had to shower him and wash his feet in particular because he wouldn't let his feet be washed. So I said: "I'm coming up." And he tells me: "What are you doing? What is a Black doing in my house? I don't agree." And he started to shout, to shout a lot. "Go away from my house, I don't like that Black people enter my house, why did you open the door to this woman?" So I tried to be patient because we need to be prepared for everything. (Mayra, 52, Ecuador, Madrid)

Given that the likelihood of being exposed to racist comments and insults is high for racialised care workers, being confronted with racial prejudice amongst residents constitutes a significant aspect of their daily work. These comments and insults need to be fully taken into account in the analysis of participants' experiences of racism and discrimination because they involve important emotional work and shape their affective perceptions of the workplace. Most importantly, how these experiences are dealt with, amongst colleagues as well as by managers and the company as a whole, reveal some of the forms taken by institutional racism. The example of older-age care demonstrates that anti-discrimination legislation does not constitute an effective tool for challenging manifestations of racism that are both specific to that occupation and common in the sector. The following section looks into the coping strategies developed by care workers and analyses the role of managers and employers in relation to residents' racist attitudes.

Differentiated Coping Strategies

Given the frequency of racist comments addressed by residents or service users to care workers, in all three sites of fieldwork participants talked about their coping strategies at the individual and collective levels.

At the individual level, being confronted with residents' racist comments triggered various coping strategies. It necessarily involved emotional labour to be able to carry on with one's job. Jacques in Paris and Mary in London described how they dealt on a personal level with such situations:

> In that moment, in two seconds in the heart, you have ideas that cross your mind, if you're not patient you could react, which leads often our colleagues to be laid off because they've touched physically the resident. Because they can't control themselves, that's it. (Jacques, 31, Cameroon, Paris)

> Personally if there is aggression, if a resident is being very aggressive personally I try to calm them down I always talk to them in a very calm manner but not demeaning and if it doesn't work I will have to leave the room

because I am human as well I might get angry so to calm myself down I need to take a second of … just go outside calm myself and step away from that atmosphere for a bit you know. (Mary, 20, Black UK, London)

In all three sites of fieldwork, participants highlighted that there was little to be done because racist beliefs were very common for this generation and that their illnesses fostered this aggressiveness. Andrea in Madrid made that point:

With elderly persons sometimes they send you back to your country, you know what I mean? "Go back to your place, I don't know what, to your country". But I don't give much importance because the mindset … they're elderly and the mindset before was like this. (Andrea, 47, Cape Verde, Madrid)

Framing the problem in these terms allows some care workers to manage racist incidents by seeing them as professional tasks and challenges. By the same token, what could have been interpreted as a negative experience of racist prejudice was turned into a matter of professionalism and emotional labour. Many participants therefore described the techniques they had developed over the years to overcome residents' and service users' prejudice. Saba in Paris and Marisol in Madrid told how they mobilised their enthusiasm and energy to overcome residents' fears and apprehensions:

So when she tells me "No, not you!" I tell her "but I'm like chocolate, my colour is like chocolate, chocolate is good to eat." I'll find small things and she'll start to laugh. I always find something. I play with it now. I play with it. If by playing with it, it doesn't help, I ask my colleague if she can help. The problem is she's Black like myself! (Saba, 41, Cameroon, Paris)

When a person rejects you, you do it with more enthusiasm, you attend to this person every day until this moment arrives when he/she starts liking you, gives in and accepts you. Because there are those who accept you, they fight but little by little they accept you. Yes, in the long run you get there, they accept you. (Marisol, 47, Ecuador, Madrid)

The emotional labour required to face and overcome residents' prejudice was often both personal, in the feelings it triggered, and collective, in that solidarity arose amongst racialised workers, as hinted at in Saba's quote. The following paragraphs explore in more detail the collective dimension of the coping strategies to which workers could resort.

Since supervisors and managers left these problems to be resolved by staff involved in direct care, workers tended to answer these challenges collectively. Eloise in Paris pointed out managers' lack of interest in dealing with these issues, and Marisol in Madrid thought that there was no other solution than to work it out amongst carers, given that they are the ones in contact with residents:

NS: What would you expect from the nurse in charge and managers? Can they be of any help?

Eloise: We don't get any feedback (laugh) it's upon us to deal with it. (Eloise, 59, Guadeloupe, Paris)

NS: The administration does something or is it dealt with amongst colleagues?

Marisol: No the administration doesn't get involved, it's an organisation amongst ourselves, so we have to make the residents accept us because we're the ones who are going to be with them every day caring for them. (Marisol, 47, Ecuador, Madrid)

Resolving it amongst colleagues most often meant asking a colleague to step in when the resident refused care by a specific worker. For Doriane, for instance, who worked in Paris, that was the only solution she envisaged:

NS: Are there any forms of support that help you facing these situations?

Doriane: No, there's nothing in any of the homes I went to, nothing, nothing…. The only thing you're told is if it doesn't work with a person, hand over to your colleague. That's it. But other than that there's no support, no. (Doriane, 59, Guadeloupe, Paris)

Antonio, who came to Spain from Cuba on the basis that his grand-parents were Spaniards, said that he frequently replaced a Black colleague in the care home where he worked:

> When we have these cases, for example I mention this colleague of mine who attends to an elderly woman who doesn't like Blacks, he tells me and I used to replace him. (Antonio, 39, Cuba, Madrid)

Being replaced by a colleague provides a pragmatic solution to a resident's refusal of care, but it does not provide support to workers. On the discursive level, it was frequently mentioned in the narratives of participants in Paris that they 'laugh about it' amongst colleagues as a way to play down these situations. Interestingly enough, none of the participants in Madrid or London mentioned resorting to humour as an informal collective approach to these experiences. The quote by Doriane is typical in this regard and resembles many other accounts:

> A woman, not so long ago, told to a colleague: "you know why they recruit you? Because you cost them less, you Black people." So you see ... "you know why they recruit you? Because you cost them less" ... We laugh about it and that's it. (Doriane, 59, Guadeloupe, Paris)

The story told by Sofia reveals furthermore the institutionalisation of detachment as appropriate behaviour in these situations. From this perspective, taking the insults seriously is almost a professional mistake:

> We had a young one who just graduated and that's when we realised that we have experience and that the young ones don't, those who just arrived. Because there was a resident who told her, who insulted her of bloody negro or slave, I don't remember ... and it traumatised her so much that she mentioned it during the handover. We told her it's no big deal ... it's nothing ... you should tell her "yes" and give her the whip if she wanted to whip you, by joking we tried to make her understand, later she understood that it was recurrent so that she shouldn't be so affected each time because that's not possible. (Sofia, 36, French, North African parents, Paris)

Encountered only in the narratives of participants in Paris, this method of removing the drama at the discursive level among care workers leaves the question of the role of care homes as institutions and of companies as employers open. This apparent detachment conceals the necessary emotional labour that these incidents trigger at the individual level, as described above. The following paragraphs thus seek to illuminate this paradox by looking at how this form of abuse is dealt with by the employing institutions.

If residents' aggressive behaviour is hardly avoidable and if racist comments and insults will continue to be directed at carers, the institution's attention to, or neglect of, this form of abuse is crucial for racialised workers' lived experiences. In this regard, several care workers in Paris mentioned the role of the psychologist with whom care workers met on a regular basis. The presence of the psychologist is not, however, a legal obligation. Elodie observed for instance that after the care home she worked in was sold to a different company, the psychologist's hours were cut down and only those dedicated to residents were maintained, because of the cost-reduction strategy followed by the new owner. Employed by a different care home, Amélie valued the support the psychologist was able to provide in her workplace:

> We have a group therapy, we get together once a week, we tell the problems, the difficulties we experience and there's a psychologist who guides us, who gives us advice, "do rather like this" or "share the information, don't keep it to yourself". (Amélie, 43, Ivory Coast, Paris)

The example of the role of the psychologist illustrates the argument that challenging racism at work cannot be limited to anti-discrimination measures because the latter are often inadequate to effectively challenge situations pervaded by racism, in which determining liabilities remains a complex task. The presence of the psychologist in the care homes visited is not related to any anti-racism measure per se but is aimed at improving workers' well-being at work. In relation to experiences of racism and discrimination, it is one of the few measures mentioned in this study, along with NGO and union membership, which was described as having a positive impact in this matter. This demonstrates the necessity of thinking about anti-racism in broader terms than anti-discrimination. Employment rights, the representation of workers' interests at work and the bargaining power of professional trade associations, all contribute in this respect to giving workers opportunities to voice their concerns and thus improve their working conditions. The collective dimension of these processes is crucial in order to avoid the depoliticisation of these situations. An individualisation of these challenges conceals the meanings of experiences of racism and discrimination and obscures its institutional dimension.

Besides the role of the psychologist in some of the Parisian care homes (and again, if relevant, this did not reflect a concern with issues of racism per se), most of the institutions visited were abuse-blind in relation to residents' racist prejudice. Mary, who worked in London, deplored for instance the non-acknowledgement of the harmful implications of such exposure to racist attitudes:

> These days nobody goes around making racist remarks but most of the residents do and there is no excuse for it, they are allowed to do it because they are residents which is a bit silly sometimes because we are not just carers we are humans as well, we do have emotions, we do have feelings, if someone called you a nasty name you would feel it you know. (Mary, 20, Black UK, London)

Mary was most affected by the indifference of the managers and their systematic compliance with residents' preferences, leaving unaddressed the harm these comments might have inflicted. In a similar vein, Bacar in Paris pointed out that the fact that these insults were coming from elderly persons did not diminish their violence and the trauma they caused:

> There are many residents who tell you: you're here to take care of me, you're paid to take care of me, you're paid, you're a domestic, you're a slave, you've left your country, you were poor over there, you came to take care of me. That's a moral violence. The nurse in charge says "no she's sick".... Whereas if it's on the street you register a complaint automatically and the person is judged, no? Isn't it? Racism is an offence, isn't it? Racist remarks, homophobic remarks, all of that is punished by French law, it's an offence. But we say it's an elderly person, it's not.... No, it's a form of psychological and moral

violence. When you work 10 or 12 hours, you come, you sweat, you take care of the person, you wash him/her, you wake him/her up, you prepare him/her for breakfast, sometimes you even feed the person, she/he can't eat alone, you turn, sometimes you're alone, your back, you bend, you sweat, you're called negro, domestic…. (Bacar, 35, Senegal, Paris)

The lack of support for the abuse suffered by care workers indicates that these companies either ignored it or regarded coping with it as care workers' duty. Sameera emphasised that the possibility of care workers being abused is left unaddressed:

What about our rights as staff? When you think about it, we don't have any rights, we just have to bear abuse. Abuse is both side, it's for us and for them also, but if abuse is happening to them, oh my god, it might be wrong, it might be something which is not big but they will make a big thing out of it. Why? Because they are vulnerable, because they are … but what about us, the staff? We are not human beings? We have to bear abuse from them? This is not fair. (Sameera, 32, Mauritius, London)

Sameera referred here the vulnerability created unwittingly by the protection regulations concerning elderly residents. In the UK, the regulatory framework makes it very easy indeed for any manager to dismiss a worker on the basis of a Safeguarding of Vulnerable Adults (SOVA) case. From the perspective of a migrant worker harassed by her manager, the SOVA procedure appears to represent an additional weapon in her employer's hands that contributes to the imbalance of power and allows for arbitrariness (for instance through unfair dismissal). Managers were themselves trapped in a customer-oriented approach that guided their priorities and imposed on them to ensure that residents would not complain to their relatives. This fostered in several cases precautionary but unfair practices, whereby employers did not respect workers' employment rights. The context of older-age care creates thus a specific situation, whereby vulnerable residents/customers and workers in precarious employment find themselves in a triangular relationship with managers and employers.

While exposure to racist comments might seem to some extent unavoidable, much harm results from the negligence and indifference to these experiences and thus the institutional context in which they take place, as demonstrated by the positive role the psychologist was able to play in a few Parisian care homes. Participants' words also demonstrated that beyond the actual support, the psychologists' presence and availability acknowledged the challenges that accompany care workers' emotional labour, including racism. An ethic of care that stresses the well-being of all who are part of a caring relationship has the potential of transforming the one-sided approach prevalent in current systems of care for the improvement of the quality of care for all. Conceiving of care as a two-way relationship, rather than a unidirectional process of the caregiver providing care to a care recipient, fundamentally transforms how care is understood. In this perspective, the decision to reduce the psychologist's hours by maintaining this support only for residents (clients in this case) and not for care workers, as Elodie observed in her care home, endangers the overall quality of care. Care ethics' emphasis on interdependency sheds light on the existing relation between care workers' and residents' well-being.

This section looked into individual coping strategies as well as the informal collective means that workers used to face frequent racist comments and insults. In the following section, I turn to another form of racist prejudice: racist attitudes amongst colleagues.

7.3   Racist Discrimination at Work: Strong Power Relationships, Limited Resources

Racist Attitudes Amongst Colleagues: Abusive Work Environments

Some participants faced additionally their colleagues' racist prejudice: several participants in Madrid and in London shared negative experiences of colleagues' racist attitudes in the workplace, but none of the participants complained about racist attitudes of work colleagues in Paris, which could be related to the fact that in the care homes visited for fieldwork racialised workers made up the great majority of the workforce (around 80–90% as indicated by the nurses in supervisory positions whom I interviewed). Facing similar racism on behalf of certain residents might have fostered solidarity amongst workers by creating a shared condition. This is not to suggest that racist attitudes do not arise amongst racialised workers. Racialisation processes are multifold, creating divisions that might equally manifest themselves amongst racialised care workers.

An obvious form of negative experience with colleagues entailed remarks directly addressed to migrant workers implying inferiorisation. Isabel, who had started a Master's degree in the Philippines, felt deeply insulted by her colleagues' comments:

> I have experience in the previous job you know there are some people you know.... Racists.... When I started there they said, one of the carer asked me, because I'm reading a newspaper in front of a resident, then she just asked me, "oh can you read English?" I said yes I can't come here if I don't know how to read English. "oh I see" ... and then I am using the remote control because one of the resident asked me to turn on the TV and set it on a program. "Oh do you know how to use that?" As if they are thinking I am ignorant or I'm illiterate because I'm foreigner I don't know.... They are just degrading you. (Isabel, 37, the Philippines, London)

In this case Isabel perceived her colleagues' remarks as demeaning and as an attempt to put her down. Often the same feelings were described in relation to more covert attitudes that did not necessarily involve any voiced interaction but had no less far-reaching implications. Pedro, who was born in Spain to Guinean parents, described Spanish society as intrinsically racist and explained how he had to learn to navigate a space of social relations systematically imbued with racist prejudice:

> In spite that you hate me I will know how to get along. That's something that I learned as a little boy, ignore, carry on, and keep on living. You can't do anything else, it's not worth it because it's not viable. You can't fight your whole life against something that vast. So at work I've observed it. You see it a lot, a lot. What happens is that then it depends on each person how do you deal with it. If you're a person who doesn't put up with this and you can't channel it and ignore it so that you focus on what's really important, then yes you can have problems. Because unfortunately they'll never tell you, very rarely they'll say it openly so that you can justify it, the key is to

prove it. So they'll say "I didn't say anything". So the best thing is to take it in, deflect it and transform it into something good. (Pedro, 25, born in Spain to Guinean parents, Madrid)

In Pedro's account, racist prejudice is diffuse, permanently present but rarely provable. It affects so many of his daily social relations that even if he is highly aware of the racist overtones of certain attitudes towards him, he feels he can do very little about it, given that this prejudice is not expressed through insults or aggression but through less obvious behaviour, which nevertheless leaves no doubt about its meaning for the person affected by it. In another care home in Madrid but in a similar vein, Marisol, who came from Ecuador, explains that Latino American workers are marginalised by Spanish workers:

There are many Latinos working, many immigrants. So we often gather, we comment on the situation and we say so the only thing we can do is to continue, to ignore these persons. So we ignore them and we continue the everyday fight but many times they look down upon us. So we've learned that these persons we have to ignore, not to pay attention to these persons. We came here to work not to make friends. (Marisol, 47, Ecuador, Madrid)

The situation presented by Marisol is different from the lived experience of Pedro in the sense that, although marginalised, Latino American workers were able to form a group that provided informal support. The following account by Sameera describes a more individualised form of bullying:

And when I was working I could feel, they wouldn't even look at you while you're sitting, they just move when you come to the staff room, you sit next to them, they move. I was thinking … what happened? I was thinking maybe I'm smelly… You know? Maybe something is wrong with me, maybe my cloth is dirty.… Me I shower every day … slowly slowly I feel the attitude. Now I start feeling what this is you know. And then there was a girl over there I will never forget, the way she treats you … how can I say. It's like you're nothing. (Sameera, 32, Mauritius, London)

These discriminatory attitudes at work deeply affected Sameera's well-being as her marginalisation became more and more apparent. Her colleagues' behaviour was not, as it might appear, a passive attitude but constituted an active form of bullying. This form of interpersonal interaction illustrates racist prejudice at the individual level. The attitude of Sameera's colleagues can be described as a form of 'aversive racism' (Byrd 2011; Gawronski et al. 2008). Negative feelings towards a racialised person are expressed by this behaviour but no opinion is voiced against egalitarian values per se. The examples given here by Isabel, Pedro, Marisol and Sameera all reflect the fact that contemporary manifestations of racism in interpersonal interactions tend to be less overt because of the stigmatisation of racism in mainstream political and societal discourse and the likelihood of it being sanctioned. As a consequence, victims of racism often feel insecure about their ability to challenge a form of racism not accompanied by racist claims. From this perspective, anti-discrimination legislation risks falling short of addressing the social phenomenon it concerns itself with, and this in spite of having reversed the burden of proof in corresponding judiciary procedures.

Another form of inter-colleagues' harmful interactions concerns issues of favouritism, either between majority-minority groups or minority-minority groups. Mary, for instance, worked in a care home where she was one of the few Black workers (she identified as 'Black British') and where migrant workers from the Philippines represented the numerical majority, including Filipino staff in most managerial positions (except for the manager of the home, who was White British):

> In a workplace where we have a lot of different minorities, Black, White, Asians, when there becomes a majority of a certain minority then it starts a little bit of unfairness going on and favouritism but … and which does happen here in (care home name) and I'm not gonna lie to you there is a lot of favouritism here. (Mary, 20, Black UK, London)

In the Spanish context, Claudia, who had been working in the same care home for ten years, explained:

At work there's sometimes discrimination, a lot of discrimination. Those who go first for breaks are the Spaniards and the Latinos go "What are you doing there?" So what happens is that they always have their breaks first, the Spaniards, best things for them and the Latinos are as always left behind. (Claudia, 53, Peru, Madrid)

Racist behaviour amongst colleagues involves employers' responsibility for ensuring a fair workplace. However, in none of the cases described above did managers provide support to victims of harassment. When discriminatory attitudes by colleagues were pervasive or took the form of favouritism, in the cases reported by participants, managers were complicit in that they tolerated it or sided with the dominant group. Workers discriminated against because of favouritism towards other groups of workers did not envisage taking action, often out of fear of retaliation, as presented in greater detail below. As a matter of fact, such apprehensions constitute a very common deterrent to the use of anti-discrimination legislation.

The following section explores managers' responsibility in relation to institutional racism as well as cases of direct harassment and discrimination by management.

Discrimination and Harassment by Managers and Employers

In this section I analyse experiences narrated by participants that describe racist practices involving supervisors, managers and/or employers. Precarious employment and work interact with experiences of discrimination and create specific sets of experiences. I here demonstrate how overarching racialisation processes bear material consequences for workers against the background of intersecting regimes. In three national contexts, the vulnerabilities created by employment and older-age care regimes generate specific consequences from the standpoint of migrant and minority ethnic workers, but along differentiated patterns for these two groups. First of all, as hinted at above, some of the ways managers dealt with (or did not deal with) discrimination perpetrated by others amounted under certain circumstances to institutionalised forms of racism. When Sameera had difficulties with one service user, she was moved out of the unit by her manager against her will, which actually made things worse for her:

> That's why most care workers just prefer to keep quiet, we talk among ourselves and we won't say anything you know. Like when I was in the other workplace I remember … they wouldn't ask me are you happy? Do you have any issues with the service users or the colleagues? At that time I had a problem with one service user and I just say yes, blah blah, I have this issue. And the next thing I know, instead of resolving that problem, he makes this ten times worse for me and I say to myself why did I even open my mouth, this has learnt me a lesson. (Sameera, 32, Mauritius, London)

This story shows that management practices might have significant discriminatory implications, regardless of the actual intentions of the manager. Similarly, in relation to colleagues' attitudes, when the issue was informally raised with a deputy manager or a manager, the response was in several cases to move the victim to another floor or unit. This, however, sent out the wrong message as to who was to blame and therefore weakened the position of the affected worker who was further marginalised. In these cases, institutional practices effectively transformed the experience of individual prejudice into a form of institutional racism, because of the way the managers' position of power was used to entrench discriminatory outcomes. Such examples illustrate empirically that addressing racism in the workplace not only requires workers' mobilisation, it also crucially requires managers' awareness and engagement in order for legal rights to be enforced. 'The transformation of racists themselves' that Balibar called for (1988, p. 29) requires the transformation of the majority group, that is, in this case, of employers' and management's practices. As outlined in Chap. 3, the focus of judiciary systems is often on racist intentions and not on the outcome, that is, on racist discrimination. This is clearly the case in France and in Spain where the concept of racism is conflated with that of racist prejudice. In the UK, the concept of institutional racism entered the public debate over two decades ago, but this has rarely been taken into account by judges in cases of individual discrimination.[1]

The commercial context of the private care homes in which participants in this study were employed, by transforming residents into customers, further exacerbated the tensions engendered by the juxtaposition mentioned above of vulnerable service users and precarious workers. The vulnerabilities created by migration policies and labour market segmentation, which weakened the position of workers, were deepened by the commercial context in which these relationships are embedded. Bacar clearly blamed this framework for exacerbating workers' vulnerability:

> In for-profit care homes, that make profits, so residents are clients, 'the client is the king' so they prefer clients to carers. Because the client makes the money go in, for the carer the employer pays out, he pays at the end of the month but clients pay in so he prefers clients, the person that makes the money go in, that's logical. So if a carer has a problem with a patient or a resident or with the family, automatically it's the carer who's sanctioned, the client is always right.

In addition, managerial practices could be directly discriminatory in themselves and ranged from unfair workloads to bullying and stigmatisation. In several cases, a combination of these practices was present. The unfair division of tasks, as identified in the UK by Alessio Cangiano and colleagues in their study, constitutes a common form of discrimination in the care sector (Cangiano et al. 2009, p. 137). This research further points out that unfair shift and annual leave distributions are equally common practices. Jade, who worked in Paris, complained about how shifts and days off were attributed:

> I would say that it [annual leave distribution] is not fair. For instance, I can ask for a day off, one time it can be accepted, the other it's not. It's not fair it's all I know it's not fair. Annual leave, absences, no, it's not fair. (Jade, 46, Ivory Coast, Paris)

---

[1] http://www.irr.org.uk/news/culture-of-disbelief-why-race-discrimination-claims-fail-in-the-employment-tribunal/. Last accessed in February 2016.

Such management practices created resentment and impacted to varying degrees on workers' well-being. The unfair distribution of the workload could have serious health implications for the workers, given the heavy bodily work involved in care (as examined in Chap. 6). Furthermore, as argued in Chap. 3, migrant workers are undoubtedly exposed to specific forms of discrimination and exploitation due to the 'institutional insecurity' created by migration policies (Anderson 2010) within the group of racialised workers as a whole. The more dependent migrant workers were on their employer to support their work permit and provide their accommodation, the more they were exposed to abuse. In the same way, a limited knowledge of their rights or a lack of language skills worsened their experiences. Isabel's first employer in the UK attempted to forcibly retain her in a job in which she faced abusive practices; she was required to work any shifts that the employer saw fit, as he had provided her with accommodation in a room adjacent to the care home, and she had her wages withheld.

The environment is not really good they are bullying, they are abusing us because they knew that we are new and that we are foreigners. So we filed a resignation but they didn't accept it, they wanted us to stay though it is our right if you're not happy you can go, yeah? We asked permission, we asked properly that we don't stay here any longer but they didn't allow us so we just leave. (Isabel, 37, the Philippines, London)

Equally a victim of abuse, Sameera described how she felt oppressed in her workplace where she experienced bullying but felt completely powerless and unable to challenge these behaviours. Her account shows that the stigma of being a migrant goes beyond legal status. As Guillaumin (1972/2002, p. 247, my translation) wrote several decades ago: 'Each individual who used to be foreigner, alienated, condemned, always bears the scars of it, and his/her status of integration and conformism always remains ambiguous and submitted to the form of good will that constitutes tolerance or the silence of the majority.' Here, Sameera did not expect the planned acquisition of British citizenship to have any impact on how she would be perceived by managers and colleagues in the workplace and thus on their abusive attitudes towards her.

And me as migrant I can't even open my mouth, you understand? How can I? Because these people is more powerful than me. You understand? Even I've got 10 years now, I'm married, my status changed, tomorrow I apply for British [passport], I will get it because my husband is British it's still … I will be considered like different level, you understand? Because of my background, where I come from, because maybe of my skin colour, you understand? This is always something which is always … how can I say … always inside you but you can't open your mouth and talk about it. Sometimes you feel you just want to shout, you want to explode. But what can you do? You're scared, you do your job. (Sameera, 32, Mauritius, London)

The vulnerable position of migrant workers left a space for employers' arbitrariness given the very low probability that their practices would be sanctioned in any way. In London, Jenifer highlighted a case of harassment of foreigners at her workplace:

And she [the manager] has been reported by several witnesses on one day, she went upstairs and was telling, because it's mostly Filipinos and a few Asian people on the first floor, she was going around and telling you're lucky you're in your jobs otherwise you could be back home, if you're not happy where you're working you should go back home to your own country. (Jenifer, 24, the Philippines, London)

This xenophobic harassment of her staff by a manager amounted to more than just xenophobia. The space for arbitrariness created by migration policies facilitated abuse in employer-employee relationships. Grace, employed in the same care home, made the point that bullying happens as a result of the specific power relationships in which migrant workers are caught:

She [the manager] doesn't do that [bullying] to the White ones who are there, like you know who can just drop everything and go. She doesn't do that to them. That's the difference she doesn't insult them like that. She does it to the foreigners. (Grace, 61, the Philippines, London)

Harassment by employers, including racist insults, was most common in the narratives of migrant workers in Madrid employed in live-in caring arrangements.[2] This employment situation produces a striking form of imbalance between the employer and the employee, whereby the rights of the employee are extremely limited, on the one hand, by employment legislation and migration regulations and, on the other, by the material conditions of the employment relationship. A quite typical quote in this regard is that of Lucia, whose employer (a member of the family of the person she cared for) got angry and attacked her after she announced that she could not travel with the family to Mallorca as planned because of a health issue:

> She insulted me. She told me that we were only coming to steal, that I was a thief because she had bought me a uniform, she had bought me supplies. Because workers who worked in the house didn't eat in the house. They had a small separate house where domestic workers ate. Until they [employers] had finished eating, everything needed to be done and then you were going to the small house to have something to eat. It was a very difficult situation there. (Lucia, 56, Nicaragua, Madrid)

The imbalance of power between the employer and the employee tends to be exacerbated in specific contexts: for instance, when privatisation increases pressures to reduce labour costs or when the employment relationship is situated in the domestic sphere. When undocumented and materially dependent on their employer, workers can be trapped in an abusive employment relationship without being able to challenge it. Several participants in Madrid went through a period of being undocumented on arrival in Spain. Due to the focus of this book on residential care, all participants possessed either a residence permit or Spanish citizenship at the time of the interview; often the employment journey from live-in caring arrangements to a job in residential care followed progressive improvements related to their migration statuses. Victoria, whose sister was undocumented for some time, recounts:

---

[2] Only a minority of participants were employed in domestic care in this research due to my focus on institutional care. Yet many respondents in Madrid were employed in domestic care prior to being recruited in residential care facilities. See Chap. 2 for an overview of the distribution of institutional versus household employers among participants.

When you don't have documents, you're not legally here, you're scared of doing it, of reporting. Because you know that without documents, documents in order it was very important, to have these documents, your resident permit, your work permit. If you don't have those, they'll deport and you go. Who's losing out is the worker. So often they kept quiet to avoid this, by necessity. (Victoria, 54, Ecuador, Madrid)

Stories told in Paris, Madrid and London in relation to managers' and employers' direct discrimination epitomise the reasons why anti-discrimination policies are de facto of very limited relevance when a large proportion of the workforce is trapped in segmented sections of the labour market due to limited rights and precarious employment terms. Even when working legally, few migrant workers can afford to invest time and money individually in lengthy judicial procedures unlikely to bring positive results, as statistics demonstrate for the UK and the absence of figures hint at in the case of Spain and France.

These negative working experiences were nevertheless resisted and fought against individually and collectively in creative ways. The following section looks at forms of resistance to harassment and discrimination by employers and management.

Challenging Racist Practices and Behaviour

If care workers can talk about residents' racist prejudice to their managers, it is rarely possible in the case of racist behaviour by colleagues and virtually impossible when the discrimination comes from management itself. When harassment and discrimination are embedded in employer-employee power relationships, workers need to seek support outside the workplace and the struggle is all the more difficult when targeted workers are denizens with limited rights (Standing 2011; De Genova 2013).

Faced with harassment by employers, it appeared that participants in Madrid mostly resorted to informal support groups and associations, while unions struggled to be present in this feminised sector of the labour market where a large share of migrant workers is present. Often, the creation of such associations is the outgrowth of a previously existing informal group. Victoria, who founded an association of migrant care workers, explained for instance how they were able to provide support to migrant care workers who had been sacked by the family they were working for, in some cases after having been insulted and abused:

> We had colleagues [not necessarily in the workplace] for whom it was very tough. They were told "what are you doing here? Go back to your country" (…) They left their jobs and they were very depressed. We've been helping, I tell you many women who came and whose situation was: "Look, they treated me like this, they told this or that." Us: "No, you have to cheer up, you're not like this and you have to carry on." And we've worked, because we always had the luck to work with professional colleagues, we have a colleague who's psychologist, others who used to be psychologists. So they've helped us with the women to make them realize that things are not as we're told. (Victoria, 54, Ecuador, Madrid)

Mayra, also of Ecuadorian origin, joined a group of domestic workers in Madrid who met twice a month. She described how these contacts provided a powerful form of solidarity:

> We have an association, a group of women where we say we empower ourselves because we learn techniques and tricks to be able to endure the situation. It's not that it's to teach us but it's the experience of each one of us, amongst ourselves we've constructed a method to take care of ourselves for things that affect us at work. (Mayra, 52, Ecuador, Madrid)

These forms of support are crucial for workers' well-being and if they sometimes ushered in support for judiciary procedures, that was not the primary function of these organisations. Unions, which could theoretically play that role, were rarely mentioned by participants in Madrid and did not act as a significant source of support in cases of harassment. The association mentioned by Mayra was, for instance, rather critical of unions' role, perceiving them as outdated organisations unable to address the specific challenges of the highly feminised care and domestic work sectors. One respondent, a victim of harassment in Madrid, thought of involving a union but her story shows that she was discouraged by the union from initiating a legal action:

NS: Were you thinking in this situation of seeking support for example from a union?

Rita: Yes, yes.

NS: What could they do in this situation?

Rita: I said I was about to denounce her for harassment because I knew that the union had to back me up. What happens is—and this is what the union told me—that if I go to court I need to be courageous. They told me "If you go to court you need to be courageous because you go to court and this woman she'll harass you even more than you can imagine, she'll harass you and harass you until she can prove that you're arrogant and instead of you winning, she'll be the one winning. Do you take the risk of going to court?" Because the trial will take years he told me. "You might have left the care home but the trial will be going on for one, two, three or more years." So I said: "No, it's not like I got to the point that … I'm not starving as much as to go to court" I said. (Rita, 54, Ecuador, Madrid)

This story illustrates that cases of racist harassment are particularly difficult to challenge legally, even for unions. The mere existence of anti-discrimination legislation does not empower racialised workers, because the path to employment tribunals is fraught with pitfalls. The reluctance of the union to start judicial proceedings seems to reflect its awareness of its limited effectiveness. At the same time it highlights again that most cases remain unchallenged (at least in legal terms) and thus unsanctioned.

In London it was mostly unions that were perceived as potentially supportive institutions, even though none of the participants actually asked a union for help, and several had joined unions after they had problems at work. For example, this was decisive for Sameera:

I joined the union first time when I had a problem but maybe my only mistake I did not involve the union when it happened because one lady she was in this category, the same thing happened to her and she involved the union in this. They make a big thing out of it and since today she's still in the same unit and nobody can even touch her, do anything to her. (Sameera, 32, Mauritius, London)

Isabel, the Filipina care worker who experienced abuse in her first workplace in the UK, also thought that unions could have effectively supported her if she had asked them for help:

> Because here in this country racism and bullying is a really big issue they don't really allow it. It's not a crime but it's really a big issue for them. (...) I can get a big support from union if I were a union member when that experience happened, when that incident happened because what I have experienced there is really racism, bullying, abuse. (Isabel, 37, the Philippines, London)

In practice though, unions faced difficulties similar to those in Madrid, in spite of the stronger regulatory framework available to them in the UK. Workers felt that it was difficult to prove discrimination, especially in cases of covert forms of racism. Furthermore, it was common amongst participants in the UK to be afraid that joining a union would be perceived negatively by management. Needless to say, when cases of discrimination did arise and the potential for confrontation through mediation by a union increased, this fear grew as well. Worry that making an allegation of discrimination would make the situation worse in future discouraged Sameera from seeking the union's support:

NS: And did you get in touch with the union?
Sameera: No, I didn't because I was thinking if I have not resolved that problem, but thank God it was fine and I don't want to involve the union for anything because then there might be a grudge against me. If something which can't be resolved at all then I involve them, if not ... but at the moment it's ok. (Sameera, 32, Mauritius, London)

The commercialisation of unions' services also played a role in diminishing the trust workers could place in unions: if union membership was a cost/benefit calculation for unions (and for workers), then the likelihood of obtaining the union's support for a costly and uncertain procedure was perceived as low. The UK is probably the place where this paradox is most prominent: in spite of the existence of well-developed anti-discrimination legislation, encompassing a wide range of possible forms of discrimination, the possibility of lodging a complaint with an employment tribunal is hampered by a series of structural characteristics of the UK employment regime, including low levels of employment protection in comparison with other European countries, costly judiciary procedures and a low probability of obtaining a union's support, given that the chances of winning discrimination cases are generally low and that unions take that variable into account. In her willingness to support her care assistant colleagues who were harassed by the manager of the care home she worked in, Grace did not assess positively the potential role of unions:

> Everybody is making money, even unions sometimes they're making money, they collect all the membership and they don't support you when you need them, they're collecting money, everything is business nowadays. So when it comes to litigations, when it comes to spending so much money, to fight your case, goodbye to you, they don't want to know. (…) Unless you're a strong person that you can go through this hassle and this trouble, forget it, because it's a very lengthy procedure and you need a lot of evidence to prove that. (Grace, 61, the Philippines, London)

It thus appears that when abuse does happen, these rights are often hardly accessible notwithstanding the level of development of the regulatory framework. Existing power relationships make it difficult for workers to be able to challenge their managers and employers. The difficulty of proving discrimination and harassment in these cases adds to the problem and to the fear of starting a procedure in vain, thus risking exposure to more abuse as in Sameera's case.

7.4 Conclusion

Looking into experiences of racism and discrimination in older-age care has shown that manifestations of racism take a great variety of forms. The nature of these experiences differs according to the power relationships in which they are embedded: being insulted by residents, being bullied by colleagues or being harassed by managers; each of these instances has different implications for workers. The analysis of various forms of racism and discrimination and of the consequent coping strategies revealed how these are in fact interrelated and the symptom of broader institutional racism.

The chapter presented first a cross-national analysis of racialised workers' experiences in relation to the racist prejudice of some residents or service users. Workers faced similar neglect on the part of employers in this matter in London and in Madrid and received limited support in Paris, in the form of the presence of a psychologist. This, however, was not systematic and was not due to an acknowledgement of the implications of racism per se. This chapter further argued that workers' individual and collective responses were symptomatic of different contexts of institutional racism. Then, the analysis of situations of harassment and abuse by colleagues illustrated common manifestations of racism and discrimination and exposed some of its implications for workers' well-being. This section also pointed out how these experiences were embedded in workplace power relationships and identified the role managers and employers played in different situations. In none of the cases analysed here did bullying and harassment by colleagues usher in disciplinary procedures or legal cases. The third aspect, that of discrimination or harassment by managers, revealed how intersecting regimes, when exacerbating precariousness, foster abuse at the workplace level. Migrant workers were in this regard most exposed to direct harassment by managers.

In assessing the shortcomings of the rights approach to combat racism in older-age care, an ethic of care suggests alternative understandings. By placing care in the centre of what matters in society, care ethics interrogate the racist outcomes of intersecting migration and care policies. The inclusiveness of a feminist democratic ethic of care (Tronto 2013) poses a major challenge to the structural aspects of the racism and discrimination experienced by care workers in the current political economy of care. A political theory inspired by care ethics advocates for relating the concept of citizenship to that of care so that care ceases to be overlooked, at best taken for granted, in the political organisation of society. Relating care to citizenship (Sevenhuijsen 1998) and democracy (Tronto 2013) carries the potential of empowering care workers through better inclusion into society and renewed consideration of the importance of care, translating into secure legal statuses, protective employment and proactive measures to ensure care workers' well-being at work.

The comparative analysis conducted illustrated indeed that by defining workers' rights, employment and migration regimes shape the conditions for workers' exposure to racist discrimination, harassment and abuse. Challenging these situations is complex and no single framework can possibly improve workers' experiences from all these perspectives. Anti-discrimination legislation appears to be of very limited efficacy for precarious workers: in spite of the numerous experiences related by participants in this research, no one actually resorted to anti-discrimination legislation. The great majority of cases go unchallenged, which suggests that it is difficult to fix structurally created unequal power relationships through individual legal action. Moreover, most abusive situations are created or exacerbated by the space for arbitrariness derived from the articulation of migration and employment policies. Therefore, overstating the relevance of anti-discrimination legislation runs the risk of equating anti-racism with anti-discrimination policies, instead of conducting a political economy analysis of the conditions under which racism and discrimination thrive. The challenge to racism and racist discrimination cannot rely solely on an anti-discrimination legislative framework. Low levels of employment protection weaken the possibility of denouncing an employer for harassment, due to the unfavourable power relationship thus established. Furthermore, workers' well-being depends on solutions adapted to workplaces as the specifics of older-age care have demonstrated: solutions which can only be designed and implemented if workers' voices are heard and taken into account through more balanced power relationships.

8

Negotiating the Future, Within and Out of Care

I think I've done here enough of what I had to do and that's time for me to return, because I don't see the situation improving, I see that each time it's worse, I've been offered to work as live-in carer for a miserable wage, honestly it both saddens me and makes me laugh when they tell you. And that's like this everywhere, so that's the current situation, it's difficult. It's very complicated for people working as carers honestly. So I plan on staying until the end of the year and return home. I'm not sure I will but I plan on going back. (Mayra, 52, Ecuador, Madrid)

Mayra was residing in Madrid for 14 years when we met. She was envisaging return as a result of the limited professional opportunities she had in Madrid. Participants' projections often reflected this negotiation between the perceived opportunity structures in the countries of origin and destination. With no specific plans for her return, the more the economic situation within care deteriorated, the more was Mayra willing to return to Ecuador. The collapse of the Spanish economy intensified the return of many Ecuadorians after 2008 (Martínez Buján 2015). Since care is at the heart of sustaining life itself, care-related activities were not surprisingly less hit by the crisis than the construction sector that employed many Ecuadorian men. However, as explored in Chap. 5, the

© The Author(s) 2019
N. Sahraoui, *Racialised Workers and European Older-Age Care*, Thinking Gender in Transnational Times, https://doi.org/10.1007/978-3-030-14397-8_8

care sector was also affected by the economic crisis in Spain with a deterioration of the level of earnings and of the working conditions. Observing the worsening of the situation, Mayra, though she had become a Spanish citizen, saw no future in Spain. This chapter explores how racialised care workers negotiated their futures. With an approach combining elements of political economy analysis and intersectionality, I examine the paths that lead to more or less inclusion, first from the legal perspective of accessing the citizenship of the country of residence and second in relation to professional training and advancement. In the first section, I examine the articulation between migration status, citizenship and employment by assessing the professional and economic implications of gaining citizenship in the country of residence. This section only includes migrant workers so that the citizenship variable is more meaningful. In order to assess if care jobs constitute a stepping-stone or an entrapment for migrant and minority ethnic workers, I further question how differentiated degrees of professionalisation shape participants' possibilities for upward mobility. In the third section, I build a comparative typology of participants' aspirations that reveals what opportunities and barriers they perceive as decisive and how they conceive of their agency within it.

8.1   Becoming a Citizen: The Migration/ Employment Nexus

Citizenship, Time Spent in the Country and Earnings

Clearly, significant differences emerged from one country to another in terms of access to citizenship for non-EU participants. As mentioned in Chap. 3, national legislations differ in this regard and the Spanish case is distinct in that nationals from Latin American countries might apply for Spanish citizenship after two years of legal residency, as opposed to ten years for most other nationalities. Given that the vast majority of non-EU migrant care workers in Madrid come from Latin American countries, and especially Ecuador and Peru in this study, this constitutes an explanatory factor in the higher proportion of participants holding Spanish citizenship, as illustrated by Fig. 8.1.

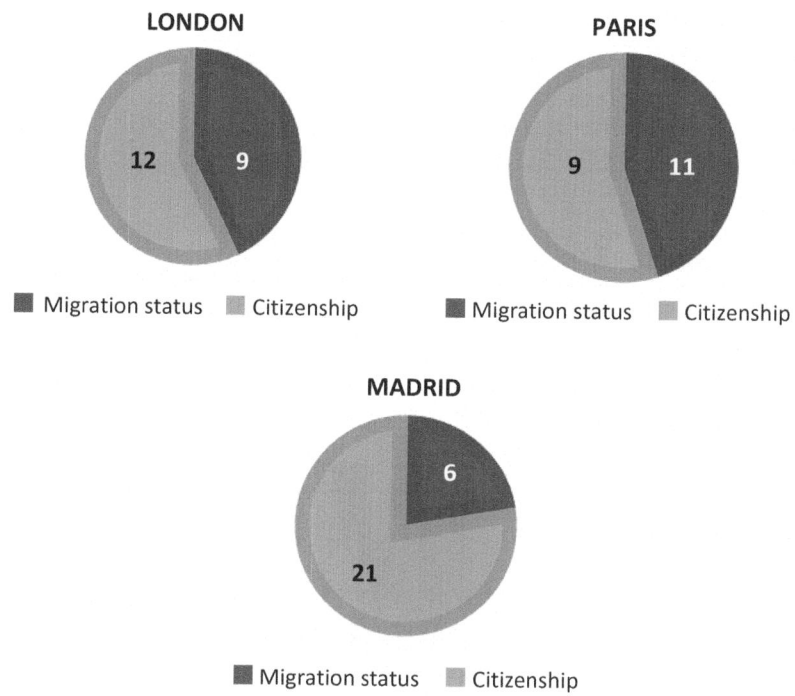

Fig. 8.1 Access to citizenship of the country of residence amongst migrant participants. Source: Own data and elaboration

In spite of these striking differences, the share of non-EU migrants holding the citizenship of the country of residence is relatively high in these three sites: almost half of participants in London, more than half in Paris and 21 out of 27 in Madrid. Obtaining citizenship does not shield one, however, from the discriminatory implications of labour market segmentation. Racialisation processes reinforce the performative power of formal distinctions and bear long-lasting effects even when one is no longer subject to migration regulations. The proliferation of borders (Mezzadra and Neilson 2013) is not overcome by accessing citizenship and it is continuity rather than rupture that characterises the experiences of non-EU migrants in terms of the social implications of labour market segmentation. Table 8.1 illustrates the time spent in the country of destination for all non-EU participants on average, as well as for those having

Table 8.1 Time spent in the country of destination according to migration status

Years in the destination country	London	Paris	Madrid
All participants, average	7.8	17.3	11.6
Migrants *without* citizenship of country of residence	5	11	7
Migrants *with* citizenship of country of residence	12	23	13

Source: Own data and elaboration

Table 8.2 Level of earnings according to migration status

	London (£)	Paris (€)	Madrid (€)
Average earnings of migrants with temporary migration status	802	1400	703
Median	940	1386	760
Average earnings of migrants with citizenship of country of residence	950	1375	802
Median	900	1400	840

Source: Own data and elaboration

gained citizenship and those who did not possess it at the time of the interview. While an obvious relationship appears between time spent in the country and access to citizenship, this table sheds additional light on the particularity of the Spanish case; the vast majority of participants had gained Spanish citizenship at the time of the interview, yet the average number of years spent in the country is only slightly higher than that spent by migrants in London and much lower than that spent in Paris.

Access to a country's citizenship theoretically improves an individual's employment prospects in that it extracts the person from the social location of being a denizen and grants the individual the full set of rights. Yet, as the following paragraphs illustrate, accessing the citizenship of the country of destination, while presenting a few immediate advantages, is for its most part inscribed into much longer processes of inclusion with limited social implications in the short term.

In terms of levels of earnings, Table 8.2 presents the average earnings of participants in this study according to whether they hold the citizenship of the country they reside in. A positive but limited correlation emerges in the case of London and Madrid. A lack of correlation in the Paris case might be caused by stronger employment regulation, as presented in Chap. 3, that limits the extent of differentiated levels of earnings for similar jobs.

In Spain, many non-EU care workers go through a period of being undocumented. The length of this period of time depends to some extent on the migrant worker's luck in securing an employer willing to sponsor his or her documentation, and thus on his or her decision to leave an employer not willing to fulfil this role. This criterion pushed Lucia, for example, to leave her job when she felt it was necessary to do so:

> At first the person who was about to do it for me did not meet the requirements. Then, it was a woman who really did not want, it was an elderly woman. I was in a difficult situation because I didn't know what to do. (…) I stayed working with her until one day I said: "That's it, no more, I'll search for an alternative because I need to get my documentation, because I haven't reached my aims yet." (Lucia, 56, Nicaragua, Madrid)

Obtaining documentation makes an immense difference to workers' position in the labour market and shelters them from the most extreme forms of exploitation. It does not, however, allow for substantial improvement in their levels of pay or career prospects and they remain confined to a highly segmented section of the labour market.

Citizenship and Employment Opportunities

Owing to differentiated regulations according to the nationality of origin in Spain, non-EU migrant workers' plans and strategies necessarily differed in relation to the acquisition of citizenship, depending on whether or not they could benefit from the reduced time of minimum legal residency. Abdel, of Moroccan origin, relates his path to Spanish citizenship:

NS: How was the journey to obtain Spanish citizenship?

Abdel: The journey was very long. With the laws between Morocco and Spain, you're a bit…. You need to have been residing 10 years here in Spain to receive Spanish nationality and you also need make sure you never had any problems with the police, no problem with people, otherwise they don't give it to you. Thanks to God I'm very home-loving, home, work, I received the nationality with no difficulty. (Abdel, 48, Morocco, Madrid)

In Madrid, in spite of the fact that most participants had Spanish citizenship, most of them did not perceive any concrete improvement or changes in relation to their employment situation apart from the fact that they had the possibility of emigrating from Spain to a different European country. For instance, Beronica remained perplexed in this regard:

> So, what can I say? If it has improved … I could travel, as a European citizen you can travel, you can go to work in a different city. But I don't know what to tell you, I haven't noticed any difference for being Spanish, for having Spanish nationality. There are some benefits but I don't have changes in my life that I would notice. (Beronica, 38, Ecuador, Madrid)

Rather than being related to better employment opportunities or the hope of better career prospects, a citizenship application was often conceived by participants in Madrid as part of a return or remigration project. Many participants spoke of plans to return, notably those of Ecuadorian origin, as I explore in further detail in the section on participants' aspirations. Accessing citizenship enabled return in that it guaranteed potential re-emigration or simply visits to Spain, while leaving without having gained Spanish citizenship tended to be perceived as a failure and waste of the time invested in Spain. A second set of reasons for obtaining Spanish citizenship is to be found in the perception that migration to Spain only constitutes a partial success and that Spanish citizenship will facilitate re-emigration to Northern European countries where earnings are higher and where prospects for children might be brighter. Claudia's words illustrate this perspective:

> I am more mobile, so the benefit of having Spanish nationality is that we can go to different countries, to France, to Portugal, any country in the European Union. I will think about it seriously, above all for the children, once they finish school so that they can start university there and leave this country, and start from scratch as we did, it could be England or any other European country. (Claudia, 53, Peru, Madrid)

In Paris, gaining French citizenship improves a non-EU migrant worker's employment opportunities (yet without an increase in terms of income as demonstrated by Table 8.2) because of the structural discrimination that reserves civil servant status, that is, permanent public employment, to French and EU nationals. This creates an over-representation of foreign workers in the private older-age care sector, where employment contracts are less stable. In spite of the prevalence of temporary contracts, the private sector constitutes the only possibility for foreign workers to secure permanent positions, as explained by Amandine:

> In the private sector, what I actually wanted, was a stable job right away because I had some plans and I really needed a permanent contract. Really. And because I don't have French nationality, I knew that in the public sector they couldn't hire me as civil servant, so I went straight to the private sector. (Amandine, 32, Ivory Coast, Paris)

In the UK, gaining British citizenship offers protection from changing migration regulations that increasingly commodify migrant workers by defining their rights according to their alleged economic (narrowly understood as financial) contribution to the British economy. Indeed, not only is one's right to stay dependent on employment; increasingly discriminatory rules define one's rights according to preset levels of earnings or financial capital as detailed in Chap. 3. Furthermore, in London the overwhelming overqualification (eight in ten participants, see Chap. 4) occurs in spite of four in ten participants holding British citizenship. What Fiona Williams calls the 'lived experience of citizenship' (2011c, p. 52) is crucial for an encompassing understanding of care workers' experiences of the intertwined paths to employment and citizenship. The trajectories of non-EU migrants demonstrate that a strictly legalistic perspective cannot account for enduring forms of disadvantage. In this regard, the Bourdieusian notion of cultural capital in its three dimensions, embodied, objectified and institutionalised, is illuminating in order to account for enduring forms of disadvantage and discrimination (Bourdieu 1979). In spite of the significant share of participants who benefit formally from the same status as non-migrants, it appears that labour market opportunities for those who gained citizenship remain to a great extent shaped by latent social processes that easily take precedence over formal equality. Migrants thus navigate the administrative spaces that migration policies create and decide on the strategies that best suit their purposes against the background of institutional constraints. Values that underpin current conceptualisations of care work, that is, its devaluation, and of citizenship, that is, work-based citizenship narrowly associated with financial remuneration, constrict these administrative spaces. Theorists of care ethics argue for the need to rethink citizenship on the basis of care relationships (Sevenhuijsen 1998; Tronto 2013). This approach shifts fundamentally the value of migrant care work (see Chap. 9) and has the potential of altering the highly gendered implications of current migration policies and of challenging the 'temporal borders' (Mezzadra and Neilson 2013) that these policies engender.

The following section maintains a focus on migrant care workers in the examination of how care workers navigate these spaces, first analysing the professional hierarchies from a comparative perspective and then turning to their professional aspirations, presented here as indicative of participants' perceptions of social mobility possibilities.

8.2   Becoming a Professional: Comparative Insights into Social Mobility

Training Requirements

The professionalisation of the occupation of care assistant varies greatly between the three cities, as presented in Chap. 3. If the tasks carried out daily by all participants in this research are similar, training requirements and career prospects have little in common. As a consequence, significant differences exist in terms of employment status and professional mobility. Differences in terms of the knowledge transmitted through different types of training are primarily due to differences in terms of depth and detail, rather than fundamental differences in terms of content and approach. Care qualifications in France and Spain, as well as National Vocational Qualifications (NVQ) in the UK, often comprise similar modules. Yet, if professionalisation shapes workers' trajectories so differently, it is because regulations attached to the acquisition of this knowledge vary greatly.

In the UK, these qualifications are not embedded in a clear career path for care workers, and completing NVQ levels serves above all to fulfil employers' duties in terms of workforce training. The completion of these NVQs does not translate into better labour market opportunities for workers, given that no prior training is formally required for the position of care assistant and that wages are kept low throughout the industry. As a consequence, incentives for workers to engage in this training remain limited. In this context, there is little scope for promotion apart from senior carer positions, and here there are no homogeneously defined criteria in terms of access and level of salary; the position itself did not exist in some of the care homes I visited.

In Spain, the 2015 reform renders training prior to employment mandatory. The official title of healthcare assistant requires a year of studies and is formally recognised. It is however not mandatory to complete the longest version of the training and in the aftermath of the reform courses offered by private schools mushroomed. In the autonomous community of Madrid, it remained unclear to workers which private schools were granted official accreditation and which were not, as participants knew of many examples where allegedly accredited schools delivered certificates that failed to be acknowledged later on by official authorities. Before the introduction of this reform, the completion of training often served the purpose of moving away from live-in employment arrangements to live-out arrangements, notably by finding employment in residential care. Attending a course provided in this regard a tool for empowerment and many participants in this study regretted having spent too much time in live-in employment, often several years, isolated and not aware of the existence of such courses.

In France, three statuses qualify a person to work in a position equivalent to that of care assistant in terms of the job description (see Table 3.4 in Chap. 3). Danièle, for instance, designed strategies according to the perceived level of difficulty of the entry exams attached to each of these qualifications and to the existing bridges between them:

Because the selection is very tough for the exam of healthcare assistant, I preferred to pass this one first (Medical/psychological assistant), it's a question of chance and also will. So I passed three exams to multiply my chances actually. Because it's possible to pass several exams at once. And given that some colleagues advised me this … because if you have the qualification as Medical/psychological Assistant, you only have to pass some additional modules to become Healthcare Assistant. (Danièle, 53, Senegal, Paris)

I now turn to the costs of different qualifications and available funding opportunities that constituted key elements in the decision-making process of non-EU migrant care workers.

Cost of Training

At first sight, it might appear that the longer the training takes, the more it amounts to a barrier to entering the sector. In practice, this correlation is not necessarily valid, and the sector's accessibility depends on the combination of regulations in terms of training, availability of training and existing financing schemes.

In the UK, given the absence of formal requirements, individuals who become care workers do not need to invest time and money in training before they are employed. Jobs are therefore very accessible but at the same time particularly segmented. The lack of training reinforces the essentialisation of care skills and entraps workers in a highly segmented section of the labour market without formal bridges and advancement paths on which to build a career. Training provided by employers does not impose additional financial costs on workers, but often no time is dedicated to that training and workers are compelled to complete it in their personal time. It thus created situations in which training was completed at home, as presented by Amal.

NS: Can you manage to do it (the online training) during your working time?

Amal: You cannot do it during work, especially this unit I am working in, the residents keep ringing the bell so I don't really think you have time for that because you are only two staff as well, you can't just go and do your e-learning, then the other person gets fed up with you … but sometimes if we have a day off we are allowed to come and just do our e-learning if the Internet is not working in my house I can just come here and do the e-learning. (Amal, 24, Somalia, London)

In Spain, given the existence of multiple types of training that do not hold the same value, participants in this study had to navigate an opaque system. The most straightforward way to obtain a recognised qualification was to benefit from training organised by local authorities, as in the case of Abdel:

I'm here since March covering someone's leave and I completed health and social work course through the city council and the work placement I did it in this care home. (Abdel, 48, Morocco, Madrid)

While Abdel could attend his training at no cost in the framework of employment policies designed for the unemployed, opportunities to be trained for free seem to have diminished and to have become increasingly restrictive. Individuals already in employment faced logistic difficulties in being able to attend training, while the greater availability of training prior to the crisis made it easier for them to combine studies and work. Flor, for instance, was looking for further training, but she experienced difficulties in finding it for free and at the same time was careful not to fall into the trap of paying for a qualification that would not be recognised:

If I could find something for afternoons, brilliant, and working in the morning. That would be great but I need to search because a friend of mine told me that the same company (name) in Madrid, they consider having classes in the afternoon. Of course if they do it in the afternoon and it's for free that would be great. That would be really good. Because they're people they want to make you pay 800, but they're private and it doesn't help because it won't be officially recognised. (Flor, 25, Peru, Madrid)

Magdalena's account below illustrates the effort it takes to make the most of available possibilities while avoiding unnecessary costs. Magdalena seems to have been particularly diligent in preparing herself for the 2015 reform. Her commitment allowed her to avoid being affected by employers' tendency to transfer the cost of training onto workers:

NS: And the courses to comply with the 2015 reform?

Magdalena: These too…. The first two modules were given by the company. And the other two I obtained them by calling all the time and searching the Internet for organisations that offer these.

NS: And these last two modules, did it have a cost for you?

Magdalena: No, the other two either. When they call from companies and they say it costs something, I don't have money to waste, so I say "we'll see I'm trying to find something I don't have to pay for it. If I can't, I still have one year, in last resort I'll pay". (…) But if I can find them for free … and I did. (Magdalena, 51, Ecuador, Madrid)

In France, as mentioned above, training is longer than in Spain and the UK. This length does not automatically translate into higher cost, given that several fully funded study schemes exist, both for the unemployed through the role of the national employment agency and for those already in employment through the support of state-funded agencies. For instance, Jade benefitted from the support of a state agency in funding her six months training to become a 'Life Assistant':

NS: How long was your training to become Life Assistant?

Jade: I completed a six months training. Six months and for two months it was possible to do internships. I did six months and two more weeks of internship and that was it.

NS: And did you have to pay for that training or the cost was covered by….

Jade: No, it was covered by the Fongécif [state agency managing a fund for individual training leave]. (Jade, 46, Ivory Coast, Paris)

On the whole, in all three countries there exists a trend towards professionalisation, though with different implications for migrant and minority ethnic workers according to the specific policies in place. In the UK, given that training does not translate into professional advancement, care assistant positions do not allow for career progression without a career break for studies which creates a certain entrapment. In Madrid, the professionalisation reform created a market for private training centres and a lot of confusion for workers as to whether they had to pay and which modules were needed. While some had achieved the required training earlier, others had to find their way through the new regulations. Similarly in Paris, workers who were willing to achieve professional advancement needed to know where to find the relevant information and how to file applications. The existence of pre-established administrative pathways towards new positions nonetheless allowed migrant and minority ethnic workers to advance their careers without having to quit their job.

In the following section, I explore participants' aspirations. These are particularly revealing as to their perceptions of social mobility opportunities and the strategies developed accordingly.

8.3   Aspirations: Agency Within Different Opportunity Structures

Non-EU Migrants

This section sheds further light on the meanings attached by participants to their work in older-age care and their projections within and out of care. Tronto highlighted the importance of migrant care workers' aspirations from the perspective of a democratic ethic of care: 'insofar as many of those who currently do this low-paid and low-status caring work are migrant workers, any real solution to the problem of care imbalances within households would also need to consider the needs and aspirations of such global care workers' (Tronto 2013, p. 176). Table 8.3 classifies non-EU migrants' narratives according to a schematic description of the projects they sketched out during the interview. The aspirations of minority ethnic workers are analysed separately in order to account for their different positionality. 'Advancement in care' groups individuals whose objective is to obtain a higher qualification within care, not only but most frequently a nursing degree. In the French case, it also includes individuals who hold one of the three qualifications that qualify them for care work and who intend to complete a second one. The group 'continuity in care' comprises individuals who plan on remaining in their current

Table 8.3 Non-EU migrants' professional aspirations

	Paris	Madrid	London
Advancement in care	15	3	8
Including overseas trained nurses	*1*		*4*
Continuity in care	2	8	2
Out of care	2	0	8
Return	0	8	3
Advancement in care AND out of care	0	1	0
Continuity in care AND/OR return	1	1	0
Advancement in care OR return	0	3	0
Out of care OR return	0	2	0

Source: Own data and elaboration

job, and who do not mention intentions to pursue upward mobility. The label 'out of care' describes those who conceive their professional future as outside the care sector and who thus await an opportunity to change their sector of employment. Under the category 'return' I have grouped all those who spoke of return as a short- or medium-term project that determined their professional future. The four remaining categories are composed of only a few participants each and correspond to the combination of several of the categories described above when the narrative did not clearly prioritise one project over the other.

Participants' aspirations differed greatly from one capital city to the other. At first sight this finding might seem surprising, given the relative homogeneity of the group of participants and their position in the labour market: non-EU migrant care workers in a European capital city employed in privately run care homes. Drawing on elements of the cross-national political economy of care illuminates these differences.

In Paris the overwhelming majority formulated wishes for professional advancement through the acquisition of additional official qualifications in the care sector. Interestingly enough, this occurs in spite of the fact that a majority of workers did not actively choose to enter the care sector, as demonstrated in Chap. 4. Typically, participants were aiming for the next level of professional qualification, either through the 'validation of knowledge acquired through experience' route or through formal education. The 'validation of knowledge acquired through experience' scheme allows workers' professional experience to be taken into account so that the curriculum to be completed is adjusted. The number of hours of formal education is reduced given the experience already acquired, and the completion of the qualification is therefore more easily compatible with full-time employment. Participants in Paris often availed themselves of this possibility. This is, for example, the route chosen by Nabila:

Nabila: For now I'm here, I'm struggling to become a healthcare assistant.
NS: And you want to achieve this through "Validation of Knowledge acquired through Experience (VKE)"?
Nabila: Yes, I'll try to get there through VKE
NS: So it's a certain number of hours you need to validate?
Nabila: Yes, yes, but I have enough hours because I'm in this occupation for more than six years. (Nabila, 40, Senegal, Paris)

Those already in the position of healthcare assistant often envisaged continuing their studies and becoming nurses. Naima, employed as a healthcare assistant, was about to start a nursing degree when I interviewed her:

So I passed my exam and I got it so now I'll start the nursing degree in September, for three years. So I'm proud, I'm happy that's what I wanted. I wanted to do something else because … I think I've done my time in this job. In my occupation as healthcare assistant I've done my time. So I think it's normal to move forward. That's what I like in this profession because we can move forward. I already had managers…. One manager used to be a hospital worker, then she became healthcare assistant, then registered nurse, and then she became a manager…. So it's a trajectory that I admire, that I like, so I hope I can follow this path. (Naima, 32, Tunisia, Paris)

Naima's case is also illustrative of another aspect frequently encountered in the narratives of participants in Paris: the impact of role models. Most participants would refer to colleagues or friends who had already achieved the professional mobility they were envisaging. These colleagues or acquaintances had realised their aspirations and at the same time served as sources of information about gaining access to these opportunities, notably in terms of knowledge of available financing schemes.

Obtaining a higher qualification within the care sector not only implied better pay but could also be part of a project to acquire professional autonomy. It is indeed possible for a nurse to open his or her own practice, becoming by the same token one's own employer. Luc clearly related his project of becoming a nurse to this possibility of gaining professional independence:

NS: And today how do you see your professional future?

Luc: I want to do something else. To become a nurse so that I can open my own practice. I want to be independent and organise my work individually. (Luc, 25, Cameroon, Paris)

Among participants in Madrid, only a minority envisaged obtaining qualifications in the care sector. First, obtaining such a qualification represented a cost because of the time off work that it required and, most importantly, it would not necessarily translate into better professional outcomes, given the limited regulation of the sector. If a care worker had already completed training in geriatric care, studying for a qualification as healthcare assistant would not have an impact on the person's employment situation in residential care (although this person could then apply to work in a hospital). Rather, one-third of participants envisaged remaining in their current occupation for a longer period. Many did not actively choose the sector but organised their lives around this employment and planned on staying in the care sector. This was for instance Soraya's case: she graduated in Law in Morocco but never worked in her profession and had already been working for 18 years as a care assistant in Madrid at the time of the interview:

NS: How do you see your professional future?

Soraya: I want to continue working in this, I want to continue. Hopefully I'll continue caring for older people, I like it, I really enjoy it. And I don't see myself doing something else. (Soraya, 45, Morocco, Madrid)

Beyond the formal qualifications structure, participants in Madrid shared a sense of immobility due to the pervasive and systematic discrimination that effectively left migrants with few illusions as to the possibility of moving up the social ladder, starting from the workplace. Claudia, who had graduated and worked as a psychologist in Peru, explained the situation she observed:

> In my case for instance, my employer knows that I have this documentation, these qualifications, the right training, but they don't give me a job as a senior care worker nevertheless. Because comes first the niece of the manager, she's got a niece working. Through the other manager there's her own niece working, through the previous manager there's a sister-in-law and so it goes. So these jobs they give it to family members. (Claudia, 53, Peru, Madrid)

These workplace power relations and broader social dynamics worked jointly with formal discrimination enshrined in migration policies to produce enduring segmentation at the labour market level and 'sticky floors' for individuals. To wit, participants' narratives in Madrid converged around the idea of return: taken together, the category 'return' and those who mentioned 'return' along with another project represent over half the participants. Return to the home country was thus on the mind of most of those I have interviewed in Madrid. Beronica's story is quite typical in this regard and many participants mentioned the financial goals they had set themselves before leaving:

> My dream is to have my own shop. (…) So I still want to work for a couple of years and see if I can make my dream happen. I would like to do that, to open a business there in my country. I would see that my life wasn't in vain here. So only with making this dream happen I would be satisfied of having worked hard here and of having something mine. A business that I could say: "I'm the manager, the employee, the owner." I would like that, that's what I'm thinking of doing. (Beronica, 38, Ecuador, Madrid)

The fact that most participants in Madrid shared this idea of return contrasts with the small group of participants in London who planned to return to their home country and the absence of participants in this category among those interviewed in Paris. To explain this trend, it is necessary to take into account both the economic and social situation in the country of residence, as well as available prospects in the country of origin. Determinants of return migration are indeed shaped to a great extent by socio-economic opportunities in the home country, and how migrants perceive them (De Haas 2007). It also illustrates how these spaces composed of constraints and opportunities were navigated and how participants' coping strategies relied on their translocational positionality (Anthias 2011). Naomi mentions the situation in Spain and in the home country and the role such factors play in her decision:

> Let's see if I can go back to my country and continue studying there, to do a nursing degree more professional, or something else, social work, I don't know. But I would like to study further and to work there in the field of what I would have studied. Here I haven't studied yet because I couldn't afford it. But that's what I want, study and work in the field I have studied, be it nursing, social work, laboratory, I don't know, something like this. That's what I want in the future. But let's see if that will be possible there, here I couldn't until now but let's see if when I go back I'll have the opportunity to study. (Naomi, 37, Colombia, Madrid)

In London, not surprisingly, over one-third of participants hoped to achieve professional mobility within the sector by becoming nurses, given that half the individuals in this group already held nursing degrees gained in their country of origin. The same proportion of participants envisioned their professional future outside the care sector. The extract below from my interview with Fadila is illustrative of the position in which highly qualified migrants find themselves while working as care assistants, awaiting professional opportunities more in line with their qualifications:

> Actually I don't have high ambitions regarding the care sector because I'm very happy with what I'm doing now but if I get a relevant job related to law or business definitely I will switch. Until I get this opportunity I'm very happy with what I am doing. I don't want to be like a deputy manager or a manager but of course if I get any scope to work in administration in a care home I don't mind I will be happy to do that because it's related to my experience I will be happy but for now it's okay. But I look for scope to enhance my professional career instead of being a care worker. (Fadila, 30, Bangladesh, London)

Conceiving of care as a temporary job was all the more common in London that the majority of participants were either highly skilled in a different sector or felt compelled to take up a job as care assistant. For the group of participants who were on student visas, the limitations that were imposed regarding the number of hours that they could work contributed to create a perception of temporariness. A smaller group was on a post-study work visa and found themselves in the contradictory position of being employed, but not in a job that could secure them the prolongation of their visa. Finally, a small group of participants in London planned on returning to the home country. This project, while emerging much less frequently than among participants in Madrid, does nevertheless illustrate again a conception of return as ensuring an upward mobility that is not foreseeable in the UK. Isabel, similarly to Beronica in Madrid, plans on going back and opening her own business in the Philippines:

NS: How do you envisage your professional future?
Isabel: Actually I'm just waiting for that visa but I think once I've got money I'll just go back home it is better to live there you know. You own your time, you are with your family, you are in your own place. (…)
NS: Why would you like to wait to get your visa?
Isabel: I need to get it so I can work more hours, stay for quite some time and then go. It's not an abrupt plan because my children are just starting going to school I'm glad because my sister is here to help us to support ourselves but that's our long-term plan to just go back home and start a small business there. (Isabel, 37, the Philippines, London)

In the following paragraphs, I focus on minority ethnic workers' aspirations, distinguishing their experiences on the basis of their different positionality and the specific motives that guided their entry into the care sector.

Minority Ethnic Workers in Paris and in London

Amongst minority ethnic workers in Paris and in London, the idea of 'advancement in care' came most to the fore in relation to participants' aspirations. It concerned six out of ten participants in Paris and two out of three participants in London. This is consistent with the motives and trajectories analysed in Chap. 4, in which, in the case of minority ethnic participants in Paris, nine out of ten articulated a professional project in the care sector. Laetitia in Paris and Mary in London both planned on pursuing a career within care. Yet, the interviews with them and several other participants in similar situations revealed some differences as compared to non-EU migrants who were also aspiring to advance their careers in the care sector. The tone of the interview revealed a higher sense of confidence in the future as to the possibility of actually pursuing their plans. The 'institutional insecurity' (Anderson 2010) so prevalent in non-EU participants' narratives seemed less present in the perceptions of young minority ethnic care workers like Laetitia and Mary.

NS: How do you see your professional future?
Laetitia: I won't lie to you, I aim at becoming a nurse, and I'll be a nurse, no matter how long it takes, but I'll become one. After that I aim at becoming a manager and I stop there. (Laetitia 29, Guadeloupe, Paris)

> If it happens and if there is a big opportunity for me in care then I would probably stick on but I'm studying to be a social worker which has something to do with care but it's not care so my future is likely linked to care but just a different sector of care, so probably to be a professional or something like that a social worker either that or a radiologist. (Mary, 20, Black UK, London)

Not all in this group, however, were satisfied with their employment. Some lamented the discrimination they faced or envisaged moving to a different place altogether. Several participants in Paris planned to move back to Guadeloupe or Martinique to continue working there or to retire, while Marc planned on starting from scratch in a different country to escape the discrimination he experienced in the French labour market where he was unable to work in accordance with his qualifications:

Marc: I was saving, because I see the hardship of the work, I see my colleagues working ... I tell to myself.... When I was 18 I could continue but now with 37 years I don't want anymore. That's why, I have my qualification in real estate management, it will be useful in the future.

NS: And now how do you see your professional future?

Marc: I would like to leave in two years. To go to Africa and start out a business, in real estate. (Marc, 37, Reunion Island, Paris)

Marc's intention to create a business in an East-African country was not only motivated by financial gains. He was also tired of the job and hoped for social upward mobility with this planned international move. A man in a feminised sector, Marc insisted on his expertise in a manner that revealed the gendered dimension of his aspirations.

8.4   Conclusion

The limited positive implications of acquiring the citizenship of the country of residence in terms of socio-economic opportunities demonstrate the long-term effects of migration policies, in other words the underpinning temporal borders (Mezzadra and Neilson 2013) and their articulation with broader racialisation processes that go beyond formal lines of division enacted by these policies. While obtaining documentation helps to limit the extent of non-EU workers' exploitation, gaining citizenship is not sufficient to substantially improve their labour market opportunities.

Against this background, looking into care workers' professional perspectives and the role of training highlighted decisive differences between the three capitals. The comparative approach demonstrated that the regulation of the care sector through professionalisation fosters better employment opportunities when accompanied by accessible financing schemes and clear career paths. The analysis of participants' narratives and a schematic classification of their projects revealed crucial differences in how care workers thought of their professional future in London, Paris and Madrid. These aspirations reflect a combination of objective and subjective labour market opportunities and perceptions. The professionalisation of the care occupation in France, and established paths for advancement, impacted on workers' professional plans in that it encouraged them to think of a career within care, even when they had not positively chosen to enter the care sector in the first place. In Madrid, the fact that fewer participants had specific qualifications than in London or Paris might explain why one-third of participants envisaged remaining in their current position. Moreover, employment in residential care in Madrid corresponds to a relatively privileged position in comparison with live-in caring arrangements and informal jobs. The projections of half the participants to return to their home country hint potentially at a temporary form of migration. In London, the existing mismatch of skills explains the high proportion of those envisaging professional mobility within or outside the sector.

The penultimate chapter in this book proposes to take a step back and turn to racialised care workers' own caring arrangements with the view of thinking about social reproduction in broader terms.

9

Social Reproduction and Care Ethics

NS: How do you manage childcare?

Sonia: When I'm working my husband looks after my child and when he is working I'm the one looking after her.

NS: What does your husband do?

Sonia: He works for the train company. (Sonia, 33, Mauritius, London)

To care for their daughter, Sonia and her partner organised their lives around opposite working shifts so that one of them is always available to look after their child. Splitting the working schedules in this manner was common for participants working in the care sector, particularly in London, to respond to their own care responsibilities and needs against the background of a privatised and expensive childcare regime. In this chapter I examine how racialised care workers in London, Paris and Madrid organised and attended to their own needs in terms of reproductive labour. I approach this theme through the lens of social reproduction, building upon Laslett and Brenner's definition whereby social reproduction entails:

the activities and attitudes, behaviors and emotions, responsibilities and relationships directly involved in the maintenance of life on a daily basis, and intergenerationally. (…) Social reproduction can thus be seen to include various kinds of work—mental, manual, and emotional—aimed at providing the historically and socially, as well as biologically, defined care necessary to maintain existing life and to reproduce the next generation. (Laslett and Brenner 1989, pp. 382–383)

In the context of the generalisation of the bourgeois model of the family first, and that of the double-income family in the second half of the twentieth century, time available to care for children and older persons within the family has progressively been squeezed. In Nancy Fraser's words, the regime of globalising financialised capitalism 'promotes state and corporate disinvestment from social welfare, while recruiting women into the paid workforce—externalising care work onto families and communities while diminishing their capacity to perform it' (2016, p. 112). The crisis of care that stems from this tension is addressed in the current political economy of the UK, France and Spain through commodification and marketisation of older-age care provision. In this configuration, care-related work remains devalued while some of the implications of its marketisation reveal care's uneasy submission to the logics of the market. As demonstrated in Chaps. 5 and 6, processes of marketisation produce employment precariousness and exacerbate work precariousness that characterises older-age care. As spending time is precisely what creates the care relationship, the marketisation of care provision enters into tension with the usual means for cost reductions that markets facilitate such as labour cost cuts and economies of scale, a point made by feminist political economy as well as care ethicists (Federici 2012; Tronto 2013). From ready meals to private care homes, social reproduction became a new site for capital accumulation. Migration and gender play a key role in this process as the racialisation of a feminised workforce is part and parcel of the marketisation and corporatisation of older-age care in Europe.

In the first section of the chapter, I engage with social reproduction theory from the specific angle of its intertwinement with migration regimes and processes of racialisation. I build in particular on social reproduction feminism to outline the broader political economy of what I refer to as the double outsourcing of social reproduction. In the second section of the chapter, I present a schematic classification and analysis of participants' care arrangements towards their children and/or parents. The section compares the different configurations of care arrangements across the three capitals and accounts for some of the differences observed against the background of a policy environment not conducive to the recognition of participants' own care needs. The unequal division of these care activities within the household is highlighted, exacerbating the gendered inequalities lived through the labour market. Finally, in the third section, I sketch out how an approach in terms of care ethics suggests a way forward for thinking and organising society's social reproduction on fairer terms in the spirit of a feminist democratic ethic of care. In these developments, I selectively focus on one point of entry that is however not exhaustive of the interplay between care ethics and social reproduction: citizenship.

9.1 The Double Outsourcing of Social Reproduction

Social Reproduction Feminism: The Political Economy of Caring Arrangements

As a matter of fact, it is not through a valorisation of household activities—as advocated by the Wages for Housework campaign in the 1970s for instance (Federici 2012)—that domestic work was included in the 'productive sphere', but through its partial marketisation (Kofman and Raghuram 2015) and increasing corporatisation (Farris and Marchetti 2017). This marketisation, as noted above, constitutes the neoliberal answer to the 'care deficit' and reflects the transformation of the role of the state under neoliberalism. David Harvey analyses how neoliberalism fosters the externalisation of the cost of social reproduction on a global scale:

Under conditions of social democracy, however, political movements drove capital to internalize some of the costs either directly (through pension, insurance and health care provision in wage contracts) or indirectly (through taxation on capital to support the state provision of services via a welfare state). Part of the neoliberal political programme and ethos in recent times has been to externalise as much as possible the costs of social reproduction on to the populace at large in order to raise the profit rate for capital by reducing its tax burden. (2014, pp. 189–190)

In a feminist-Marxist perspective, Susan Ferguson elaborates this argument further and integrates an intersectional dimension in her analysis. The core of her approach lies in the conversation she develops between a political economy analysis in terms of social reproduction and the intersectional attention to intertwining processes of oppression, what she refers to as social reproduction feminism:

In demonstrating that state, household and market are integrally linked (in contradictory but necessary ways) in the process of reproducing the capitalist social formation as a whole, social-reproduction feminism is a powerful analytic framework that avoids the difficulties of an additive account. (2016, p. 50)

The strength of Susan Ferguson's approach is that it theorises the relation between productive and reproductive labour while integrating gender and racialisation, drawing on intersectionality, in the core of the theory. Much of her demonstration revolves around the need for conducting a process-centred intersectional analysis (rather than one centred on a given social location) of social relations as embedded in capitalism. Her argument emphasises the shortcomings of intersectionality if the latter remains disconnected from the analysis of 'a unified (capitalist) whole, but one that is also differentiated and contradictory' (2016, p. 47). The point being that social theory needs to integrate capitalist power relations and social processes in order to account for the complexity of lived experiences against the background of intersectional oppressions (Ferguson 2008, 2016). Admittedly, class tends to be under-theorised within intersectionality, notably in relation to gendered migrations (Kofman and Raghuram 2015, p. 163). With social reproduction feminism, the analysis of class is revitalised in that the relation between reproductive and productive labour is soundly theorised. The following section elaborates on the articulation between social reproduction and migration.

Conceptualising the Social Reproduction/Migration Nexus

If ironically the commodification and marketisation of certain forms of housework inserts it into the productive sphere, it also misses the point brought to the fore by both feminist moral philosophy and feminist political economy as both strands advocate a revalorisation of housework and care, that is, a recognition of the very activities that sustain life in opposition to the sexist and racist hierarchies that the market enacts (Tronto 2013; Perez Orozco 2014). The restructuring of social reproduction led indeed to a revisited international division of reproductive work in order to keep labour costs low, rather than to significant changes in gender roles: 'marginal status in immigration regimes reflect an undervaluing of female embodied labour whilst ensuring social reproduction at the cheapest for the receiving society' (Kofman and Raghuram 2015, p. 149). This however constitutes a 'private solution to a public problem' as phrased by Arlie Hochschild, who highlights the historic continuity of this flow from the Global South to the Global North: 'The notion of extracting resources from the Third World in order to enrich the First World is hardly new. It harks back to imperialism in its most literal form: the 19th century extraction of gold, ivory and rubber from the Third World. (…) Today as love and care become the "new gold", the female part of the story has grown in prominence' (2003, p. 194). As identified by the literature on 'global care chains' (Hochschild 2000; Parreñas 2000), migrant workers fulfil a specific role within global social reproduction processes, and their migration trajectories tend to follow postcolonial paths (Marchetti 2014). Their status as non-citizens facilitates the externalisation of costs attached to social reproduction, given that dominant discourses and legislation define migrants' rights in relation to their employment status and alleged economic utility (see Chaps. 3 and 4). This utilitarian approach underpins the disconnect between one's labour and one's social reproduction; as argued by Anderson 'the migrant worker is framed by immigration legislation as a unit of labour, without connection to family or friends, a unit whose production costs (food, education, shelter) were met elsewhere, and whose reproduction costs are of no concern to employer or state' (Anderson 2000, p. 108). The fact that these costs are of 'no concern' to both the employer and the state is produced by migration and employment policies: 'Specific entitlements, such as the right to bring in family members, the right to settlement and citizenship and access to welfare, are attached to each of these categories of skills and temporality and have implications for the conditions of social reproduction in receiving and sending countries' (Kofman and Raghuram 2015, p. 154). By being employed to sustain the social reproduction of families—and thus that of societies—in the Global North, migrant workers find themselves at the crossroads of double outsourcing as European migration regimes tend increasingly to deny workers' own caring responsibilities and needs with restrictions on family reunification and precarious temporary work permits. Within a neoliberal political economy, these trends are exacerbated in that migrants are on the frontline of welfare state retrenchments (Lonergan 2015). However, if migrant workers came to epitomise these dynamics, minority ethnic workers are also affected, as illustrated by their over-representation in the sector and by former state and corporate policies of overseas recruitment in the healthcare sector. The following section looks empirically at how migrant and racialised care workers organise their lives around the need to care for their own children and parents.

9.2   Migrant Care Workers' Own Caring Arrangements

Fragile Arrangements of Care

Table 9.1 presents a schematic classification of care workers' own caring arrangements. Their narratives reveal more complex situations than these labels can reflect and often several forms of care arrangements were combined. This table provides nevertheless a cross-national overview of

Table 9.1 Categorisation of participants' caring arrangements

	London	Paris	Madrid
No caring responsibility	10	15	9
Opposite shifts	9	3	1
Caring responsibilities back home (children or parents)	3	0	8
Paid private care	0	2	1
Public nursery and school hours cover most of working hours	0	5	3
Support from other family members or neighbours	0	4	4
Caring responsibility left mostly to partner	0	0	1
NA	1	1	0

Source: Own data and elaboration

certain trends based upon the form of care provision participants empha-sised most to account for how they looked after their children or parents. Under 'opposite shifts' are grouped those parents who worked different hours in order to be able to look after their children, a practice possible in the context of shift work in place in the older-age care sector. Participants in the third group have transnational caring responsibilities towards children, parents or extended family to whom they send remit-tances. It does not mean that participants in other groups do not have transnational caring responsibilities, but this third category captures those participants for whom this constitutes their main caring responsi-bility (outside of employment). Some parents recruited child-minders (fourth category); others relied mostly on public nurseries and school hours when these could cover most of their working hours (fifth category). At times, some additional support was needed from a relative or a child-minder to make it work, but on the whole participants in this group considered that these facilities provided an essential part of the childcare they needed. In the narratives of participants in the second-to-last group, it is the time that family, friends and neighbours were able to dedicate to childcare that was most crucial in making paid employment possible for participants. The last category covers situations in which caring responsi-bilities are mostly dealt with by the partner of the respondent.

On the whole, a significant share of workers did not have direct caring responsibilities: half of the participants in Paris, a little less than half in London and a third in Madrid. Those who did have caring responsibilities organised their lives around their work shifts. In this regard, they were confronted with different opportunity structures according to, on the one hand, the working patterns prevalent in the sector, as these varied between the cities, and, on the other, to the characteristics of the welfare state and its childcare regime (e.g. in relation to the availability of public nurseries or the extent of school hours). The absence of public nurseries accessible at reduced cost in London explains why this was not an option for participants working in the London Region. The data in Table 9.1 reflect furthermore the demographic characteristics of participants themselves; for example, the average age of participants was higher in Paris and in Madrid (41 and 42 respectively vs. 37 amongst participants in London) where some of them had grown-up children for whom they no longer needed to provide face-to-face or financial care. The following paragraphs analyse the different types of caring arrangements while being attentive to their implications in terms of work-life balance (or the absence of it).

In London, all participants with caring responsibilities in their place of residence (as opposed to transnational responsibilities) worked opposite shifts to their partners in order to be able to look after their children. Splitting their schedules appeared to be the only possibility to respond to their care responsibilities while the rest of the participants either had transnational caring responsibilities, that is, children back home, or did not have such responsibilities. The experiences of this group of participants thus shed light on the daily challenges faced by many migrant and minority ethnic care workers in London. Working opposite shifts concerned a smaller share of participants in Paris and in Madrid, but some did resort to this as well. In the first quote, Jade for instance worked opposite shifts to her husband, a nurse by profession.

NS: How do you organise yourself?
Jade: I can say that it's okay. Because with my husband we work different hours. Because he's also in this sector, we have different hours. (Jade, 46, Ivory Coast, Paris)

One of the implications for the lives of these workers was that working opposite shifts did not allow for family time and the schedule was carefully studied to ensure that children could always be looked after by one of the partners at all times. This type of arrangement was often regarded as a favour by the employer to the benefit of the worker, especially when both parents worked in the same care home, given that private childcare was unaffordable. However, it affected care workers' 'work-life' balance because of the fatigue that results from such a strained daily life. Alma, who was employed in London, lamented:

> My eldest goes to school by herself because she's already in year seven, so if I'm working and my husband is here, works here, works night I have to bring my daughter here and he brings her to school. But when I'm not working it's fine I can be the one to drop her to school. But if we're both working that's the only … and also you know when I'm tired from work I don't have time to read with them, to teach them and it's frustrating for me as well. (Alma, 41, the Philippines, London)

It appeared that among the different forms of care that emerged from the narratives, working opposite shifts brought the role of the partner most to the fore. The role of the partner was otherwise only mentioned as additional support to another primary arrangement relying on other family members or school hours. Most participants were women and their family lives were as gendered as their working lives: no female participant relied on the partner for most of childcare; only male participants did so. Aimée, employed in Paris, accounted for the role of her husband as a form of additional support:

NS: Do you encounter difficulties to combine childcare with your working hours?

Aimée: Their dad works in the town hall of my city, so he's nearby. If there's a problem he is the one to be called. Except if it's more serious and that the children call me, then I drop everything and I go. (Aimée, 44, Guinea, Paris)

Many women I have met described the double/triple shifts required of them to be able to attend to their children and their paid employment. Amandine, a mother of a four-year-old and a nine-year-old, talked about 'another day'. In the second quote, Claudia's words show how she managed work and caring responsibilities over time by switching from one shift to another until she opted for night shifts in order to do housework and care for the children during the day:

Once I get home, I need to put on the hat of the mum. And I need to 'take off' the fact that I'm tired, and I need to look after the children. It's really, it's another ... it's another day that starts after that let's say. (Amandine, 32, Ivory Coast, Paris)

I had my mother who helped me, she used to help me a lot, at home and everything. She passed away already. And I switched to the afternoon shift, because the course was in the mornings. It was school hours from 8:00 am to 2:00 pm, like going to college, being there every day. So I obtained that and I stayed in the afternoon shift. But when my mum fell ill I said "I'll switch to night shift". Because in the mornings I had house-work to do and in the afternoons things to do with the children. So I couldn't stop working either, I started night shifts. (Claudia, 53, Peru, Madrid)

For another group of participants, their primary caring responsibilities were transnational. Victoria, for instance, was supporting her children in Ecuador until she could bring them to Madrid, while Analyn's children stayed in the Philippines and she needed to support them as well as her grandchildren:

Yes, while my children were there I was sending money to their father, to my sisters, because my son stayed with my sister and my daughters stayed with their father. So I was sending money from here so that they continue supporting them, that they continue their education because they stayed at school. Until I brought them here. (Victoria, 54, Ecuador, Madrid)

Analyn: I send every month, my children, my grandchildren. I support them every month. Because the money there is not enough to support themselves and they are still studying.

NS: How old are your children?

Analyn: My elder is 24 still studying, the other one is 23, he graduated already as a nurse and they have kids and still looking for a job it's difficult to get a job there that's why I am supporting them even graduated in the Philippines it's very hard to get the job even when they have a degree. (Analyn, 50, the Philippines, London)

To one-third of participants in Madrid, their caring responsibilities were primarily transnational as they were sending remittances to children and parents and needed to organise the care provided for their dependents back home. These responsibilities exerted financial pressure upon workers; many undertook multiple jobs to sustain themselves and their dependents. Understanding the lived experience of care labour cannot neglect the question of who assumes the cost of social reproduction for those employed as care workers given that the externalisation of these costs contributes to the fragility of their position in the labour market. Parreñas' study of Filipina care workers in Rome and Los Angeles (2000) demonstrated how the emigration of women from the Philippines required other women, most frequently relatives or internal migrants, to take up the reproductive labour that emigrants were not able to fulfil anymore, what she called the international division of reproductive labour. Migrant care workers experienced in this perspective a 'conflicting class mobility' (ibid., p. 574) as they were confronted with processes of deskilling and social marginalisation in the country of destination (see Chap. 4 in this book) but simultaneously experienced an upward social mobility as regards their community of origin on the basis of the financial capital acquired through migration, means that were often sufficient to employ domestic and care workers for the reproductive labour of their own households. The global care chains literature uncovered the globalisation of care provision (Hochschild 2000; Parreñas 2000, 2012). The marketisation of older-age care in the 'global North' further shapes this trend. With a focus on the 'double outsourcing' of social reproduction in the country of destination, the international dimension of the division of reproductive labour remains here analytically in the background though I acknowledge the importance of these transnational interdependencies. The selective focus on the conditions for racialised care workers' reproductive labour illuminates the workings of several fields of policy, namely migration, care and employment in the capital cities studied here.

Migration regimes, notably through the tightening of family reunification possibilities (Kofman 2008), play a major role, as discussed in Chap. 3. From the standpoint of paid care, work-related immigration rules such as the £18,600 minimum income threshold for family reunification in the UK have deeply gendered consequences for migrant workers. A devalued and deskilled sector, older-age care is characterised by low earnings as analysed in Chap. 5. Female migrant care workers are thus disproportionately affected by this legislation. Amal, for example, who came to the UK from Somalia ten years ago, and was pregnant at the time of the interview, was unable to support her Kenyan husband for him to join her in the UK due to the financial conditions imposed by immigration policies:

> My husband isn't here, he is in Kenya. (…) To be honest, I try to apply for him because I had my savings as well so I tried to apply … but the rules now … you have to have £18,600 and my job doesn't have that money…. So…. (Amal, 24, Somalia, London)

The difficulties Amal was confronted with represent a case in point of how gendered inequalities are enacted and widened by migration policies as a result of precarious employment in older-age care. The gendered devaluation of care labour specifically, and the biased conceptualisation of production as detached from reproduction more broadly, underpin such utilitarian migration policies that become the vehicles of the reproduction of gendered inequalities.

Moving on to the fourth category in Table 9.1, for a minority of participants public nurseries and schools accounted for the childcare needed, often in combination with some support from other children or the partner, in the form of bringing children to school or picking them up. These situations were not mentioned by participants in London (since they relied on opposite shifts as analysed above) but concerned a couple of parents in Paris and in Madrid. This was for instance the case for Nabila, who had five children:

NS: The opening hours of the nursery and the school are they compatible with your job?

Nabila: No, school hours no, because I start at 8:30 am, I can't drop her off at 8:30, so it's my husband who drops her off and it's my daughter who picks her up at 6:00 pm. (Nabila, 40, Senegal, Paris)

Of similar importance was the support that family members or other acquaintances could provide. In this regard, minority ethnic workers could rely more extensively on their families and in-laws, while migrant workers' options were more limited, all the more that the family members who resided nearby or with them were often themselves spending many hours at work. Amélie, who came from the Ivory Coast, relied for instance on her neighbour to pick up her son from school.

NS: You mentioned earlier your child, was it difficult for you to reconcile childcare and your working hours?

Amélie: It has been difficult, very difficult even, but luckily I have a neighbour who is great, she picked him up in the evening and sometimes when I came he had already eaten, he had taken his shower and I would find him asleep on the couch, it has been very difficult. (Amélie, 43, Ivory Coast, Paris)

Those who would have needed family or friends' support for childcare but could not access it resorted to private paid care in Paris and in Madrid. When the responsibility of childcare was on one person only (amongst participants this situation concerned only women), recruiting a child-minder became unavoidable, as in the case of Camille in Paris or Rebecca in Madrid:

NS: Do you have any difficulty in organising your time?

Camille: Many difficulties, many difficulties, being alone, and responsible for a child, with our working hours, especially working hours that we have here, it's very difficult. Very very difficult. One day, the woman who looked after her [the daughter], her nanny, she travelled, I had to cancel all of my temping jobs because I couldn't find anyone to look after her. (…) So part of the salary goes into childcare. (Camille, 45, Cameroon, Paris)

My children grew up mainly in the hands of third persons, because I paid these persons so that they look after my daughter, after my son. Why?

Because I didn't have time, because I had to come to work and if I didn't work I didn't earn money. (Rebecca, 46, Peru, Madrid)

The question of the distribution of care responsibilities in society at large can be posed in terms of work-life balance. The material conditions for participants' reproductive labour reveal the double outsourcing of social reproduction that characterises the political economy of care in the three capital cities. Their daily experiences reveal that the current relation between paid employment and reproductive labour is heavily permeated by the care-capital tension. The care ethics paradigm questions the centrality of paid work and if such a conceptual revolution might seem distant to the daily experiences of migrant and minority ethnic care workers, sketching out new horizons contributes to constructing the conditions for such social change to take place:

If work-life balance is actually to mean balance, then instead of paid work being the starting point and the question being how, as a society we are to fit our life around our paid work, we put it the other way round and ask: how do we fit our work around our life? (Williams 2004, p. 77)

This ambition supposes a fundamental redefinition of gender roles. Amongst the situations described above, men's narratives are to be found primarily under the label 'opposite shifts' highlighting their absence from the daily tasks of childcare when the care configuration did not rely on opposite working shifts. The following section focuses on how migrant and minority ethnic men accounted for their caring responsibilities.

Male Care Workers and Caring Responsibilities at Home

Most participants were women and patterns for childcare arrangements were strongly gendered. While this unequal distribution of reproductive labour exacerbated the experience of precariousness for migrant and minority ethnic women, male care workers' discourses illustrated that, far from being taken for granted, these inequalities were in their perception due to employment precariousness in the sector. I pointed out earlier that the role of male partners in this matter came most to the fore when the partners were working opposite shifts. These cases were mirrored in the narratives of several male participants, as in the case of Abdel, who came from Morocco and worked in Madrid:

NS: How did you combine work and family life?

Abdel: I reconcile both, in the morning I take care of the girls, I bring them to school, I prepare the food, my wife works in the morning, she has a couple of hours in the morning, I look after them in the morning and I bring them to school, then I pick them up, she doesn't work afternoons, so it's her turn to look after the girls and I come here to work. So one is there in the morning and the other in the afternoon, so there are no problems. (Abdel, 48, Morocco, Madrid)

A significant difference in this narrative, as compared to the stories told in London, is that 'opposite shifts' means here mornings and afternoons, while for workers in London it implied day and night shifts, as most of them were working so-called long days, often from eight to eight. When not working opposite shifts, experiences shared by male workers in this study confirmed their role as 'secondary support' that women's narratives hinted at. Their discourses revealed, however, that, far from accepting this situation, they lamented the unsocial working hours of the care sector and the absence of work-life balance. David, who worked in London, complained about not seeing his daughter, and Antonio, who worked in Madrid, described how his schedule left him little time to see his children:

But it's sometimes not easy, the attention will become less because the working patterns and the hours, those two things, the hours and the working patterns. (…) To eat your own food, after midnight, so what about family? You want to know your child, what he is doing. (David, 40, Uganda, London)

Due to my job, I hardly have time to look after them, except on the days I have off. For example when I'm off in the morning, but they are at school and when they come back from school I go to work. And when I come at night they are already asleep because they have to go to school. So it means I see them when I'm off in the afternoon or on weekends. (Antonio, 39, Cuba, Madrid)

The invisibilisation of the cost of social reproduction, relegating it to the 'private sphere', affects both women and men, albeit differently. The gender regime accounts for the unequal distribution of care responsibilities whereby women work several shifts, combining paid employment, at times multiple jobs, with most of house-related work. Men play a secondary role and do not bear primary responsibility for childcare, except when caring arrangements are equally distributed due to opposite work schedules. Analysing these inequalities through the lens of the unequal distribution of care responsibilities (Tronto 2013), as suggested by feminist moral philosophy, highlights the non-viability of time allocation between the so-called productive and reproductive spheres. Beyond the emphasis on gendered inequalities in the distribution of reproductive labour, for-profit older-age care provision being a site of capital accumulation, the analysis needs to interrogate the broader conditions under which social reproduction activities are carried out. In the following section, I relate the insights presented in this chapter to the question of care workers' voices within a democratic polity, examining what is being foreclosed by the exclusion of non-citizen care workers from political representation and how their inclusion would help to envisage alternative understandings of the place of care and thus of processes of social reproduction.

9.3   Beyond Better Conditions: Achieving Better Distribution Through Louder Voices

The unequal distribution of care responsibilities is but one of the symptoms of the crisis of care, which Nancy Fraser analyses as resulting from a structural capital-care contradiction, not unique to neoliberalism, but

heightened by financialised capitalism (Fraser 2016). Feminist econo-
mists have long pointed out the biased understanding of production that
fails to theorise reproduction and the relation between the two. Some
have further argued that the neoliberal version of capitalist accumulation
is particularly at odds with ensuring life sustainability (Perez Orozco
2014). Because of this fundamental tension, the critique of the marginalisation of care activities cannot limit itself to the ambition of improving
material conditions for care. Instead, uncovering the workings of the
exploitative relations that produce such conditions bears the promise of
achieving more just social relations. Drawing on care ethics I sketch out
in the following paragraphs empirical and theoretical paths to rethink the
distribution of care responsibilities within society.

In the current political economy, neoliberal political participation
relies on a 'market-oriented model of citizenship' (Bakker 2003, p. 66) or
'neoliberal model of citizenship' (Lonergan 2015). This model of citizenship defines, under current Western political economy, one's belonging
and, consequently, one's voice within society. In line with a market-
oriented definition of individuals' position within society, utilitarian
migration policies grant rights in relation to migrants' alleged economic
utility as explored in Chaps. 3 and 4. The care ethics literature, relying on
an alternative relational ontology, contains the possibility for a different
understanding of citizenship, one that acknowledges interdependency
beyond the market. Tronto exposes the ways in which neoliberalism, as a
political project, is fundamentally at odds with the idea of a 'caring
democracy'. The marginalisation of care activities, and consequently also
of those who are assigned to carry them out, is produced by the gendered
understanding of production and of citizenship, both reflecting what
'matters' according to the dominant hierarchies of values. An approach in
terms of care ethics illuminates the political struggle necessary for the
reduction of care workers' marginalisation starting with the political consideration of their voices.

Not only is the current political economy of care most distant from the
care ethics perspective, the double outsourcing of reproductive work to a
gendered and racialised workforce covers up the capital-care contradictions (Fraser 2016) in that workers' voices are easily discarded in the current configuration of power. Their exclusion from the polity silences their

political voices and 'resolves', on the surface, the fundamental conflict between capitalism and life sustainability (Perez Orozco 2014). The marginalisation of those who are in charge of most of care provision thus facilitates the reproduction of exploitative social relations. The 'feminist democratic ethic of care' (Tronto 2013) paradigm offers a theoretical space within which these inequalities are politicised and translated into a fundamental question of social justice. I argue in this regard that for such a 'feminist democratic ethic of care' to acquire transformative potential, it is necessary to link back the 'feminist voice', originally identified by Gilligan (1982/2003), with the empirical study of care work. Bringing care workers' voices to the centre of the democratic debate about the place of care in society bears the potential of shifting current understandings of care and achieving better conditions for society's social reproduction.

A way to start challenging the current political economy of care is thus to acknowledge the centrality of care workers' experiences and voices so as to work towards making these contradictions apparent. This task supposes fostering care workers' participation in the polity on democratic grounds and consequently rethinking liberal understandings of citizenship. A few care ethicists have engaged with this debate, notably Selma Sevenhuijsen, who identified the need for 'locating the ethics of care within notions of citizenship, if it is to acquire a significant political meaning' (1998, p. 15). Citizenship, as the main vehicle of legitimate belonging and participation, needs to be thought through from the perspective of a relational ontology, and consequently interdependency and care, to achieve fairer social relations based on equality of participation.

9.4   Conclusion

This chapter demonstrated how racialised care workers' own reproductive work is endangered by a combination of migration, social care and employment policies within neoliberal polities. Building on social reproduction theory and in particular on social reproduction feminism, I explored what participants' own caring responsibilities and arrangements revealed as to broader processes of social reproduction in a cross-national perspective. Between a third and half of participants across the three cities were not providing care to children or parents while they were providing care to elderly persons in one of these European capitals, revealing migrant workers' fragile position as 'units of labour' (Anderson 2010). Among those who had such caring responsibilities, both women and men deplored the lack of a work-life balance, yet women's experiences of care responsibilities at home remained highly gendered. The role of the men was most visible within care arrangements that involved working opposite shifts, a quite common labour pattern, that did not however allow for family life. The double outsourcing of social reproduction, which translates into a highly unequal distribution of care responsibilities and precarious employment conditions for those employed to provide care, is to be observed across these capital cities and constitutes a prevalent feature of the current political economy of older-age care. The challenges faced by racialised care workers to respond to their own care responsibilities across the three contexts are symptomatic of the social implications of policies that deny the existence of such needs, most clearly for migrant workers. In the final section of the chapter I explored how the theoretical devices developed by care ethicists contribute to shape alternatives to the highly unequal distribution of care labour. Other chapters have argued across different themes for a valorisation of care work building on the ethic of care that emerged from care workers' discourses. I do not advocate for a blindly egalitarian distribution of care responsibilities as a burden to be fairly shared. Rather, I argue that only a renewed understanding of care and a genuine consideration of care activities as important and significant to life sustainability can achieve fairer social relations and patterns of social reproduction. Drawing on the work of care ethicists, this chapter emphasised that care workers' voices need to be heard and considered within democratic processes for meaningful social change to take place. The marginalisation of racialised care workers, and their exclusion from the polity in the case of migrant workers, forecloses such possibility and ensures that the care-capital contradiction remains silenced. Achieving better distribution of reproductive labour and sustainable social reproduction requires no less than rethinking the notion of citizenship and redefining belonging to the polity.

10

Conclusion

The introduction to this book opens with Fouzia's words: 'What I do, it's not little, it's really something.' I hope that the different chapters have illustrated and demonstrated the power of this statement, in spite of its apparent simplicity. Throughout the chapters, I have attempted to convey how the narrated experiences of participants sustained the theoretical reflections in productive ways, with the theory being voiced by participants and not only introduced by the analysis. Drawing on a gendered political economy of care, I explored racialised care workers' trajectories and experiences, from entering the older-age care sector to several dimensions of their daily labour to their aspirations and projections for the future. Their discourses led me to engage with care ethics and the two approaches enriched the proposed understanding of care workers' experiences on the one hand and of the place of care in contemporary European societies on the other.

If care workers' voices are generally not listened to and remain unheard, this is not because they do not speak as this book has illustrated. Rather, not many are around to listen and not those in positions of power. The analytical tools of a gendered political economy reveal the processes that produce this marginalisation and care ethics indicate the inflection points

© The Author(s) 2019
N. Sahraoui, *Racialised Workers and European Older-Age Care*, Thinking Gender in Transnational Times, https://doi.org/10.1007/978-3-030-14397-8_10

potentially leading to social change. I therefore see these two perspectives as highly complementary for transformative politics. In these concluding remarks, I do not go back to the arguments developed in the individual chapters but draw on the presented insights across topics and fieldwork sites. I first outline particular themes whereby the care ethics paradigm produces alternative understandings for a political economy of care. I then turn to some specific insights that empirical research on care labour offers to thinking about the ethics of care. Linking back to the voices expressing an ethic of care leads to revisit contested themes within feminist moral philosophy. Finally, I conclude this pendular movement from care labour to care ethics and back with a few reflections on the potential of care ethics as a militant commitment. The very last section describes a grassroot initiative that translates such feminist ethics into local and transnational activism, providing a rare but powerful example of organised voices of care ethics within society.

10.1   Bringing Care Ethics to a Gendered Political Economy: Sketching Out Potentialities

By no means are the themes explored here exhaustive of what a conversation between care ethics and political economy can produce. I go back here to two major themes developed in this book across several chapters: that of precarious employment and work and that of the distribution of care responsibilities. This section illustrates how the philosophical tenets of care ethics feed into alternative understandings of these questions with major social and political implications.

Starting with a relational ontology as put forward by care ethics, the implications of the very precariousness of life become apparent. From there, I formulated a critique of classical conceptualisations of precarious employment and work and suggested approaches that include not only the meanings attached to the lived experience of precariousness but also the ambiguity of this precariousness in the context of care. While precarious employment conditions produce material deprivation, a qualitative understanding of the concept of precarious employment is necessary to effectively challenge such material marginalisation. Attention to the content of care labour further questions the contrasted meanings of precariousness. Moving away from the dominant figure of the autonomous individual and emphasising human existence as inscribed into a net of relationships sheds a different light on care labour and work altogether. I have argued in this book that older-age care provision, as currently organised in the private residential sector, obscures the relational dimension of care. Such biased understanding of care fosters a daily precariousness in the labour experiences of racialised care workers. At the same time, care workers' confrontation with the very precariousness of life—while it does not alleviate the socially organised vulnerabilities of care employment and work—strengthens the conviction of doing something that matters. It is in this latter sense that acknowledging a shared ontological precariousness entails a potential for empowerment.

Another theme that runs through the different chapters concerns the (re)distribution of caring responsibilities. Of topical importance to a political economy of care, the question of the organisation of care-related activities acquires additional depth when informed by care ethics. The two approaches are here complementary in that the analysis of intersecting regimes produces a gendered critique calling for social change. Yet, for fairer social relations to emerge a direction of flight needs to be defined and the alternative moral philosophy of care ethics offers sound tools to think about policies and institutions that would work towards a redistribution of care responsibilities within society. A gendered political economy of older-age care reveals the conflicting interests that lie ahead of such transformative politics, the paradigm shift operated by care ethics responds however to this challenge with the possibility of an alternative organisation of labour, work and production at large. The place of care in society cannot be improved without such fundamental transformations. The invisibilisation of care has sustained the dominant neoliberal capitalist economy and its displacement can only shake the established equilibrium. The main tenets of care ethics offer in this regard a renewed understanding of social justice. Given that the current organisation of older-age care provision in Europe and North America is particularly distant from a feminist democratic ethic of care (Tronto 2013), paths towards acknowledgement and recognition need to be carved out. There are potentially many points of entry for this enterprise and I have identified several ones through these chapters. For instance, a profession-alisation informed by care ethics will avoid the gendered bias most training programmes entrench, contributing to reproduce the devaluation of central aspects of care labour. Professionalisation under current terms that value technical skills over emotional dimensions of care activities is not up to the challenge of sustainably improving perceptions around care work and its distribution. The shortcomings of the liberal apparatus of anti-discrimination legislation in the face of structural racism constitute yet another point of inflection for renewed approaches to social justice. The daily experiences of racialised care workers clearly demonstrate that a rights framework remains insufficient to combat intersecting inequalities. The vulnerabilities produced by the workings of several fields of policy require a more comprehensive approach. (Re)starting from a relational ontology bears in this regard the promise of more inclusive avenues for social participation, and thus, less unequal distributions of care. A final example of how care ethics might serve as the horizon to the critique built from a political economy perspective concerns the recognition of care as a political matter. The dominant model of the neoliberal citizenship defines a hierarchy of values governing one's belonging to society. With masculinised formal paid employment at the top of such a hierarchy, racialised care workers find themselves multiply excluded from the venues of recognised social, and political, participation. The precariousness of migrant workers' legal statuses combines here with the marginalisation of care labour as a degraded sector of the labour market, whereby earnings within the sector prove oftentimes insufficient to administratively legitimate residency, as is the case for migrant care workers in the UK. Care and reproductive labour need thus to be politicised and its relevance to citizenship acknowledged to fight for racialised care workers' social, legal and political inclusion.

10.2   Revisiting Care Ethics Walking an Empirical Path

If care ethics constituted an eye-opening tool to enhance the political economy critique with transformative potential, my empirical material also speaks to the tenets of care ethics while this feminist moral philosophy tended to grow detached from its empirical origins. One of them is to posit care as practice. The trajectories of racialised care workers demonstrate in this regard how caring attitudes follow from practising care. In their overwhelming majority participants' employment in older-age care did not result from an optimal choice but a very constrained one, in the context of strong labour market segmentation as well as migration and employment policies that entrench the channelling of racialised, and even more so migrant, workers into the care sector. And yet, their narratives revealed an ethic of care that emerged through practice, an ethic of care that proved essential for them to be able to carry out their work. The contribution that this point makes to the care ethics literature is to demonstrate how attentiveness to care needs is materially constructed and how indifference is so too.

The argument that follows from this observation is that gender could have little to do with attentiveness to care but has everything to do with it under a patriarchal version of neoliberal capitalism. Given that the most resilient critique to care ethics lies in the supposed essentialisation that it operates (as summarised by Hankivsky 2004), it is important to unpack this point. The risk, goes the argument, is to assume that all women possess a set of care-related skills, not only entrenching the current social distribution of gender roles but effectively reproducing the marginalisation of women. Such a reading—facilitated by an abstract understanding of care ethics uprooted from empirical research—glosses over key nuances of care ethics. Shifting the focus from women to racialised care workers, this book demonstrates that an ethic of care is voiced in the context of paid employment within the older-age care sector. If the workforce remains feminised as an ineluctable consequence of the historic clout of patriarchy and the workings of various fields of policy, the intersectional dimension of these processes also explicates the significant presence of migrant men in the sector. The daily care labour carried out by participants I have met produced moral discourses on care, which were certainly entangled with gendered performances; yet they clearly went beyond conservative gender roles and revealed how taking up care responsibilities produces caring attitudes. Drawing on the material presented in this book, I thus argue that the voices of care ethics cannot be easily associated and reduced to women's voices. Rather, women and men involved in care emphasise that care and relationships matter.

An acknowledgement that women have played a key role in care and the reproduction of societies should not obscure shifting gender boundaries, roles and aspirations. Only by apprehending these complexities, is it possible to do justice to the core claim of care ethics of placing care in the centre of society. Contrary to the assignation of women to care work, stating loud and clear that care work matters, as done by Fouzia with confidence and pride, and maybe a bit of anger, represents the only possible way to achieve recognition and combat the reduction of care to fixed gender identities.

10.3   From Care Labour to Care Ethics and Back: Thinking Care Ethics as a Militant Commitment

At the juncture of care labour and care ethics, *Territorio Domestico*, a grassroots association located in Madrid and animated by Spanish, South American and North African women, fights every day for making care more visible, one artistic performance, legal case or international meeting at a time. Their daily commitments best illuminate the social changes that underpin the idea of a 'caring democracy' (Tronto 2013). As the organisation mostly comprises domestic workers, I have not included the experiences of this group in the data analysed in this book, given my primary focus on private residential care. Their activism however needs to be foregrounded from the perspective of care ethics' transformative potential and material implications. These women are collectively engaging with a feminist political economy of domestic and care work, what they relate to as feminist economics, and turn it into powerful tools for mobilisation expressed through creative means, such as theatrical happenings, performed in the streets of the city, out in the public space. One of their slogans, 'without us, the world doesn't move anymore', illustrates their fundamental struggle: to bring care, including all dimensions of domestic work, into the centre of society, because it sustains life and enables all other societal activities to be carried out. If they also fulfil the role of a support network to the women involved in the movement, their struggle differs from that of most other migrant associations. Their commitment to value care as such fills the horizon of a less unequal distribution of care with meaning. Achieving a fairer distribution of care responsibilities aims at placing care at the centre of society's social relations so that its members can provide care in ways that acknowledge an ontological interdependency and value these relationships. Activists of *Territorio Domestico* have deployed their struggles at different yet interconnected levels of oppression and make their voices heard from the streets of Madrid to international fora on domestic work. They are the harbingers of the social transformations that many care ethicists aspire to.

Bibliography

ACAS. (2011). The Equality Act – What's New for Employers? Retrieved from http://www.acas.org.uk/media/pdf/n/8/Equality_Act_2010_guide_for_employers-accessible-version-Nov-2011.pdf.

Alberola, E., Gilles, L., & Tith, F. (2011). *Les services à La personne: un Levier d'insertion pour Les publics éloignés de l'emploi ?* Paris: Crédoc.

Aldeghi, I., & Loones, A. (2010). *Les emplois dans les services à domicile aux personnes âgées. Approche d'un secteur statistiquement indéfinissable.* Paris: Crédoc. Retrieved from http://www.credoc.fr/pdf/Rech/C277.pdf.

Alvesson, M., & Sköldberg, K. (2009). *Reflexive Methodology New Vistas for Qualitative Research.* London: Sage.

Anderson, B. (2000). *Doing the Dirty Work? The Global Politics of Domestic Labour.* London: Palgrave Macmillan.

Anderson, B. (2010). Migration, Immigration Controls and the Fashioning of Precarious Workers. *Work, Employment & Society, 24*(2), 300–317.

Anderson, B., & Shutes, I. (2014). *Migration and Care Labour Theory, Policy and Politics.* London: Palgrave Macmillan.

Andolfatto, D., & Labbé, D. (2006). La transformation des syndicats français. Vers un nouveau "modèle social"? *Revue française de science politique, 56*(2), 281–297.

Andrews, T. (2012, June). What Is Social Constructionism? *Grounded Theory Review, 11*(1). Retrieved from http://groundedtheoryreview.com/2012/06/01/what-is-social-constructionism/.

Anthias, F. (2011). Intersections and Translocations: New Paradigms for Thinking About Cultural Diversity and Social Identities. *European Educational Research Journal, 10*(2), 204–217.

Anthias, F. (2012). Intersectional What? Social Divisions, Intersectionality and Levels of Analysis. *Ethnicities, 13*(1), 3–19.

Anthias, F., & Yuval-Davis, N. (1992). *Racialized Boundaries: Race, Nation, Gender, Colour and Class and the Anti-racist Struggle*. London: Routledge.

Anton José, I., Munoz de Bustillo, R., & Carrera, M. (2010). Labor Market Performance of Latin American and Caribbean Immigrants in Spain. *Journal of Applied Economics, XIII*(2), 233–261.

Anttonen, A., & Haïkiö, L. (2011). Care 'Going Market': Finnish Elderly-Care Policies in Transition. *Nordic Journal of Social Research, 2*(Special Issue), 70–90.

Aspinall, P. J. (2002). Collective Terminology to Describe the Minority Ethnic Population: The Persistence of Confusion and Ambiguity in Usage. *Sociology, 36*, 803.

Avril, C. (2009). Une mobilisation collective dans l'aide à domicile à la lumière des pratiques et des relations de travail. *Politix, 2*(86), 97–118.

Ayres, L. (2008). Semi-Structured Interview. In L. M. Given (Ed.), *The Sage Encyclopedia of Qualitative Research Methods* (pp. 811–812). Thousand Oaks, CA: SAGE Publications.

Bakker, I. (2003). Neo-liberal Governance and the Reprivatization of Social Reproduction: Social Provisioning and Shifting Gender Orders. In I. Bakker & S. Gill (Eds.), *Power, Production and Social Reproduction*. London: Palgrave Macmillan.

Balibar, E. (1988/2012). Y a-t-il un "néo-racisme"? In E. Balibar & I. Wallerstein (Eds.), *Race, nation, classe. Les identités ambiguës*. Paris: Editions La Découverte.

Balibar, E., & Wallerstein, I. M. (1988). *Race, nation, classe: les identités ambiguës*. Paris: Ed. La Découverte.

Barbier, J.-C. (2002). *A Survey of the Use of the Term précarité in French Economics and Sociology*. Centre d'Etudes de l'Emploi. Retrieved from http://www.cee-recherche.fr/fr/fiches_chercheurs/texte_pdf/PRECARITE2BARBIER.pdf.

Barbier, J.-C. (2005). La précarité, une catégorie française à l'épreuve de la comparaison internationale. *Revue française de sociologie, 46*(2), 351–371.

Becker, G. S., & Tomes, N. (1994). Human Capital and the Rise and Fall of Families. In *Human Capital: A Theoretical and Empirical Analysis with Special*

Reference to Education (3rd ed., pp. 257–298). New York: The University of Chicago Press.

Bedolla, L. G. (2007). Intersections of Inequality: Understanding Marginalization and Privilege in the Post-Civil Rights Era. *Politics & Gender, 3*(2), 232–248.

Berger, P., & Luckmann, T. (1966/1991). *The Social Construction of Reality. A Treatise in the Sociology of Knowledge.* London: Penguin Books.

Bertossi, C. (2007). *French and British Models of Integration. Public Philosophies, Policies and State Institutions.* ESRC Centre on Migration, Policy and Society, Working Paper (46). Oxford: University of Oxford.

Bettio, F., Simonazzi, A., & Villa, P. (2006). Change in Care Regimes and Female Migration: The 'Care Drain' in the Mediterranean. *Journal of European Social Policy, 16*(3), 271–285.

Bourdieu, P. (1979, Novembre). Les trois états du capital culturel. *Actes de la recherche en sciences sociales, 30,* 3–6. L'institution scolaire.

Bourdieu, P. (1998). *Contre-feux. Propos pour servir à la résistance contre l'invasion néo-libérale.* Paris: Editions Raisons d'Agir.

Bourne, J. (2001). The Life and Times of Institutional Racism. *Race & Class, 43*(2), 7–22.

Boyatzis, R. E. (1998). *Transforming Qualitative Information: Thematic Analysis and Code Development.* Thousand Oaks, CA: Sage Publications.

Brah, A., & Phoenix, A. (2004). Ain't I A Woman? Revisiting Intersectionality. *Journal of International Women's Studies, 5*(3), 75–86.

Browne, P. L. (2010). The Dialectics of Health and Social Care: Toward a Conceptual Framework. *Theory and Society, 39*(5), 575–591.

Brugère, F. (2011). *L'éthique du "care".* Paris: Presses Universitaires de France.

Burawoy, M. (1975). The Functions and Reproduction of Migrant Labor: Comparative Material from Southern Africa and the United States. *American Journal of Sociology, 81*(5), 1050–1087.

Butler, J. (2009/2016). *Frames of War. When Is Life Grievable?* London: Verso.

Byrd, C. (2011). Conflating Apples and Oranges: Understanding Modern Forms of Racism. *Sociology Compass, 5*(11), 1005–1017.

Cabrero, G. R., & Gallego, V. M. (2013). Long-Term Care in Spain: Between Family Care Tradition and the Public Recognition of Social Risk. In C. Ranci & E. Pavolini (Eds.), *Reforms in Long-Term Care Policies in Europe.* New York: Springer.

Cachon Rodriguez, L. (2008). La Integracion de y con lon inmigrantes en Espana: debates teoricos, politicas y ideversidad territorial. *Politica y Sociedad, 45*(1), 205–235.

Cangiano, A. (2014). Elder Care and Migrant Labor in Europe: A Demographic Outlook. *Population and Development Review, 40*(1), 131–154.

Cangiano, A., Shutes, I., Spencer, S., & Leeson, G. (2009). *Migrant Care Workers in Ageing Societies: Research Findings in the United Kingdom Report*. Report on Research Findings in the UK (Vol. 44).

Cano, E. (2004). *Formas, percepciones y consecuencias de la precariedad. Mientras Tanto, Invierno, 93*, 67–82.

Cantle, T. (Chair.). (2001) *Community Cohesion: A Report of the Independent Review Team*. Home Office. Retrieved from http://resources.cohesioninstitute.org.uk/Publications/Documents/Document/DownloadDocumentsFile.aspx?recordId=96&file=PDFversion.

Cantle, T. (2008). *Parallel Lives – The Development of Community Cohesion. Citizenship, Cohesion and Solidarity* (pp. 9–20). London: Smith Institute.

Carmichael, S., & Hamilton, C. V. (1967/1992). *Black Power. The Politics of Liberation*. New York: Vintage Books.

Carrera, S. (Ed.). (2009). *In Search of the Perfect Citizen? The Intersection Between Integration, Immigration, and Nationality in the EU*. Leiden: Martinus Nijhoff Publishers.

Castel, R. (1995). *Les métamorphoses de la question sociale*. Paris: Gallimard.

Castles, S. (2006). Guestworkers in Europe: A Resurrection? *International Migration Review, 40*(4), 741–766.

Choo, H. Y., & Ferree, M. M. (2010). Practicing Intersectionality in Sociological Research: A Critical Analysis of Inclusions, Interactions, and Institutions in the Study of Inequalities. *Sociological Theory, 28*, 129–149.

Christensen, H., & Guldvik, I. (2014). *Migrant Care Workers. Searching for New Horizons*. Dorchester: Ashgate.

Colectivo Ioé. (2003). Experiencias de Discriminación de Minorías Étnicas en España. Retrieved from http://www.colectivoioe.org/uploads/edb969a5b5bb4f6aaf3f9afb865cf396533d9315.pdf.

Condon, S. (2000). Migrations Antillaises en métropole. *Les cahiers du CEDREF* [En ligne], 8–9. Retrieved from http://cedref.revues.org/196.

Cook, K. (2008). In-Depth Interview. In L. M. Given (Ed.), *The Sage Encyclopedia of Qualitative Research Methods* (pp. 423–424). Thousand Oaks, CA: SAGE Publications.

Corkill, D. (2001). Economic Migrants and the Labour Market in Spain and Portugal. *Ethnic and Racial Studies, 24*(5), 828–844.

Crenshaw, K. W. (1989). Demarginalizing the Intersection of Race and Sex: A Black Feminist Critique of Antidiscrimination Doctrine, Feminist Theory and Antiracist Politics. *University of Chicago Legal Forum, 140*, 139–167.

Cruickshank, J. (2011). *The Positive and the Negative. Assessing Critical Realism and Social Constructionism as Post-Positivist Approaches to Empirical Research in the Social Sciences*. IMI Working Papers, Paper 42. Oxford: International Migration Institute.

Cuban, S. (2013). *Deskilling Migrant Women in the Global Care Industry*. London: Palgrave Macmillan.

Datta, K., McIlwaine, C., Evans, Y., Herbert, J., May, J., & Wills, J. (2006). *Work, Care and Life Among Low-Paid Migrant Workers in London: Towards a Migrant Ethic of Care*. London: Queen Mary, University of London.

De Genova, N. (2013). Spectacles of Migrant 'Illegality': The Scene of Exclusion, the Obscene of Inclusion. *Ethnic and Racial Studies, 36*(7), 1180–1198.

De Haas, H. (2007). Between Courting and Controlling: The Moroccan State and 'Its' Emigrants. *Working Paper No 54*. Oxford: Centre on Migration, Policy and Society, University of Oxford.

De Lizarrondo Artola, A. M. (2009). La integración de inmigrantes en España: el modelo patchwork. *Migraciones, 26*, 115–146.

Delphy, C. (2013). *L'Ennemi Principal. Economie Politique du Patriarcat*. Paris: Editions Syllepse.

Department for Business Innovation and Skills. (2014). Findings from the Survey of Tribunal Employment Applications 201. Research Series No. 177. Retrieved from https://www.gov.uk/government/uploads/system/uploads/attachment_data/file/316704/bis-14-708-survey-of-employment-tribunal-applications-2013.pdf.

Devetter, F., & Messaoudi, D. (2013). Les aides à domicile entre flexibilité et incomplétude du rapport salarial: conséquences sur le temps de travail et les conditions d'emploi. *La Revue de l'Ires, 3*(78), 51–76.

Doeringer, P., & Piore, M. J. (1971). *Internal Labor Markets and Manpower Adjustment*. New York: DC Heath and Company.

Duggan, L. (2003). *The Twilight of Equality. Neoliberalism, Cultural Politics and the Attack on Democracy*. Boston: Beacon Press Books.

Ehrenreich, B., & English, D. (1973). *Witches. Midwives and Nurses: A History of Women Healers*. Old Westbury: Feminist Press.

ENAR. (2013). Racism and Related Discriminatory Practices in Employment in Spain. Retrieved from http://www.enar-eu.org/IMG/pdf/spain.pdf.

England, K., & Dyck, I. (2012). Migrant Workers in Home Care: Routes, Responsibilities, and Respect. *Annals of the Association of American Geographers, 102*(5), 1076–1083.

Engster, D. (2007). *The Heart of Justice. Care Ethics and Political Theory*. Oxford: Oxford University Press.

Erel, U. (2010). Migrating Cultural Capital: Bourdieu in Migration Studies. *Sociology, 44*(4), 642–660.

Ernst and Young Advisory. (2008). Etude sur le marché de l'offre de soins, d'hébergement et de services destinés aux personnes âgées dépendantes. Retrieved from http://www.senat.fr/rap/r07-447-2/r07-447-2-scan1.pdf.

Esping-Andersen, G. (1990/2013). *The Three Worlds of Welfare Capitalism.* Hoboken, NJ: John Wiley & Sons.

Fargues, P. (2008). Circular Migration: Is It Relevant for the South and East of the Mediterranean? *CARIM Analytic and Synthetic Notes,* No. 40. San Domenico di Fiesole: European University Institute.

Farris, S., & Marchetti, S. (2017). From the Commodification to the Corporatization of Care: European Perspectives and Debates. *Social Politics, 24*(2), 109–131.

Fassin, D., & Fassin, E. (2006). *De la question sociale à la question raciale. Représenter la société française.* Paris: La Découverte.

Federici, S. (2006). Precarious Labor: A Feminist Viewpoint. In the Middle of a Whirlwind. Retrieved January 10, 2016, from https://inthemiddleofthewhirlwind.wordpress.com/precarious-labor-a-feminist-viewpoint/.

Federici, S. (2012). *Revolution at Point Zero: Housework, Reproduction, and Feminist Struggle.* New York: PM Press.

Ferguson, S. (2008). Canadian Contributions to Social Reproduction Feminism, Race and Embodied Labor. *Race, Gender & Class, 15*(1/2), 42–57.

Ferguson, S. (2016). Intersectionality and Social-Reproduction Feminisms Toward an Integrative Ontology. *Historical Materialism, 24*(2), 38–60.

Folbre, N. (2012). Should Women Care Less? Intrinsic Motivation and Gender Inequality. *British Journal of Industrial Relations, 50*(4), 597–619.

Foucault, M. (1978/2002). *Sécurité, Territoire, Population. Cours au Collège de France 1977–1978.* Paris: École des hautes études en sciences sociales, Éditions Gallimard et Éditions du Seuil.

Frade, C., Darmon, I., & Laparra, M. (2004). *Precarious Employment in Europe: A Comparative Study of Labour Market Related Risks in Flexible Economies.* ESOPE Project. Final Report. Brussels: European Commission. Retrieved February 2015, from https://www.researchgate.net/publication/242731766_Precarious_employment_in_Europe_a_comparative_study_of_labour_market_related_risk_in_flexible_economies/download.

Fraser, N. (2016, July–August). Contradictions of Capital and Care. *New Left Review, 100,* 99–117.

Froy, F., & Pyne, L. (2011). *Ensuring Labour Market Success for Ethnic Minority and Immigrant Youth.* OECD Local Economic and Employment Development (LEED) Working Papers, 2011/09. Paris: OECD Publishing.

Gallo, E., & Scrinzi, F. (2016). *Migration, Masculinities and Reproductive Labour. Men of the Home.* London: Palgrave Macmillan.

Garner, H., & Lainé, F. (2013). *Service à la personne: constats et enjeux.* Commissariat Général à la Stratégie et à la Prospective.

Gawronski, B., et al. (2008). Understanding the Relations Between Different Forms of Racial Prejudice: A Cognitive Consistency Perspective. *Personality & Social Psychology Bulletin, 34*(5), 648–665.

Gilligan, C. (1982/2003). *In a Different Voice.* Cambridge, MA: Harvard University Press.

Gilligan, C., Hochschild, A. R., & Tronto, J. C. (2013). *Contre l'indifférence des privilégiés. A quoi sert le care* (P. Molinier & P. Paperman, Eds.). Paris: Payot.

Gilroy, P. (1987/2002). *There Ain't No Black in the Union Jack.* London: Routledge.

Glendinning, C. (2013). Long Term Care Reform in England: A Long and Unfinished Story. In C. Ranci & E. Pavolini (Eds.), *Reforms in Long-Term Care Policies in Europe.* New York: Springer.

Guillaumin, C. (1972/2002). *L'idéologie raciste.* Paris: Editions Folios Essais.

Hall, S. (1978). 'Racism and Reaction' in Five Views of Multi-Racial Britain (pp. 23–35). London: Commission of Racial Equality.

Hankivsky, O. (2004). *Social Policy and the Ethic of Care.* Vancouver and Toronto: University of British Columbia Press.

Harding, S. (1997, Winter). Comment on Hekman's "Truth and Method: Feminist Standpoint Theory Revisited": Whose Standpoint Needs the Regimes of Truth and Reality? *Signs, 22*(2), 382–391.

Hardt, M., & Negri, A. (2000). *Empire.* Cambridge, MA: Harvard University Press.

Hardy, J., Eldring, L., & Schulten, T. (2012). Trade Union Responses to Migrant Workers from the 'New Europe': A Three Sector Comparison in the UK, Norway and Germany. *European Journal of Industrial Relations, 18*(4), 347–363.

Hartsock, N. (1997, Winter). Comment on Hekman's "Truth and Method: Feminist Standpoint Theory Revisited": Truth or Justice? *Signs, 22*(2), 367–374.

Harvey, D. (2014). *Seventeen Contradictions and the End of Capitalism.* New York: Oxford University Press.

Headley, C. (2000). Philosophical Approaches to Racism: A Critique of the Individualistic Perspective. *Journal of Social Philosophy, 31*(2), 223–257.

Heath, A. F., & Cheung, S. Y. (2007). *Unequal Chances: Ethnic Minorities in Western Labour Markets* (Vol. 137). Oxford: Oxford University Press.

Held, V. (2005). *The Ethics of Care: Personal, Political, and Global.* Oxford: Oxford University Press Scholarship Online.

Hemerijck, A. C., Palm, T. P., Entenmann, E., & Van Hooren, F. J. (2013). *Changing European Welfare States and the Evolution of Migrant Incorporation Regimes.* Working Paper. University Amsterdam. Retrieved from https://www.compas.ox.ac.uk/wp-content/uploads/PR-2013-IMPACIM_Background_Welfare_States.pdf.

HM Revenue & Customs. (2013). National Minimum Wage Compliance in the Social Care Sector. Retrieved February 2015, from https://www.gov.uk/government/uploads/system/uploads/attachment_data/file/262269/131125_Social_Care_Evaluation_2013_ReportNov2013PDF.PDF.

Hochschild, A. R. (1983/2003). *The Managed Heart. Commercialization of Human Feeling.* Berkeley: University of California Press.

Hochschild, A. R. (2000). Global Care Chains and Emotional Surplus Value. In A. Giddens & W. Hutton (Eds.), *On the Edge: Living with Global Capitalism* (pp. 130–146). London: Jonathan Cape.

Hussein, S., & Manthorpe, J. (2005). An International Review of the Long-Term Care Workforce. *Journal of Aging & Social Policy, 17*(4), 75–94.

Hussein, S., Manthorpe, J., & Stevens, M. (2011). Social Care as First Work Experience in England: a Secondary Analysis of the Profile of a National Sample of Migrant Workers. *Health and Social Care in the Community, 19*(1), 83–97.

Hyman, R. (2001). *Trade Union Research and Cross-National Comparison* [online]. London: LSE Research Online. Retrieved from http://eprints.lse.ac.uk/archive/00000757.

Ikuenobe, P. (2010). Conceptualizing Racism and Its Subtle Forms. *Journal for the Theory of Social Behaviour, 41*, 2.

ILO International Labour Organization. (2012). *From Precarious Work to Decent Work: Outcome Document to the Workers' Symposium on Policies and Regulations to Combat Precarious Employment'.* Geneva: International Labour Organization. Retrieved from http://www.ilo.org/wcmsp5/groups/public/@ed_dialogue/@actrav/documents/meetingdocument/wcms_179787.pdf.

IMSERSO. (2005). *Cuidado a la dependencia e Inmigracion, Informe de Resultados.* Coleccion Estudios Serie Dependencia Instituto de Mayores y Servicios Sociales. Madrid: Instituto de Mayores y Servicios Sociales.

Jany-Catrice, F. (2013). Mise en visibilité statistique des emplois dans les services à la personne. *La Revue de l'Ires, 3*(78), 25–49.

Jayaweera, H., & Anderson, B. (2008). Migrant Workers and Vulnerable Employment: A Review of Existing Data. Report for TUC Commission on Vulnerable Employment. Retrieved February 2015, from http://www.vulnerableworkers.org.uk/wp-content/uploads/2008/08/analysis-of-migrant-worker-data-final.pdf.

Jefferys, S., & Ouali, N. (2007). Trade Unions and Racism in London, Brussels and Paris Public Transport. *Industrial Relations Journal, 38*(5), 406–422.

Jenkins, S. (2004). *Gender, Place, and the Labour Market*. Aldershot: Ashgate.

Jivraj, S. (2013). *How Has Ethnic Diversity Grown 1991–2001–2011? The Dynamics of Diversity: Evidence from the 2011 Census*. Manchester: Centre on Dynamics of Ethnicity (CoDE).

Kalleberg, A. L. (2009). Precarious Work, Insecure Workers: Employment Relations in Transition. *American Sociological Review, 74*(1), 1–22.

Kofman, E. (2008). Managing Migration and Citizenship in Europe: Towards an Overarching Framework. In C. Gabriel & H. Pellerin (Eds.), *Governing International Labour Migration: Current Issues, Challenges and Dilemmas*. New York: Routledge.

Kofman, E., & Raghuram, P. (2015). *Gendered Migrations and Global Social Reproduction*. London: Palgrave Macmillan.

Köhler, H.-D., & Calleja Jiménez, J.-P. (2012). Transformations in Spanish Trade Union Membership. *Industrial Relations Journal, 43*(3), 281–292.

Korczyk, S. (2004). *Long-Term Care Workers in Five Countries: Issues and Options*. AARP Public Policy Institute. Retrieved from http://assets.aarp.org/rgcenter/health/2004_07_care.pdf.

Kymlicka, W. (2002). *Contemporary Political Philosophy*. New York: Oxford University Press.

Lada, E. (2011, Juillet–Septembre). Les associations jouent un role ambivalent dans la professionalisation des emplois et des salariées du secteur d'aide à domicile. *La documentation Française Formation Emploi, 115*: 9–23.

Lanoix, M. (2013, Winter). Labor as Embodied Practice: The Lessons of Care Work. *Hypatia, 28*(1), 85–100.

Laslett, B., & Brenner, J. (1989). Gender and Social Reproduction: Historical Perspectives. *Annual Review of Sociology, 15*, 381–404.

Le Bihan, B., & Martin, C. (2010). Reforming Long-Term Care Policy in France: Private–Public Complementarities. *Social Policy & Administration, 44*(4), 392–410.

Lentin, A., & Titley, G. (2011). *The Crises of Multiculturalism: Racism in a Neoliberal Age*. New York: Zed Books Ltd.

León, M. (2010). Migration and Care Work in Spain: The Domestic Sector Revisited. *Social Policy and Society, 9*, 409–418.

Leontaridi, M. (1998). Segmented Labour Markets: Theory and Evidence. *Journal of Economic Surveys, 12*(1), 103–109.

Lethbridge, J. (2011). *Care Services for Older People in Europe – Challenges for Labour*. Greenwich: PSIRU, Business School. Retrieved from https://www. epsu.org/sites/default/files/article/files/Care_Services_Older_People_ Europe_report_final.pdf.

Lewchuk, W., & Clarke, M. (2011). *Working Without Commitments: The Health Effects of Precarious Employment*. Montréal: McGill-Queen's University Press.

Lonergan, G. (2015). Migrant Women and Social Reproduction Under Austerity. *Feminist Review, 109*, 124–145.

Lorey I. (2010). Becoming Common: Precarization as Political Constituting. *E-flux*, no. 17. Retrieved October 4, 2018, from http://www.e-flux.com/journal/17/67385/becoming-common-precarization-as-political-constituting/.

Lorrey, I. (2015). *State of Insecurity. Government of the Precarious*. London: Verso.

Low Pay Commission. (2014). *National Minimum Wage*. Report 2014. Retrieved February 2015, from https://www.gov.uk/government/uploads/system/ uploads/attachment_data/file/288847/The_National_Minimum_Wage_ LPC_Report_2014.pdf.

Lutz, H. (Ed.). (2008). *Migration and Domestic Work: A European Perspective on a Global Theme*. Aldershot: Ashgate.

Lutz, H., & Palenga-Möllenbeck, E. (2011). Care, Gender and Migration: Towards a Theory of Transnational Domestic Work Migration in Europe. *Journal of Contemporary European Studies, 19*(3), 349–364.

Machin, S. (2000). *Union Decline in Britain*. London: London School of Economics. Retrieved from http://eprints.lse.ac.uk/20191/1/Union_ Decline_in_Britain.pdf.

Macpherson. (1999). The Stephen Lawrence Inquiry. Retrieved from https:// www.gov.uk/government/uploads/system/uploads/attachment_data/ file/277111/4262.pdf.

Mahon, R., & Robinson, F. (Eds.). (2011). *Feminist Ethics and Social Policy: Towards a New Global Political Economy of Care*. Vancouver: UBC Press.

Marchetti, S. (2014). *Black Girls. Migrant Domestic Workers and Colonial Legacies*. Leiden and Boston: Brill.

Marie, C.-V., & Temporal, F. (2011). Les DOM: Terres de migrations. *Espace populations sociétés* [En ligne], 2011/3. Retrieved from http://eps. revues.org/4652.

Martin, C. (2008). Qu'est-ce que le social care? Une revue de questions. *Revue Française de Socio-Économie, 2*(2), 27–42.

Martínez Buján, R. (2015). Gendered Motivations for Return Migrations to Bolivia from Spain. *Journal of Immigrant & Refugee Studies, 13*(4), 401–418.

Martiniello, M. (2013). *Penser l'ethnicité. Identité, culture et relations sociales.* Liège: Presses Universitaires de Liège.

McCall, L. (2005). The Complexity of Intersectionality. *Journal of Women and Culture in Society, 30*(3), 1771–1800.

McKay, S., et al. (2012). *Study on Precarious Work and Social Rights.* London: Working Lives Research Institute, London Metropolitan University.

McLoughlin, S., & Münz, R. (2011). *Temporary and Circular Migration: Opportunities and Challenges.* Working Paper No. 35. Brussels: European Policy Center.

Meardi, G. (2012). *Social Failures of EU Enlargement: A Case of Workers Voting with Their Feet.* New York: Routledge.

Menz, G., & Caviedes, A. (2010). *Labour Migration in Europe.* London: Palgrave Macmillan.

Mezzadra, S., & Neilson, B. (2013). *Border as Method, or, the Multiplication of Labor.* Durham: Duke University Press.

Miles, R. (1993). *Racism After 'Race Relations'.* London: Routledge.

Mills, C. W. (2007). White Ignorance. In S. Sullican & N. Tuana (Eds.), *Race and Epistemologies of Ignorance.* Albany, NY: State University of New York.

Ministère de l'Intérieur. (2013). *Les données de l'immigration professionnelle et étudiante.* Paris: Direction de l'immigration.

Ministry of Justice. (2012). Employment Tribunals and EAT Statistics, 2011–12. Retrieved from https://www.gov.uk/government/uploads/system/uploads/attachment_data/file/218497/employment-trib-stats-april-march-2011-12.pdf.

Molinier, P. (2013). *Le travail du care.* Paris: La Dispute/Snédit.

Molinier, P., Laugier, S., & Paperman, P. (2009). *Qu'est ce que le care? Souci des autres, sensibilité, responsabilité.* Paris: Éditions Payot & Rivages.

Montiel Perez-Nievas, S., & Vintila Daniela, C. (2011). La Reagrupación Familiar en España y En Europa. *Anuario de la Facultad de Derecho Universidad Autónoma de Madrid, 15*, 143–167.

Moré, P. (2018). 'Here, We Don't Only Receive Orders': (Dis)Empowering Care Labour in Madrid and Paris. In M. Amrith & N. Sahraoui (Eds.), *Gender, Work and Migration: Agency in Gendered Labour Settings.* Oxford: Routledge.

Mouriaux, R. (2013). *Le syndicalisme en France depuis 1945.* Paris: La Découverte.

Nakano Glenn, E. (2010). *Forced to Care. Coercion and Caregiving.* Cambridge, MA: Harvard University Press.

Nguyen Minh, T. N., Zavoretti, R., & Tronto, J. (2017). Beyond the Global Care Chain: Boundaries, Institutions and Ethics of Care. *Ethics and Social Welfare, 11*(3), 199–212.

Noiriel, G. (1988). *Le creuset français*. Paris: Éd. du Seuil.

OECD. (2013). *International Migration Outlook*. Paris: OECD Publishing.

OECD. (2015). *International Migration Outlook*. Paris: OECD Publishing.

OECD. (2017). *"Long-Term Care Expenditure", in Health at a Glance 2017: OECD Indicators*. Paris: OECD Publishing.

Okin, S. M. (1989). *Justice, Gender and the Family*. Princeton: Princeton University Press.

Palys, T. (2008). Purposive Sampling. In L. M. Given (Ed.), *The Sage Encyclopedia of Qualitative Research Methods* (pp. 698–699). Thousand Oaks, CA: SAGE Publications.

Pardini, B. (2013). *Diagnostic emploi formation relatif aux aides-soignants, aides médico-psychologiques et auxiliaires de vie sociale*. Paris: Défi Métiers. Retrieved from http://www.defi-metiers.fr/sites/default/files/docs/rapports-etudes/diagnostic_emploi_formation_as_amp_avsl_0.pdf.

Parreñas, R. (2000). Migrant Filipina Domestic Workers and the International Division of Reproductive Labor. *Gender & Society, 14*(4), 560–580.

Parreñas, R. (2001). *Servants of Globalization*. Stanford, CA: Stanford University Press.

Parreñas, R. (2012). The Reproductive Labour of Migrant Workers. *Global Networks, 12*(2), 269–275.

Paugam, S. (2009). *Le salarié de la précarité. Les nouvelles formes de l'intégration professionnelle*. Paris: Quadrige.

Paugam, S., Le Blanc, G., & Rui, S. (2011). Les nouvelles formes de précarité. Regards croisés entre la philosophie et la sociologie. *Sociologie, 2*(4), 417–431.

Peck, J. (1996). *Work-Place: The Social Regulation of Labor Markets*. New York: Guilford Press.

Perez Orozco, A. (2014). *Subversion feminista de la economia. Aportes para un debate sobre el conflicto capital-vida*. Madrid: Traficantes de suenos.

Puissant, E. (2011, Juillet–Septembre). Le rôle ambivalent des associations d'aide à domicile dans la professionnalisation des emplois et des salariées. *Formation emploi*, 115: 37–50.

Rass, C., & Wolff, F. (2018). What Is in a Migration Regime? Genealogical Approach and Methodological Proposal. In A. Pott et al. (Eds.), *Was ist ein Migrationsregime? What Is a Migration Regime?* Osnabrück: Springer VS.

Rattansi, A. (2011). *Multiculturalism: A Very Short Introduction* (Vol. 283). Oxford: Oxford University Press.

Robinson, F. (2011). *The Ethics of Care. A Feminist Approach to Human Security*. Philadelphia, PA: Temple University Press.

Robinson, F. (2013). Global Care Ethics: Beyond Distribution, Beyond Justice. *Journal of Global Ethics, 9*(2), 131–143.

Rocha Sánchez, F. (2012). *Youth Unemployment in Spain. Situation and Policy Recommendations*. Berlin: Friedrich Ebert Stiftung. Retrieved from http://library.fes.de/pdf-files/id/09469.pdf.

Rodgers, G., & Rodgers, J. (1989). Precarious Work in Western Europe: The State of the Debate. In G. Rodgers & J. Rodgers (Eds.), *Precarious Jobs in Labour Market Regulation: The Growth of Atypical Employment in Western Europe*. Geneva: International Institute of Labour Studies.

Rodríguez Cabrero, G., & Marbán Gallego, V. (2013). Long-Term Care in Spain: Between Family Care Tradition and the Public Recognition of Social Risk. In C. Ranci & E. Pavolini (Eds.), *Reforms in Long-Term Care Policies in Europe*. New York: Springer.

Rodríguez Rodríguez, V. (Ed.). (2012). *Inmigración y cuidados de mayores en la Comunidad de Madrid*. Bilbao: Fundacion BBVA.

Rodriquez, J. (2011). *Labors of Love. Nursing Homes and the Structures of Care Work*. New York and London: New York University Press.

Rodriquez, J. (2014). *Labors of Love: Nursing Homes and the Structures of Care Work*. New York: New York University Press.

Romero, B. A. (2012). Towards a Model of Externalisation and Denationalisation of Care? The Role of Female Migrant Care Workers for Dependent Older People in Spain. *European Journal of Social Work, 15*(1), 45–61.

Romero, M., Preston, V., & Giles, W. (Eds.). (2014). *When Care Work Goes Global: Locating the Social Relations of Domestic Work*. Farnham, UK: Ashgate.

Roy, O. (2008). *La sainte ignorance*. Paris: Seuil.

Sahraoui, N., Polkowski, R., & Karolak, M. (2018). Migration Policies and Their Threats: Going Beyond Polarization of the EU vs. Non-EU Migration Policies and Its Exceptions. In O. Fedyuk & P. Stewart (Eds.), *Inclusion and Exclusion in Europe: Migration, Work and Employment Perspectives* (pp. 57–78). London: Rowman & Littlefield International Ltd.

Samers, M. (2008). At the Heart of 'Migration Management': Immigration and Labour Markets in the European Union. In C. Gabriel (Ed.), *Governing International Labour Migration: Current Issues, Challenges and Dilemmas* (Vol. 26, pp. 128–144). London: Routledge.

Saumure, K., & Given, L. (2008). Nonprobability Sampling. In L. M. Given (Ed.), *The Sage Encyclopedia of Qualitative Research Methods* (pp. 563–564). Thousand Oaks, CA: SAGE Publications.

Scrinzi, F. (2013). *Genre, migrations et emplois domestiques en France et en Italie*. Paris: Editions Petra.

Serrano, A., Artiaga, A., & Davila de Leon, M. (2013). Crisis De Los Cuidados, Ley de Dependencia y Confusión Semántica. *Revista Internacional de Sociología, 71*(3), 669–694.

Settersten, R. A., & Angel, J. L. (2011). *Handbook of Sociology of Aging.* New York: Springer.

Sevenhuijsen, S. (1998). *Citizenship and the Ethics of Care. Feminist Considerations on Justice, Morality and Politics.* New York: Routledge.

Shutes, I. (2011). *Social Care for Older People and Demand for Migrant Workers.* Oxford: The Migration Observatory, University of Oxford.

Shutes, I. (2014). A Right to Care? Immigration Controls and the Care Labour of Non-Citizens. In B. Anderson & I. Shutes (Eds.), *Migration and Care Labour Theory, Policy and Politics.* London: Palgrave Macmillan.

Simien, E. M. (2007). Doing Intersectionality Research: From Conceptual Issues to Practical Examples. *Politics & Gender, 3*(2), 264–270.

Simonazzi, A. (2009). Care Regimes and National Employment Models. *Cambridge Journal of Economics, 33*(2), 211–232.

Sivanandan, A. (1985). RAT and the Degradation of Black Struggle. *Race Class, 26*, 1.

Slote, M. (2007). *The Ethics of Care and Empathy.* New York: Routledge.

Smith, D. E. (1987). *The Everyday World as Problematic: A Feminist Sociology.* Boston: Northeastern University Press.

Smith, D. E. (1997, Winter). Comment on Hekman's Truth and Method: Feminist Standpoint Theory Revisited. *Signs, 22*(2), 392–398.

Smith, D. E. (2005). *Institutional Ethnography: A Sociology for People.* Oxford: Altamira Press.

Smith, P., & Mackintosh, M. (2007). Profession, Market and Class: Nurse Migration and the Remaking of Division and Disadvantage. *Journal of Clinical Nursing, 16*, 2213–2220.

Solari, C. (2006). Professionals and Saints: How Immigrant Careworkers Negotiate Gender Identities at Work. *Gender and Society, 20*(3), 301–331.

Solé, C., & Parella, S. (2003). The Labour Market and Racial Discrimination in Spain. *Journal of Ethnic and Migration Studies, 29*(1), 121–140.

Standing, G. (2011). *The Precariat: The New Dangerous Class.* London: Bloomsbury Academic.

Stasiulis, D. (2008). Revisiting the Permanent-Temporary Labour Migration Dichotomy. In C. Gabriel & H. Pellerin (Eds.), *Governing International Labour Migration: Current Issues, Challenges and Dilemmas.* New York: Routledge.

Stevens, M., Hussein, S., & Manthorpe, J. (2012). Experiences of Racism and Discrimination Among Migrant Care Workers in England: Findings from a Mixed-Methods Research Project. *Ethnic and Racial Studies, 35*(2), 259–280.

Tribalat, M. (2004). Une estimation des populations d'origine étrangère en France en 1999. *Population, 59*(1), 51–81.

Tronto, J. C. (1993). *Moral Boundaries. A Political Argument for an Ethic of Care.* London: Routledge.

Tronto, J. C. (2011a). A Feminist Democratic Ethics of Care and Global Care Workers. Citizenship and Responsibility. In R. Mahon & F. Robinson (Eds.), *Feminist Ethics and Social Policy: Towards a New Global Political Economy of Care.* Vancouver: UBC Press.

Tronto, J. C. (2011b). Privatizing Neo-Colonialism: Migrant Domestic Care Workers, Partial Citizenship and Responsibility. In M. H. Dahl, M. Keränen, & A. Kovalainen (Eds.), *Europeanization, Care and Gender.* London: Palgrave Macmillan.

Tronto, J. C. (2013). *Caring Democracy. Markets, Equality, and Justice.* New York: New York University Press.

TUC Trades Union Congress. (2007). Hard Work, Hidden Lives. Retrieved from http://www.vulnerableworkers.org.uk/files/CoVE_full_report.pdf.

Ungerson, C. (2003). Commodified Care Work in European Labour Markets. *European Societies, 5*(4), 377–396.

UNISON. (2013). Time to Care. A UNISON Report into Home Care. Retrieved from https://www.unison.org.uk/content/uploads/2013/11/On-line-Catalogue220152.pdf.

UNRISD. (2010). *Combating Poverty and Inequality. Social Change, Social Policy and Politics.* Geneva: UNRISD.

Virdee, S. (2000). A Marxist Critique if Black Radical Theories of Trade-Union Racism. *Sociology, 34*(3), 545–565.

Vosko, L. F. (2006). *Precarious Employment: Understanding Labour Market Insecurity in Canada.* Montreal and Kingston: McGill-Queen's Press.

Vosko, L. F., & Clark, F. L. (2009). Gendered Precariousness and Social Reproduction. In L. F. Vosko, M. MacDonald, & I. Campbell (Eds.), *Gender and the Contours of Precarious Employment.* New York: Routledge.

Walby, S. (2007). Complexity Theory, Systems Theory, and Multiple Intersecting Social Inequalities. *Philosophy of the Social Sciences, 37*, 449.

Warmington, J., Afridi, A., & Foreman, W. (2014). *Is Excessive Paperwork in Care Homes Undermining Care for Older People?* York: Joseph Rowntree Foundation. Retrieved from https://www.jrf.org.uk/report/excessive-paper-work-care-homes-undermining-care-older-people.

Wihtol de Wenden, C. (2010). *La question migratoire au XXIème siècle. Migrants, réfugiés et relations internationales*. Paris: Presses de la Fondation Nationale des Sciences Politiques.

Williams, F. (2004). *Rethinking Families*. London: Calouste Gulbenkian Foundation.

Williams, F. (2011a). Migration and Care Work in Europe: Making Connections Across the Transnational Political Economy of Care. Context: University of Oxford, 14–15th April 2011. Retrieved from http://www.social-policy.org.uk/lincoln2011/Williams%20F%20P2.pdf.

Williams, F. (2011b). Towards a Transnational Analysis of the Political Economy of Care. In R. Mahon & F. Robinson (Eds.), *Feminist Ethics and Social Policy: Towards a New Global Political Economy of Care* (pp. 21–38). Vancouver: UBC Press.

Williams, F. (2011c). Care, Migration and Citizenship: Migration and Home-Based Care in Europe. In M. H. Dahl, M. Keränen, & A. Kovalainen (Eds.), *Europeanization, Care and Gender*. London: Palgrave Macmillan.

Williams, F. (2012). Converging Variations in Migrant Care Work in Europe. *Journal of European Social Policy, 22*(4), 363–376.

Williams, F. (2014). Making Connections Across the Transnational Political Economy of Care. In B. Anderson & I. Shutes (Eds.), *Migration and Care Labour Theory, Policy and Politics*. London: Palgrave Macmillan.

Williams, F., & Gavanas, A. (2008). The Intersection of Childcare Regimes and Migration Regimes: A Three-Country Study. In H. Lutz (Ed.), *Migration and Domestic Work. A European Perspective on a Global Theme*. Aldershot, UK: Ashgate.

Winker, G., & Degele, N. (2011). Intersectionality as Multi-level Analysis: Dealing with Social Inequality. *European Journal of Women's Studies, 18*(1), 51–66.

Yeates, N. (2009). *Globalizing Care Economies and Migrant Workers: Explorations in Global Care Chains*. London: Palgrave Macmillan.

Yinger, J. M. (1981). Towards a Theory of Assimilation and Dissimilation. *Ethnic Studies, 4*(2), 20–23.

Index[1]

---

[1] Note: Page numbers followed by 'n' refer to notes.

© The Author(s) 2019
N. Sahraoui, *Racialised Workers and European Older-Age Care*, Thinking Gender in Transnational Times, https://doi.org/10.1007/978-3-030-14397-8

The manufacturer's authorised representative in the EU is Springer
Nature Customer Service Centre GmbH, Europaplatz 3, 69115 Heidelberg,
Germany. If you have any concerns regarding our products, please
contact ProductSafety@springernature.com

Printed and bound by CPI Group (UK) Ltd, Croydon, CR0 4YY

29/04/2026

02099478-0011